Public Intellectuals

Rights and Responsibilities:
Communitarian Perspectives
Series Editor: Amitai Etzioni

Public Intellectuals

An Endangered Species?

Edited by
Amitai Etzioni and Alyssa Bowditch

ROWMAN & LITTLEFIELD PUBLISHERS, INC.
Lanham • Boulder • New York • Toronto • Oxford

ROWMAN & LITTLEFIELD PUBLISHERS, INC.

Published in the United States of America
by Rowman & Littlefield Publishers, Inc.
A wholly owned subsidary of The Rowman & Littlefield Publishing Group, Inc.
4501 Forbes Boulevard, Suite 200, Lanham, Maryland 20706
www.rowmanlittlefield.com

PO Box 317
Oxford
OX2 9RU, UK

British Library Cataloguing in Publication Information Available

Library of Congress Cataloging-in-Publication Data

Public intellectuals, an endangered species? / edited by Amitai Etzioni and
Alyssa Bowditch.
    p. cm.
  Includes bibliographical references.
  ISBN 0-7425-4254-8 (cloth : alk. paper) — ISBN 0-7425-4255-6 (pbk. : alk. paper)
  ISBN 978-0-7425-4254-9   ISBN 978-0-7425-4255-6
  1. Intellectuals-United States. 2. Specialists—United States. 3. Social
influence—United States. 4. Political planning—United States. I. Etzioni,
Amitai. II. Bowditch, Alyssa, 1982–
  HN90.E4.P83 2006
  305.5′520973—dc22   2005027694

Printed in the United States of America

∞™ The paper used in this publication meets the minimum requirements of
American National Standard for Information Sciences—Permanence of Paper
for Printed Library Materials, ANSI/NISO Z39.48-1992.

Contents

Chapter 6. Speaking Truth to Power

Introduction

Are Public Intellectuals an Endangered Species?

Amitai Etzioni*

For fifty years Americans have been warned that public intellectuals (PIs) are an endangered species, that the remaining ones are poor copies of the true (earlier) ones, and that one ought to be troubled by their demise because, as a result, society is lacking. To examine this thesis one must first ask, who qualifies as a PI? Have their ranks thinned out and their qualities diminished? The examination then turns to inquire, what is that special service that PIs are supposed to render for the body politic? And—is society being shortchanged?

1. WHAT MAKES A PI?

Before a nose count can be attempted, one clearly needs to list the defining attributes of the species. There is some agreement on what are several key attributes of PIs, but there are also some telling differences among various students of PIs as to what qualifies one as a PI. Agreed is that PIs opine on a wide array of issues, are generalists rather than specialists, concern themselves with matters of interest to the public at large, and do not keep their views to themselves. People who are "well-traveled and broadly educated men of letters who [can] speak on a myriad of topics and [are] listened to by important sectors of the public, thereby shaping public opinion and, in the case of some who [gain] access to political powerbrokers, public policy" is the way two communications professors,

---

* I am indebted to Deirdre Mead and Anne Hardenbergh for research assistance.

1

Daniel C. Brouwer and Catherine R. Squires, put it.[1] And, they write, "public intellectuals should be able to speak about a wide range of topics, but they should also address serious or grand issues and should do so with exquisite depth of knowledge."[2]

Russell Jacoby, whose book on disappearing PIs is often cited as having sounded the alarm warning that PIs are declining, concurs: PIs are people who have "a commitment not simply to a professional or private domain but to a public world—and a public language, the vernacular."[3] Richard A. Posner, who most recently joined the list of those who come to bury rather than praise PIs, writes that a PI "expresses himself in a way that is accessible to the public, and the focus of his expression is on matters of general public concern of (or inflected by) a political or ideological cast."[4] (Similar definitions have been provided by journalist Robert S. Boynton,[5] professor Kitty Calavita,[6] author Joseph Epstein,[7] professor Frances Ferguson,[8] sociologist Charles Kadushin,[9] professor J. Hillis Miller,[10] and author Rick Perlstein.[11]) It is this definition that is followed here.

There is less consensus on one key attribute of PIs, which will become clear shortly and has a great influence on the societal service PIs are expected to render: whether they must be critical and, above all, to what extent they ought to be critical. Epstein puts it carefully: "The intellectual . . . functioned best as a critic."[12] The Enlightenment philosopher Marquis de Condorcet stated that public intellectuals should be devoted to "the tracking down of prejudices in the hiding places where priests, the schools, the government and all long-established institutions had gathered and protected them."[13] Edward Said held that intellectuals should be the "ones to question patriotic nationalism, corporate thinking, and a sense of class, racial or gender privilege."[14] C. Wright Mills argued that "the intellectual ought to be the moral conscience of his society,"[15] which contrasts sharply with the notion that "intellectuals need to be nonpartisan and non-ideological,"[16] a position favored by Brouwer and Squires.

Even a cursory scanning of those considered PIs, for instance the 546 lined up by Posner,[17] shows that PIs are typically critical, though they vary a great deal in the extent and scope of their criticism. Some are critical merely of select policies or conventions, while others are severely critical of whole political or belief systems. Drawing on Posner's list, some of the more critical PIs include Richard Falk, Paul Krugman, and Noam Chomsky.[18] We shall see that PIs cannot do their societal service without being critical, although they surely need not be nearly as one-sided, extreme, or holistic as the extreme practitioners of this art.

Closely related is the disagreement over whether PIs are, or ought to be, engaged in matters of moral judgment. Posner is disdainful of public intellectuals who introduce considerations of morality into their analyses. For Posner, "claims of moral authority are nearly always hypocritical, coercive, or both. 'Moralism' is a greater enemy than any of the sins it proposes to suppress, and discussions of morality never settle anything, nor change anyone's mind."[19] Following in the footsteps of Oliver Wendell Holmes, Jr., a so-called legal-realist, Posner yearns to divest discussions of the law from their ancient associations with "moral philosophy."[20] He views it as "theology without God," a "preachy . . . solemn . . . dull" business, equaled in its perniciousness only by "theology with God."[21] Posner instead seeks to rely on economic analysis for what are, in effect, value judgments, without realizing that he, of course, is a public intellectual engaged in moral judgments, built into his preference of seeing things through the dollar sign.[22]

Paul Johnson goes further:

> The belief seems to be spreading that intellectuals are no wiser as mentors, or worthier as exemplars, than the witch doctors or priests of old. I share that skepticism. A dozen people picked at random on the street are at least as likely to offer sensible views on moral and political matters as a cross-section of the intelligentsia. But I would go further. One of the many principal lessons of our tragic century, which has seen so many millions of innocent lives sacrificed in schemes to improve the lot of humanity, is—beware intellectuals.[23]

Actually, even academic scholars, when they comment publicly about matters concerning their narrow area of specialization, from what is referred to as a "technical viewpoint," cannot avoid making normative statements. For instance, when scholars comment on the proper size of the deficit, which may seem like a judgment based solely on the science of economics, they are actually concerning themselves with such issues as the level of burden this generation may legitimately impose on future ones, whether one ought to endanger the financing of Social Security and hence violate our social contract with senior citizens, and so on. These and other such normative issues are evident in the economic tomes of Robert Solow, Milton Friedman, and James Tobin, among many others. Whatever the subject—affirmative action, the size and shape of tax cuts, school vouchers, grants to faith-based institutions, campaign financing, or environmental policies—moral issues are involved.[24]

In short, PIs must engage in moral deliberations because all major public and social policies that they routinely criticize have important moral dimensions.

For some earlier observers of PIs, being a PI was associated with railing against the prevailing regime, ideology, and social structure. Indeed, in earlier decades, especially between the 1930s and 1970s, many of the most-cited PIs were on the left or liberals.[25] However, as of the 1970s, with the rise of the neo-conservative PIs,[26] a growing number of PIs became critical of the Left, of government excesses, and of people who are self-indulgent, rather than of the prevailing economic, social, or political system.[27] And, in the last decades, there has been a significant increase in conservative think tanks (such as the Heritage Foundation, founded in 1973; the Competitive Enterprise Institute, formed in 1984; and the Progress & Freedom Foundation, founded in 1993) and in foundations that underwrite conservative PIs (such as the John M. Olin Foundation and Phyllis Schlafly's Eagle Forum). There is also an association of conservative scholars, some of whom are PIs, the National Association of Scholars, founded in 1987. None of these is uncritical, nonpartisan, and non-ideological. In short, being critical and normatively prescriptive, although not necessarily in a holistic way, and surely not in a left or liberal sense, are inherent attributes of PIs.

There is a group of people who have many of the attributes of PIs, who quack like PIs, but who do not qualify as PIs, precisely because their role is to form conceptions that support their employer, rather than to be critical. These people, sometimes referred to as "spin doctors," do address the public, on a broad array of issues, in the vernacular rather than in technical terms, but are a distinct species, because they are retained by the powers that be, or volunteered to serve them as their advocates. These include propagandists or PR experts such James Carville and Mary Matalin, as well as some who served as PIs before and after their advocacy service, but who, while in the advocacy role, clearly toe the line of those who employ them, seeking to justify policies that are transparently failing (e.g., the war in Vietnam), trying to make bad judgments seem like savvy moves (e.g., justifying tax cuts that have led to debilitating deficits), and so on. They might be referred to as "house intellectuals." In the Old Testament a similar division is found between true prophets who spoke truth to power and false ones who blessed whatever the king did, especially characterizing his wars as just.

It is important to note that being a PI is not a regular job or vocation. Rather, it belongs to a small category of roles that carry only a temporary social accreditation. (Reference is to "social" because the accreditation involved is neither legal nor technical, but rather informal.) Like movie stars and leading sports figures, PIs must continuously prove that they still qualify for their title. Thus, just as movie stars who have not had a role in a movie for, say, a decade will be considered extinct or dimming, so PIs who have not written or spoken publicly or otherwise made their voices heard on significant public issues for long stretches of time will lose their title. Many a PI who shone brightly in some periods is barely discernable in others.

Moreover, for many, serving as a PI is a phase in their life's work, and not a lifelong vocation. Just as many natural scientists "burn out" young and become academic administrators or college teachers, so academics may become PIs for some years and then return to scholarship or vice versa, or even switch back and forth several times. C. Wright Mills, often cited as one of the most important PIs of the 1940s and 1950s, started as a more or less run-of-the-mill sociologist, doing survey research (in *Small Business and Civic Welfare*, 1946). He then wrote books that are more intellectual but less based on social science (compare *Character and Social Structure: The Psychology of Social Institutions*, 1953, to *The Power Elite*, 1956), and ended up composing a work that is mainly one of advocacy if not sheer ideology (in *Listen, Yankee: The Revolution in Cuba*, 1960). The following analysis hence focuses not on the people involved but on the role of the public intellectual. Those who occupy it may come and go, their personal attributes may change, but the role of the PI does not.

2. WHICH PUBLIC?

In assessing the influence of PIs, if one applies a simplistic democratic approach—one of nose counting—one is sure to come up short, not because PIs' effectiveness is low or has declined, but because of the ways one goes about assessing their influence. Indeed, most assessments of the societal impact of PIs at least implicitly assume that a PI addresses a public; moreover, such an assumption is built into the very definition of the PI's role. However, both a major social science finding and a major social science insight are overlooked if one takes the term public in the simple and monolithic way it is often used. First, one must take into account the well-known finding that the public is divided into various layers in terms of the extent to which it is attentive to public affairs, the kind of issues PIs typically address. Gabriel A. Almond distinguishes among the "general" and the "attentive" public.[28] Studies of local communities have shown that a considerable part of the public has no national or society-wide cognitive map, nor a political one, but instead is preoccupied with making a living, tending to family matters, and watching TV.[29] All this means that a PI can have a great influence without reaching the majority of the population. I am not advocating the layering of society, but rather reporting that such layering is strongly entrenched and greatly affects the issue at hand—namely, how much influence do PIs have these days? Do they fulfill their societal role?

Second, the analysis of the influence of PIs benefits if one applies Paul F. Lazarsfeld's famous insight that communications do not flow directly from the media to the masses, but typically flow from the media to what he called opinion leaders and from them to the people.[30] PIs often reach the relatively highly attentive publics, which include local opinion leaders, elected officials, community leaders, and clergy, among others. These attentive publics, in turn, process whatever communications they have absorbed, render them new, and pass the reprocessed messages to those attentive to them—but not to PIs. Hence, those who study PIs should not assume that "the public," all 300 million citizens, is reached by even the most articulate PIs, but they should also not assume that the many millions of people who have never heard PIs' names or ideas will not be influenced by them, albeit indirectly. For example, millions who have become moral relativists,[31] or embraced various notions of political correctness, may well have never heard the names nor read the books of Richard Rorty or Stanley Fish and others of this ilk, but they may still have been influenced by them.

In short, a simple nose count of those who are familiar with the work of this or that PI, or even all of them together, will underestimate their power. An assessment of the number of people who embrace their concepts, ideas, and values is more to the point. It requires a monumental study to determine how many of the concepts that PIs have introduced gain such currency, and if their number—and import—has increased or decreased over the last decades. However, one can readily come up with examples of such concepts that have gained a very wide following. These include neo-conservative notions about excessive government in the 1980s; communitarian ideas in the 1990s;[32] and libertarian reactions to the Patriot Act over the last few years. These examples lend some support to the thesis that PIs' influence did not decline.

3. SOCIETAL FUNCTIONS: REALITY TESTING AND REFRAMING

One major societal service PIs perform concerns the "communities of assumptions" that governing elites, as well as the more attentive publics, tend to develop. These are shared worldviews, judgments about challenges faced and ways to deal with them, and much more.[33] These assumptions typically serve as frameworks that influence the ways numerous specific public and private policies are received and evaluated.

Once ensconced, which sometimes requires years of public deliberations, the validity of these assumptions is taken for granted. For example, as of 1947, the governing elites, and increasingly the attentive public, came to view the Communist camp, led by the USSR, as a major menacing power and agreed that the United States had to dedicate itself to containing this "evil empire." Thousands of specific policy items found their rationale in this conceptual framework, from the amount of public funding dedicated to teaching foreign languages to pressuring Bolivia not to grant the USSR airline landing rights, from the position of troops around the world to the size of the defense budget.

When events took place that did not fit the Cold War community of assumptions, elites and large segments of the public tended to deny that these events took place or held that they were insignificant. For instance, for years on end the breakup of the Communist camp, especially the rift between the USSR and the People's Republic of China, was considered at first feigned, and then its significance was downplayed, because it threatened the simplistic, bipolar, us-against-them worldview that was at the heart of the prevailing community of assumptions at the time. It was left to PIs, as Henry Kissinger was during his tenure at Harvard, to argue for a drastic change in this community of assumptions. It was this change that ultimately led to the "opening" of China, which brought the United States and China much closer together and undermined the notion that the world was bipolar and all which that entailed. Another case in point is the successful challenge neo-conservative PIs—including Irving Kristol, Daniel Bell, Nathan Glazer, and James Q. Wilson—posed to the liberal framework that used to justify scores of social programs that together made up the Great Society, which presumed that government could be highly effective in curing a large variety of social ills.

About an earlier era Jean Bethke Elshtain notes:

> Reinhold Niebuhr was one such [party pooper] when he decided that he could no longer hold with his compatriots of the Social Gospel movement, given what he took to be their dangerous naïveté about the rise of fascism in Europe. He was widely derided as a man who once thought total social transformation in the direction of world peace was possible, but who had become strangely determined to take a walk on the morbid side by reminding Americans of the existence of evil in the world. On this one, Niebuhr was clearly right.[34]

A personal account of attempts to question the assumptions that led the United States to be mired in the war in Vietnam and to glorify space exploration is included in my memoirs.[35]

In challenging obsolete communities of assumptions and paving the way for new, more current ones, PIs serve to enhance the reality testing of societies. There is a need for people whose special role is to try to pry open communities of assumptions and frame new ones, because old assumptions tend to resist examination and framing new ones is a daunting task. As Anthony Grafton put it, "The new intellectuals have exercised a great deal of influence, since they think through and confront foreign and domestic, social and cultural issues that the rest of us would rather ignore."[36]

There are two underlying reasons for the often intense resistance to subjecting communities of assumptions to critical review. First, elites and the public invest a considerable amount of effort in developing communities of assumptions. This often entails years of public dialogue. Hence, once such a community is well established, it is costly in terms of human mental labor to reexamine what has finally come to be taken for granted. Second, given the complexity of reality, it is often very difficult to determine what the facts are (e.g., how powerful China is) and hence there is an innate preference to adhere to any shared set of assumptions given the confounding state of the world.[37]

This resistance to reexamining well-established communities of assumptions is reflected in the criticism faced by the PIs who directly take them on. Sometimes their loyalty is suspected, as was the fate of those who questioned, during the 1950s and beyond, the prevailing view that the USSR was an expansionist power bent on taking over the world. In other times, PIs are mocked or ignored, as were, for decades, those who questioned the need for ever higher levels of nuclear armaments and new means of delivery, until President Reagan embraced an arms reduction policy in 1986.[38]

Elected officials are often called upon to act as "leaders," that is, to convince the public that the time has come to abandon one community of assumptions and work to adopt a new one, by those who see the obsolescence of the assumptions long before others, or by those who have a vested interest in the change (e.g., those who are keen to trade with Cuba). However, elected officials typically find that such changes are highly risky to their political future. Hence, as a rule, they wait until PIs pave the way and legitimate the change in course. Finding pathways through such political minefields is a primary societal mission for PIs.

A society that prevents PIs from functioning freely, whose PIs are of a declining quality, or in which PIs are ignored by the governing elites, will be lacking in reality testing, be slower in adapting its policies and viewpoints to external as well as domestic changes, and be more "ideological." Such a society will tend to adhere to the community of assumptions even if these have grown ever further away from reality and cause increasing damage. This can be validated by observing that totalitarian societies and theocracies (such as the Taliban regime in Afghanistan and the Ayatollahs in Iran) have a significantly lower level of reality testing than democratic societies. A case in point are the assumptions Saddam and his cohorts made in 2003 that Iraq could win the war against the United States by drawing on world public opinion, Iraqi armed forces, and the support of the governments of Russia, China, Germany, and France.[39]

Democracies, too, especially during nationalist periods, may seek to suppress PIs rather than examine their communities of assumptions. For instance, for decades those who questioned the U.S. view of the USSR (and the war in Vietnam) were considered Communist lackeys and traitors. As a result, the United States adhered to a course of action long after it became highly unrealistic.

As obsolete communities of assumptions are pried open, there is often a keen demand for PIs to frame new ones, because their absence is a source of multiple tensions. This is in part the case because communities of assumptions serve as a basis for resolving differences and provide a common ground on which conflicting political parties must meet if they are to have a chance to win an election. Lacking such common ground causes gridlock and conflicts that resist resolution. For instance, because there are no shared assumptions about when life begins, pro-life and pro-choice groups have been unable to resolve their differences. Similar difficulties, for the same basic reason, are also faced by those who would allow experiments on human clones for therapeutic purposes and those who would ban them.

Also, millions of people find that when communities of assumptions are not available, their world is unsettled, cluttered with details, and lacking organizing principles and an overarching, integrating picture. (Thomas Kuhn showed the same pattern in the world of scientific paradigms.[40]) PIs play a key role not only in the dialogues that lead to the destruction of the old communities of assumptions but also in the formulation of new ones. For example, Betty Friedan and several other leading feminist PIs both undermined the old, male-led community of assumptions and fostered the quest for a new formulation of the basic ways relations between the genders are considered. Rachel Carson opened the dialogues that led to a whole new set of assumptions concerning society and individual obligations to the environment. In both cases, numerous specific matters of policy and personal conduct were also considered, many of which are not yet fully settled. However, the frameworks in which they take place have been recast. A similar effort has been made in Europe to provide a whole new way of thinking about the relationship between minorities (including immigrants) and the majority in the societies involved, referred to as "diversity within unity."[41]

Now that the significant societal functions of PIs have been outlined, the next step is to examine the validity of the arguments that PIs are in decline. It has been argued for several decades that PIs in the United States have been dying out and hence ever fewer are left to provide the needed societal services. Others who see a decline in PIs maintain that those who are still with us are of diminished quality and that their ideas are ignored by both the governing elites and the attentive publics. Before these arguments can be considered, a distinction must be made between two major types of PIs.

4. STRUCTURAL DIFFERENCES:
ACADEMIC VS. BOHEMIAN PUBLIC INTELLECTUALS

It is a commonplace social science understanding that a person's beliefs, cognitions, and feelings (perspectives for short)—and the societal service they can yield—are all significantly affected by their position in the social structure, although there are great differences in the ways various social scientists define and measure these structural positions and how much weight they accord them in terms of their effects on a person's perspectives.[42] In a colloquial way it is suggested that where you stand depends on where you sit. Intellectuals are held to be the main exception. Karl Mannheim already advanced the thesis that intellectuals are much freer than other members of society to develop perspectives that diverge from those one would expect a person to have based on their income, prestige, race, and so on.[43] This relative freedom of PIs from structural constraints explains why they are able to see the obsolescence of communities of assumptions before others do, and are freer to frame new ones than other people. However, *not all PIs are equally able to render this service—precisely because they have different structural positions.*

We already saw the difference between those who are beholden to an employer and are retained as advocates ("house intellectuals") and those who act as unencumbered critics. It is useful to draw one more distinction, dividing the true PIs into two groups based on their structural positions, which in turn affect the ways they fulfill their societal roles. The first group includes those who are academically based and the second, those who are free-standing, making a living as writers, freelance editors, columnists, and so on. Because historically many of the second kind lived in places such as Greenwich Village in New York City and on the Left Bank in Paris, and had some of the behavioral attributes of bohemians, I shall refer to them as bohemian (or free-standing) public intellectuals, and to the first group as academic public intellectuals.

The differences between the structural positions of the two groups are clear; their implications, though, are highly contested. The job security of academic PIs on average is significantly higher than that of the bohemians; full-fledged tenure is almost completely the property of the first group. Academic intellectuals hence tend to consider it an article of faith that it is much easier for them to maintain a considerable measure of intellectual, ideological, and political independence—essential for their societal roles—as compared to the bohemians. This, however, is not necessarily the way everyone sees it. For instance, Jacoby argues that academics conform to university norms and seek to be "mainstream" rather than independent.[44] Others claim that "the university is unable to facilitate or sustain publicly relevant work; thus public intellectuals are primarily or exclusively to be found outside academe."[45]

As I see it, there is no evidence that those most critical of the American polity or society in recent decades are to be found more among free-standing, bohemian PIs than among those who are campus based. Mills, who is often celebrated as a grand critic, wrote as a tenured professor at Columbia University. Other academically based critics include Noam

Chomsky, Lani Guinier, Joseph Stiglitz, Cornel West, and Howard Zinn. And most would agree that despite the fact that Senator Joseph McCarthy cowed many PIs both on and off the campus, those who were free-standing were much more likely to be driven out of jobs and silenced by him than the academic ones. In short, academic PIs seem to be able to serve as independent critics at least as well as free-standing ones, if not more readily, especially in testy periods.

5. "FUNCTIONAL" CROSS-FIRE

Public intellectuals face two dangers: becoming too academic and losing their influence with the relevant public and the governing elites, as well as becoming too "popular," sacrificing their ability to provide reality testing. As those who stray in either direction are under incessant criticism, both by pure academics and each by the other brand of PIs, they tend to stray less than they would otherwise. All this deserves some elaboration.

As a result of the structural differences between bohemian and academic PIs, the former group is under much less pressure to maintain academic standards in their intellectual work than the academically based group. Also, the specific vocations of the two groups differ: the bohemians are much more likely to write and edit as their main activities, while the academics are more likely to conduct research; the first group publishes, on average, more frequently than the second, and their works are often shorter and more popular. For instance, free-standing PIs, such as George Will and William Safire, write short opinion pieces that are published weekly and their books are often compilations of their columns. (There are though quite a few exceptions, the works of Susan Sontag, for instance.) On the academic side, Jürgen Habermas and Pierre Bourdieu mainly publish heavy tomes, though again there are exceptions—for instance, Robert Reich, who is heard regularly on radio stations. In sum, bohemians are especially likely to be "too popular" and not provide reliable reality testing and academic PIs are more likely to be "too academic" and hence not provide usable reality testing.

Within the academy, individual PIs and PIs as a group are often strongly criticized for over generalizing, under documenting, and being politically and ideologically biased.[46] As Jacoby reports: "The worst thing you can say about someone in an academic meeting or when you're discussing tenure promotion is, 'Oh, his work is kind of journalistic.' Meaning, it's readable. It's journalistic, it's superficial. There's an equation between profundity and originality."[47] Stephen Carter agrees:

> You know that in the academy the really bad word is "popularizer"—a mere popularizer, not someone who is original, which of course means obscure, or

someone who is "deeply theorized," which is the other phrase. And to be deeply theorized, you understand, in academic terms today, means to be incapable of uttering a word such as "poor." No one is poor. The word, the phrase now, as some of you may know, is "restricted access to capital market." That's deeply theorized, you see. And some of us just say poor, and that makes us popularizers.[48]

Posner accuses PIs of being "often careless with facts and rash in predictions."[49] Elshtain writes that intellectuals "[possess] a worldview whose logic promises to explain everything, and perhaps, in some glorious future, control and manage everything."[50]

Specific PIs have been criticized along these lines. For instance, about John Kenneth Galbraith, *The New Yorker* wrote, "even some of those economists who personally like Galbraith dismiss him with the usual tags— 'popularizer,' 'gadfly,' or, worst of all, 'journalist.'"[51] Cornel West was savaged by *The New Republic*, which wrote that his books were "monuments to the devastation of a mind by squalls of theory," full of pomposity and demonstrating "a long saga of positioning."[52] Carl Sagan, after he died, was described as a "cunning careerist" and, the ultimate put-down, "compulsive popularizer."[53] The *National Review* excoriated Alan Dershowitz, writing that his "lawyerly obfuscating and moral grandstanding and professorial posturing testify all too powerfully to a reckless disregard for the truth that has become an increasingly common feature of the professor in his role as public intellectual."[54]

PIs have responded, maintaining that pure academics (not to be confused with PIs based in academia) learn more and more about less and less, study trivia, write in ways that cannot be comprehended ("jargon"), and, above all, that their works are "irrelevant" to the burning social issues of the day. Posner writes, "academics are not tuned to political reality . . . [and] tend to be unworldly."[55] Irving Howe argued that no one "can accept the notion that the academy is the natural home of intellect."[56] Mark Krupnick writes of academics who, "[a]s their critical idiom has become more and more technical and specialized, they have exercised less and less influence on the general culture."[57] Patrick Saveau faults intellectuals in universities who "are content to remain within their university cliques, disseminating their ideas in a void they fail to notice because it engulfs them."[58]

Academic public intellectuals have defended themselves against these charges, holding that their work is relevant and that the use of specialized language is legitimate.[59] They hold that their discipline, skills, and insights can contribute to a public debate and that they "can indeed grapple with the issues and problems of the real world."[60] In fact, some hold that public intellectuals can "contribute to a more just social order," something in which academics "have yet to realize their full potential."[61] Walter Dean Burnham correctly points out "[t]here are quite a few political scientists who believe that better and more precise understanding of the political world presents work enough for a lifetime. One could refer to some among these scholars as 'scientists,' or would-be scientists, or, more pejoratively perhaps, as 'ivory-tower' intellectuals who have neither the gifts nor the interest to become 'public intellectuals.'"[62]

Mills dedicated much of his book, *The Sociological Imagination*, to making these points. He stated, for instance, that "Surely it is evident that an empiricism as cautious and rigid as abstracted empiricism eliminates the great social problems and human issues of our time from inquiry"[63] and that

> [t]he basic cause of grand theory is the initial choice of a level of thinking so general that its practitioners cannot logically get down to observation. They never, as grand theorists, get down from the higher generalities to problems in their historical and structural contexts. This absence of a firm sense of genuine problems, in turn, makes for the unreality so noticeable in their pages. One resulting characteristic is a seemingly arbitrary and certainly endless elaboration of distinctions, which neither enlarge our understanding nor make our experience more sensible. This in turn is revealed as a partially organized abdication of the effort to describe and explain human conduct and society plainly.[64]

One can look at these observations, by both sides, not merely as empirical observations that claim to reveal serious defects in both academic PIs and "pure" academics, but as reflecting a built-in tension in the PI role, especially in those that are academically based. These PIs—as with several other roles that require two words to denote them, "working mothers" for instance—have, so to speak, a foot in two camps: the intellectual and the public.[65] As the standards and expectations of these two realms are highly incompatible, those whose role it is to bridge these two realms experience the tensions that result from the building conflict.

There is a tendency to view tension as negative. Medical literature typically views tension as a form of illness that ought to be treated because otherwise tensions may cause a variety of psychosomatic illnesses. Societal tensions are often considered a social malaise that may lead to violence, for instance tensions between two racial groups. And international tensions are considered dangerous because they may lead to war. One hence tends to overlook that tensions often have a positive function; indeed they are sometimes part of the very constitution of the constellation one is observing. To provide but two metaphors: the tension among the bricks that compose an arch, in earlier ages when no bonding agents were used, is what kept the arch standing. Tension in the wires that make up the stays of the mast of a sailboat is what keeps the mast erect.

The tension that is built into the role of PIs, especially academic PIs, is essential for sustaining this role, although it does have some negative side effects. My key hypothesis is that the fact that PIs are under constant pressure to generalize less, document more, and so on, helps to keep them more intellectually responsible than they would be if not exposed to such pressures, protects them from turning more ideological, being commercially bought, seeking to ingratiate themselves to governing elites, or playing to the public, all temptations they face from the other element of their role, the public side.[66] (Determining whether PIs also have an effect on pure academics, making them more attentive to social issues, less jargon-driven, etc., is well beyond the scope of this examination of PIs.)

One way to test the validity of the stated hypothesis is to interview academic PIs. One expects their initial reaction to academic pressures and criticism to be defensive, denying that they are not living up to academic standards in their works and pronouncements, accusing their critics of being jealous of their fame, and so on. However, at the same time, many academic PIs who have been chided by their colleagues react by adhering more closely to academic standards. (Exceptions to the rule would be those who leave academia or those relatively few who remain but openly defy all its rules, as Mills did toward the latter part of his career and Noam Chomsky does in his ideological writings as distinct from his linguistic work.)

Another way to test this hypothesis is to compare the writings of academic PIs to those of bohemian, free-standing PIs. The latter are less subject to the pressures of academia because their jobs, tenure, and raises are not controlled by academics. And bohemians are much less woven into social circles that contain pure academics. They are more dependent on the public for their income, audience, and influence.

In any case, the fact that there is considerable tension built into the role of PIs should not be viewed as a sign of decay or as a built-in societal or intellectual problem. It seems largely to serve to keep PIs honest.

6. ARE PUBLIC INTELLECTUALS AN ENDANGERED SPECIES?

Alarms have been sounded that PIs are vanishing—and grave concerns have been expressed about the ill societal effects of their demise—for many decades,[67] which itself suggests that like many other such predictions about the "ending" of this or that, these alarms often reflect various concerns rather than empirical reality. Writing in 1953, Donald Davie stated "the professional poet has already disappeared from the literary scene, and the professional man of letters is following him into the grave."[68] Jacoby dates the decline of public intellectuals to the 1950s: "If the western frontier closed in the 1890s, the cultural frontier closed in the 1950s."[69] Bruce Bawer, writing in 1998, proclaimed that public intellectuals are an endangered species, writing that "serious ideas and culture are struggling to flourish outside the academy. Independent bookstores are dying; poetry has retreated to the universities and the university presses; literary fiction is doing the same. In mainstream publishing, the words 'essay' and 'criticism' are now the kiss of death."[70] Carter claims we are in an era of "relatively little serious intellectual endeavor."[71] Elshtain believes that the existence of public intellectuals is at risk.[72] Boynton writes that the one thing "most intellectuals will agree on is that the age of the public intellectual is over."[73] Still, Posner, himself a prophet of the decline and fall of PIs, lists hundreds of them in a book published at the onset of the twenty-first century. Numerous other observers have cited a fair number of PIs quite recently.[74] Carlin Romano blames the media for any seeming decline, writing, "'prestige' mass media . . . do an appalling job of reporting and representing the flourishing intellectual culture of the United States."[75] In short, PIs have hardly vanished, nor is there is evidence that their number has declined.

7. IS THE QUALITY OF PUBLIC INTELLECTUALS DECLINING?

Some argue that while PIs may not have disappeared, the quality of the remaining ones is much lower than that of previous generations. Jacoby writes that thinkers after the end of the 1950s were not "fired by the same caliber of imagination, boldness—or writing" as their predecessors.[76] Epstein holds that the traditional intellectual (which today's public intellectuals are not) was distinguished by "a certain cast of mind, a style of thought, wide-ranging, curious, playful, genuinely excited by ideas for ideas' sake."[77] Epstein further argues that "Unlike so many of today's public intellectuals, [the traditional intellectual] was not primarily a celebrity hound, a false philosopher-king with tenure, or a single-issue publicist. An elegantly plumed, often irritating bird, the traditional intellectual was always a minuscule minority."[78]

Elshtain blames the decline of PIs on the rise of therapeutic culture and the decline of the two main political parties.[79] Carter attributes the decline to the rise of political correctness and the need to be thought to be in the right "camp."[80] Posner argues that specialization is "threatening to the quality and impact of intellectuals' interventions in public debates."[81] Blaming the academy for the decline of intellectuals has become so popular that it "has reached near dogma."[82] Epstein places part of the blame on the university and specialization in academia, but believes "it was really the decade of the 1960s that finished off the old intellectual life."[83]

For Jacoby, the causes of this decline run the gamut from PIs' increasing presence in universities[84] (where they do not seek a larger public[85]) and the pressure of conformity,[86] to the decline of bohemia,[87] the expansion of suburbia,[88] and the inability to make a living without affiliating with an institution.[89] David Brooks, himself a very successful PI, writes that the quest for money and comfortable life has corrupted PIs.[90] Posner reports that the quality of public intellectual work is declining because of intellectuals' attempts to be original and the lack of "quality controls in the public-intellectual market."[91]

Several critics argue that intellectuals of fifty years ago were part of a small and select group who kept themselves apart from the masses.[92] Today's intellectuals have broadened to include more people and "[the term] has almost lost its meaning as so many different types lay claim to it."[93] Further, intellectuals today "tend to minimize or deny the gap between themselves and everyone else, not defend it."[94]

Several of these critics refer to the difference between what some have called private intellectuals[95] and public intellectuals. Public intellectuals, by definition, try to teach the public. But the fact that they exist, even if it is true that more intellectuals these days are public than used to be (for which no evidence is presented), does not mean that there are no longer private intellectuals, who write wide-ranging, profound, and influential books, without seeking to speak to the public at large—John Rawls, for instance. Although Martha Nussbaum and Amartya Sen appear on Posner's list of PIs, they are not well known even to attentive publics and largely write in ways accessible mainly to their academic colleagues, and hence serve as additional examples of private but very accomplished intellectuals.

8. QUANTITATIVE EVIDENCE

As far as the author was able to establish, there is only one major study that provides quantitative data to demonstrate that the quality of PIs has declined.[96] The data, presented by Posner have been severely criticized.[97] He does admit that his list of 546 public intellectuals was basically chosen arbitrarily; it seems to include names that simply came to his mind.[98] (No sour grapes; here the author is included.) Posner does not claim that his list encompasses the universe of PIs or that it constitutes a representative sample of them. (In a post hoc, he reports that he has since added more names to his list of PIs—both names that occurred to him and names that were suggested to him—and increased the list to 607, further indicating the arbitrary nature of his universe.[99]) Keeping these limitations in mind, Posner's data clearly lay to rest the notion that PIs have died out. In fact,

67 percent of the PIs on his list are living.[100] But has their quality decreased? And has society, culture or the polity suffered as a result?

To measure scholarly quality Posner counts the frequency of scholarly citations during the publication years 1995 through 2000 in three databases compiled by the Institute for Scientific Information.[101] (Posner admits this is a problematic measure.[102]) Thus, the data he gathered are affected by the level of specialization and the size of one's field rather than quality of the academic work. Thus, a professor of English who studies Shakespeare is much more likely to be cited by other academics than one who studies mathematical sociology, a highly esoteric and tiny field. However, for the sake of this analysis, it will be taken for granted that there is some kind of correlation between the frequency of citation and scholarly quality.

Posner uses the number of web hits and media mentions (between 1995 and 2000) as a proxy for an individual's prominence as a public intellectual.[103] (Posner defines a public intellectual, for the purpose of his analysis, as "a person who, drawing on his intellectual resources, addresses a broad though educated public on issues with a political or ideological dimension."[104]) Public intellectuals whose work was completely overshadowed by other aspects of their career are excluded (e.g., William Sloane Coffin, Albert Einstein, Newt Gingrich, Ernest Hemingway, Pablo Picasso, and Woodrow Wilson), as are journalists and activists who are not very "intellectual" (e.g., Maureen Dowd, Charlton Heston, and Ralph Nader).[105]

Posner next whittles his list of 546 public intellectuals into a list of the one hundred most often cited public intellectuals by media mention and the one hundred most often cited public intellectuals by scholarly citation. He finds that there are more living people in his list of the top one hundred public intellectuals by media mention than in his list of the top one hundred public intellectuals by scholarly citation.[106] It is a less than completely surprising fact that a larger percentage of living public intellectuals would appear on the list of the top one hundred public intellectuals by media mention, given that they are in a considerably better position to comment on current events than those who have died. Moreover, Posner finds that the fifty academics who appear in the list of the top one hundred public intellectuals by media mention account for only 16.7 percent of the total number of scholarly citations received by all of the academics in his list of public intellectuals (354 of the 546 public intellectuals were classified as academics).[107] Far from showing that the quality of public intellectuals has declined, Posner has shown that they are not academic stars. (And of course most academics, including some of the best, are not PIs.) There is a division of labor between academics and public intellectuals, although some people have a foot in both camps, or in some phases of their lives are more of an academic or more of a PI. Posner's data are akin to showing that the top movie stars are not the top Broadway actors, or that the best hockey players are not the best football players.

When Posner analyzes the fifty academics who appear in his list of the top one hundred public intellectuals by media mention, he finds a relatively weak negative correlation between media mentions and scholarly citations (though the correlation is stronger than the one between scholarly citations and web hits).[108] Posner does point out in the text (but not in the table itself, as is customary among academics) that the correlations are not statistically significant.[109]

In short, there seems to be no quantitative evidence that the quality of current PIs is lower than it was in earlier periods. And whatever data are presented show that if there is a difference, it is so small that it is statistically, intellectually, and socially insignificant.

9. NEW SUB-CATEGORIES

One should not conclude from the fact that new kinds of PIs have risen, even if their quality is lower rather than merely different from earlier types, that the quality of PIs in general is declining. For instance, much has been made of "talking heads" and the "chattering classes" or "pundits" on TV, who superficially comment each evening on some topic, using sound bites that last nine seconds or less.[110] Obviously these did not exist before 1950, before the advent of television, although they were not unknown on radio.

Many of these "talking heads" do not qualify as PIs because they do not meet the criteria used to define this role, and hence reflect no decline of that species. However, some, who receive considerable chunks of air time, say on National Public Radio, C-Span, and public television, which enable them to explore serious matters in a serious fashion, do meet the criteria of the definition of PIs cited above. Thus, for example, "The Power of Myth," a series of several dialogues between Joseph Campbell and Bill Moyers recorded in the 1980s, and aired on public television, may well not be lower in quality than, say, public lectures presented at the 92nd Street Y in earlier decades.

True, television may not provide the same opportunity for interaction with an audience (although the technology and opportunities for such interactions are improving), but television does provide PIs with many opportunities that were unavailable earlier, including the ability to reach a huge national and even transnational audience who can use new technologies such as tapes, CDs, and downloading to hear and view these presentations as often as desired, at the pace and at the time of their own choosing.

In short, many of the criticisms of contemporary PIs, which are supposed to show their declining quality, actually either refer to people who act to some extent as if they are PIs (e.g., those who comment on the news) but are not, or constitute new breeds of PIs, with profiles of their own, but not necessarily a weaker breed. Moreover, the rise of "pundits" and TV PIs is paralleled by an abundance of other PIs, as Posner's long list shows. In short, *the new breeds—whatever their qualities—have not replaced the earlier ones.*

10. SPEAK TO POWER?

The role PIs can play in a given society is greatly affected by the extent to which the "public" is receptive to their ideas, which in turn affects their access to governing elites. And their access to the governing elites affects their public following and the impact of their criticism. As has been often observed, "the American temperament invites wariness toward intellectuals."[111] Moreover, the United States differs from many other societies in that, in earlier eras, the governing elites were highly segregated from PIs. This segregation limited the influence of PIs in the United States as compared to other countries—and after this segregation diminished, as of the Kennedy Administration, PIs' influence increased. To document these preceding observations would require a multi-volume history of American intellectuals.[112] All that can be provided here are some preliminary indications that lend some limited support to the arguments here advanced.

Some intellectuals visited Washington—and a selected few even served in presidential administrations—before the Kennedy era. For instance, Fannie Hurst in the first half of the 1900s, "was as likely to appear in the pages of leading newspapers as she was in the conference rooms of the White House, where her friends the Roosevelts gave her an open invitation."[113] Woodrow Wilson and Theodore Roosevelt could themselves be considered intellectuals (the first earned a Ph.D. at Johns Hopkins and the second wrote books) and may have consulted intellectuals informally and on an ad hoc basis, but in these early administrations of the twentieth century, "intellectuals had no *official* role to play"[114] (emphasis added). Franklin Delano Roosevelt is believed to have been the first president in this century to have brought intellectuals to the White House, which "contributed to an opening and an increased role for intellectuals in politics."[115] However, the intellectuals in FDR's administration (called the "brain trust") were not particularly influential. In this early period, many American politicians considered being associated with PIs as damaging to their political success and their attempts to present themselves as common folks. For instance, one of the main difficulties of Adlai Stevenson,

when he was seeking the presidency, was that he was considered somewhat of a PI himself.

Washington differed in these early periods from other capitals, such as
Paris, Moscow, and Jerusalem, in that it did not have a major university
and bohemia was very limited. The *Washington Post* was not nearly as
highly regarded as it is today. Most publishing houses and small magazines (e.g., the influential *Partisan Review*) were located elsewhere, especially in New York City. Hence the kind of frequent, easy, and informal
contacts between PIs and the political elites common in other capitals
(e.g., having dinners in each other's homes, attending the same seminars)
were not common, although far from unknown, in Washington, in the
decades before the Kennedy era. Thus, for the most part, governing elites
and PIs remained segregated until the mid-twentieth century. Then, the
developments that began with FDR "culminated in the 1960s, [when] intellectuals attained stature and presidents felt that they needed a liaison
to the increasingly important intellectual community."[116]

Kennedy was the first president in recent history who brought aca-
demically based PIs, largely from Harvard, into the White House in any
significant way. Kennedy "realized and capitalized on the potential of
America's intellectuals."[117] These academics included such names as
Arthur Schlesinger, Jr., and Richard Neustadt, the author of *Presidential
Power*. Kennedy was deeply influenced by Michael Harrington's book,
The Other America.[118] The Kennedy Administration provided a model for
the inclusion of public intellectuals in government. Kennedy appointed
PIs to important posts in "a higher proportion . . . than any other president in history."[119] These intellectuals left a profound legacy. As Tevi Troy
writes, "Since 1960, intellectuals have become increasingly important,
shaping the millions of words written about presidents that determine
presidential support and reputations. Consequently, every president
[since that time] has had to deal with the intellectual community."[120]

From Kennedy on, various PIs worked in the White House. Lyndon
Johnson, Richard Nixon, Jimmy Carter, Ronald Reagan, and Bill Clinton
had PIs working in the White House (e.g., Henry Kissinger, Zbigniew
Brzezinski, Samuel Huntington, Daniel Patrick Moynihan, Amitai Etzioni) and many others were invited to Camp David for consultations.[121]
While the segregation of PIs and governing elites decreased, it did not
end. (When I served in the White House in 1979–1980, I was told to address Zbigniew Brzezinski, at the time a Columbia University professor
on leave, as Mister and not as Doctor or Professor. Doctor or Professor, I
was told, smacked of being academic rather than bestowing legitimacy.)

The George W. Bush Administration is not necessarily following this
tradition. True, it has been reported that President Bush read Eliot Co-
hen's *Supreme Command* and was indirectly influenced by Bernard Lewis's

What Went Wrong? and *The Last Lion* by William Manchester.[122] However, no PIs work in his White House. It seems, as Troy noted, that "on the whole . . . [George W.] Bush showed little interest in reaching out to the so-called mainstream intellectual community."[123] However, this is an exception to the pattern that prevailed for more than forty years, although a closer examination would show that there were ups and downs in the PI–White House relationships during that period.

PIs' increased access is helped by the fact that in recent years more of them have been nearby. Although Washington still has no Harvard, its universities have improved over the last decades; many think tanks have sprung up; the *Washington Post's* quality has greatly increased; and several small magazines are published in Washington (including *Foreign Policy*, *The National Interest*, *The Public Interest*, and *The Weekly Standard*, all launched after 1960). Informal contact between elites, while not as rich as in other countries, is greater than in earlier eras.[124]

The effect of the increased contacts among PIs and the governing elites remains to be studied—in both directions. To what extent have PIs directly affected the communities of assumptions of the governing elites and their specific policies versus indirectly affecting the assumptions held by the public? And, to what extent did the increasing involvement of PIs in Washington weaken their critical power as they became anxious to be heard and invited to the White House?

Until such studies are undertaken, it seems safe to suggest, on the basis of the limited observations listed above, that (a) PIs have far from disappeared, (b) their contact with governing elites has increased and so, it seems, has their influence, and (c) while such contact may have weakened criticism from PIs who work or want to work closely with the powers that be, there is no shortage of outsiders who strongly challenge those in power.

NOTES

1. Daniel C. Brouwer and Catherine R. Squires, "Public Intellectuals, Public Life, and the University," *Argumentation and Advocacy* 39 (2003): 204.

2. Brouwer and Squires, 204.

3. Russell Jacoby, *The Last Intellectuals: American Culture in the Age of Academe* (New York, NY: Basic Books, 1987), 235.

4. Richard A. Posner, *Public Intellectuals: A Study of Decline* (Cambridge, MA: Harvard University Press, 2001), 35.

5. "A writer, informed by a strong moral impulse, who addressed a general, educated audience in accessible language about the most important issues of the day." Robert S. Boynton, "The New Intellectuals," *Atlantic Monthly*, March 1995, 53.

6. "One who commands a broad audience and is thus something of a cultural icon" and "One who engages intellectually in public" rather than serves as "the conveyor of Absolute Truths." Kitty Calavita, "Engaged Research, 'Goose Bumps,' and the Role of the Public Intellectual," *Law & Society Review* 36 (2002): 12.

7. "The natural penchant of the intellectual was not to go deeper but wider." Joseph Epstein, "Intellectuals—Public and Otherwise," *Commentary*, May 2000, 48.

8. Intellectuals "do *not* have a pre-established body of knowledge, set of facts, or specific constituency" (emphasis in original). Frances Ferguson, "Forum," *PMLA* 112 (1997): 1125.

9. "One who is an expert in dealing with high-quality general ideas on questions of values and esthetics and who communicates his judgments on these matters to a fairly general audience." Charles Kadushin, *The American Intellectual Elite* (Boston, MA: Little, Brown, 1974), 7.

10. "An intellectual was a distinguished specialist in some field . . . who also wrote for a broad educated public that shared a common culture." J. Hillis Miller, "Forum," *PMLA* 112 (1997): 1138.

11. "Writers and thinkers who address a general audience on matters of broad public concern." Rick Perlstein, "Thinkers in Need of Publishers," *The New York Times*, 22 January 2002, A19.

12. Epstein, "Intellectuals—Public and Otherwise," *Commentary*, May 2000, 48.

13. Quoted in Kenan Malik, "The Death of Ideas," *New Statesman*, 22 April 2002, 53.

14. Edward Said, *Representations of the Intellectual* (New York, NY: Pantheon Books, 1994), xiii; see also his Reith Lectures, in particular, Edward Said, "The Reith Lectures: Speaking Truth to Power," *The Independent (London)*, 22 July 1993, 12.

15. C. Wright Mills, "On Knowledge and Power," in *Power, Politics & People: The Collected Essays of C. Wright Mills*, ed. Irving Louis Horowitz (New York, NY: Oxford University Press, 1963), 611.

16. Brouwer and Squires, 204.

17. Posner, *Public Intellectuals: A Study of Decline*, 194–206 (Table 5.1).

18. Whom I would have classified as a combination of academic, when he deals with linguistics, and ideologue-propagandist, when he deals with other issues, but not as a PI.

19. Analysis of Wilfred M. McClay, "Pseudo-intellectual," *The Public Interest* 147 (2002): 110.

20. Wilfred M. McClay, "Pseudo-intellectual," *The Public Interest* 147 (2002): 110.

21. Quoted in Wilfred M. McClay, "Pseudo-intellectual," *The Public Interest* 147 (2002): 110.

22. Amitai Etzioni, *The Moral Dimension: Toward a New Economics* (New York, NY: The Free Press, 1988).

23. Paul Johnson, *Intellectuals* (New York, NY: Harper & Row, 1988), 342.

24. For more discussion see Amitai Etzioni, *The Limits of Privacy* (New York, NY: Basic Books, 1999); and Amitai Etzioni, *My Brother's Keeper: A Memoir and a Message* (Lanham, MD: Rowman & Littlefield, 2003).

25. John Lukacs notes that American public intellectuals were dominated by leftists between the 1930s and 1950s particularly, with the first conservative iden-

tifications beginning in the 1960s and conservative dominance beginning in the 1980s. John Lukacs, "The Obsolescence of the American Intellectual," *The Chronicle of Higher Education*, 4 October 2002, 7.

26. See, for example, Irving Kristol, *Neoconservatism: The Autobiography of an Idea, Selected Essays 1949–1995* (New York, NY: Free Press, 1995).

27. Posner, *Public Intellectuals: A Study of Decline*, 163–64.

28. Gabriel A. Almond, *The American People and Foreign Policy* (New York, NY: Frederick A. Praeger, 1960 [1950]), 138.

29. See numerous books by Robert E. Lane, particularly *Political Thinking and Consciousness: The Private Life of the Political Mind* (Chicago, IL: Markham, 1969).

30. Paul Lazarsfeld, Bernard Berelson, and Hazel Gaudet, *The People's Choice: How the Voter Makes Up His Mind in a Presidential Campaign*, 3rd ed. (New York, NY: Columbia University Press, 1968), 151.

31. Alan Wolfe, *Moral Freedom: The Search for Virtue in a World of Choice* (New York, NY: W.W. Norton, 2001).

32. Amitai Etzioni, *My Brother's Keeper: A Memoir and a Message* (Lanham, Md.: Rowman & Littlefield, 2003).

33. See particularly chapters 7 and 8 in Amitai Etzioni, *The Active Society: A Theory of Societal and Political Processes* (New York: Free Press, 1968).

34. "The Future of the Public Intellectual: A Forum," *The Nation*, 12 February 2001, 28.

35. Amitai Etzioni, *My Brother's Keeper: A Memoir and a Message* (Lanham, MD: Rowman & Littlefield, 2003).

36. Anthony Grafton, "The Public Intellectual and the American University: Robert Morss Lovett Revisited," *American Scholar* 10 (2001): 44.

37. For an insightful discussion of reality testing and the role of PIs in it, during the Eisenhower and Johnson Administrations, see Fred I. Greenstein and John P. Burke, "The Dynamics of Presidential Reality Testing: Evidence from Two Vietnam Decisions," *Political Science Quarterly* 104 (1989–90): 557–80.

38. Amitai Etzioni, *My Brother's Keeper: A Memoir and a Message* (Lanham, MD: Rowman & Littlefield, 2003).

39. For additional discussion of authoritarian governments and reality testing, see Betty Glad, "Why Tyrants Go Too Far: Malignant Narcissism and Absolute Power," *Political Psychology* 23 (2002): 1–37.

40. Thomas Kuhn, *The Structure of Scientific Revolutions* (Chicago, IL: University of Chicago Press, 1962).

41. "Diversity within Unity: A New Approach to Immigrants and Minorities," *Responsive Community* 13, no. 1 (Winter 2002/2003): 24–40.

42. Bernard Berelson and Gary A. Steiner, *Human Behavior: An Inventory of Scientific Findings* (New York, NY: Harcourt, Brace & World, 1964).

43. Karl Mannheim, *Man and Society in an Age of Reconstruction* (New York, NY: Harcourt, Brace and Company, 1951 [1940]), 83, and Karl Mannheim, *Ideology and Utopia: An Introduction to the Sociology of Knowledge* (New York, NY: Harcourt, Brace and World, Inc., 1951 [1936]), 153–64.

44. See Russell Jacoby, *The Last Intellectuals: American Culture in the Age of Academe* (New York, NY: Basic Books, 1987), 135–39.

45. Brouwer and Squires, 205.

46. See, for instance, two recent critiques of public intellectuals: Richard A. Posner, "In Over Their Heads," *Boston Globe*, 27 January 2002, C1; and Richard A. Posner, "The Professors Profess," *Atlantic Monthly*, February 2002, 28.

47. "The Future of the Public Intellectual: A Forum," *The Nation*, 12 February 2001, 26.

48. "The Future of the Public Intellectual: A Forum," *The Nation*, 12 February 2001, 28–29.

49. Posner, *Public Intellectuals: A Study of Decline*, 35.

50. Jean Bethke Elshtain, "Why Public Intellectuals?" *Wilson Quarterly* 25, no. 4 (2001): 43.

51. John Cassidy, "Height of Eloquence," *The New Yorker*, 30 November 1998, 70–75.

52. Leon Wieseltier, "All and Nothing at All," *The New Republic*, 6 March 1995, 31.

53. Thomas Mallon, "Billions and Billions," *The New Yorker*, 22 November 1999, 196.

54. Peter Berkowitz, "Reckless Disregard," *National Review Online*, 22 July 2001: LexisNexis.

55. Posner, *Public Intellectuals: A Study of Decline* (Cambridge, MA: Harvard University Press, 2001), 73.

56. Irving Howe, "This Age of Conformity," *Partisan Review* 21 (Jan/Feb. 1954), 14.

57. Mark Krupnick, "Why Are English Departments Still Fighting the Culture Wars?" *The Chronicle of Higher Education*, 20 September 2002, 16.

58. Patrick Saveau, "Forum," *PMLA* 112 (1997): 1127.

59. See, for instance, Sidney I. Dobrin, "Race and the Public Intellectual: A Conversation with Michael Eric Dyson," *JAC: A Journal of Composition Theory* 17 (1997): 155.

60. "The Future of the Public Intellectual: A Forum," *The Nation*, 12 February 2001, 30–31.

61. Ellen Cushman, "The Public Intellectual, Service Learning, and Activist Research," *College English* 61 (1999): 329.

62. Walter Dean Burnham, "Lions Under the Throne, Dissenters, Prophets, and Plain Academics: What (If Anything) Does American Political Development Have to Say to External Publics?" *Polity* 32 (2000): 309.

63. C. Wright Mills, *The Sociological Imagination* (New York, NY: Grove Press, 1959), 73.

64. Mills, *The Sociological Imagination* (New York, NY: Grove Press, 1959), 33.

65. Herbert Gans describes this dilemma for the sociologist. See Herbert Gans, "Sociology in America: The Discipline and the Public," *American Sociological Review* 54 (1989): 1–16.

66. Lewis Coser sees opportunities for both academic and bohemian public intellectuals to ensure the quality of their work and faults the rise of the "celebrity intellectual" for loosening controls over public intellectual work. Lewis Coser, "The Intellectual as Celebrity," *Dissent* 20 (Winter 1973): 46–56.

67. Alarm about the decline of public intellectuals extends back to the beginning the twentieth century (see Harold Stearns, "Where Are Our Intellectuals?" in

America and the Young Intellectual, ed. Harold Stearns [New York, NY: George H. Doran, 1921], 46–51) and concern was particularly acute in the 1950s. See, for instance, Irving Howe, "This Age of Conformity," *Partisan Review* 21 (Jan/Feb. 1954): 7–33; H. Stuart Hughes, "Is the Intellectual Obsolete? The Freely Speculating Mind in America," *Commentary* 22 (1956): 313–19; Merle Kling, "The Intellectual: Will He Wither Away?" *New Republic*, 8 April 1957, 14–15.

68. Donald Davie, "Academicism and Jonathan Swift," *The Twentieth Century* 154 (1953): 217.

69. Russell Jacoby, *The Last Intellectuals: American Culture in the Age of Academe* (New York: Basic Books, 1987), 19.

70. Bruce Bawer, "Public Intellectuals: An Endangered Species?," *Chronicle of Higher Education*, 24 April 1998, A72.

71. "The Future of the Public Intellectual: A Forum," *The Nation*, 12 February 2001, 29.

72. "The Future of the Public Intellectual: A Forum," *The Nation*, 12 February 2001, 28.

73. Robert S. Boynton, "The New Intellectuals," *Atlantic Monthly*, March 1995, 53.

74. James Atlas still sees an intellectual atmosphere in New York, although it is different from the atmosphere of the 1940s and 1950s, James Atlas, "The Changing World of New York Intellectuals," *New York Times Magazine*, 25 August 1985, 71. Howard Young agrees that culture and technology are different today, but argues that intellectuals are alive and well, Howard Young, "Forum," *PMLA* 112 (1997): 1126; Herbert Gans has commented that while public intellectuals today are different from those in the past, there are still "lots of them" today, "The Future of the Public Intellectual: A Forum," *The Nation*, 12 February 2001, 30.

75. Carlin Romano, "The Dirty Little Secret about Public Intellectuals," *The Chronicle of Higher Education*, 19 February 1999, B4.

76. Jacoby, *The Last Intellectuals*, 56.

77. Joseph Epstein, "Intellectuals—Public and Otherwise," *Commentary*, May 2000, 51.

78. Epstein, "Intellectuals—Public and Otherwise," *Commentary*, May 2000, 51.

79. "The Future of the Public Intellectual: A Forum," *The Nation*, 12 February 2001, 28.

80. "The Future of the Public Intellectual: A Forum," *The Nation*, 12 February 2001, 29.

81. Posner, *Public Intellectuals: A Study of Decline*, 52.

82. Alan Wolfe, "The Calling of the Public Intellectual," *Chronicle of Higher Education*, 25 May 2001, 20.

83. Joseph Epstein, "Intellectuals—Public and Otherwise," *Commentary*, May 2000, 50.

84. Jacoby, *The Last Intellectuals*, 73.

85. Jacoby, *The Last Intellectuals*, 6.

86. Jacoby, *The Last Intellectuals*, 72.

87. Jacoby, *The Last Intellectuals*, 31; see also Paul Berman, "Intellectuals After the Revolution," *Dissent* 36 (1989): 89.

88. Jacoby, *The Last Intellectuals*, 42–43.

89. Russell Jacoby, "Graying of the Intellectuals," *Dissent* 30 (1983): 237.

90. David Brooks, *Bobos in Paradise: The New Upper Class and How They Got There* (New York, NY: Simon & Schuster, 2000), chapter 4, particularly pp. 174–186.

91. Posner, *Public Intellectuals: A Study of Decline*, 71–82.

92. Irving Howe argues that the independent intellectual of the 1950s was absorbed into the government power structure, which led intellectuals to criticize those in power less than they had before. See Irving Howe, "Intellectuals, Dissent, & Bureaucrats," *Dissent* 31 (1984): 306.

93. Brooks, *Bobos in Paradise*, 148.

94. Brooks, *Bobos In Paradise*, 147.

95. See, for instance, Cynthia Ozick, "Public and Private Intellectuals," *The American Scholar* 64 (1995): 353–358.

96. Posner, *Public Intellectuals: A Study of Decline* (Cambridge, MA: Harvard University Press, 2001). In another recent study, a similar methodology was used to examine the correlation between the scholarly and public reputation of legal scholars. See, Richard A. Posner and William M. Landes, "Citations, Age, Fame, and the Web," *Journal of Legal Studies* 29, no. 1 (January 2000): 319–341.

97. See, for instance, Gertrude Himmelfarb, "Judging Richard Posner," review of *Public Intellectuals*, by Richard A. Posner, *Commentary* 113, no. 2 (February 2002): 33–44; Jon Jewett, "Thinking Out Loud and Louder," review of *Public Intellectuals*, by Richard A. Posner, *Policy Review*, April/May 2002, 81–90; and Alan Wolfe, "The Fame Game, review of *Public Intellectuals*, by Richard A. Posner," *New Republic*, 7 January 2002, 34.

98. Posner says that he included the all of the intellectuals named in Charles Kadushin's [*The American Intellectual Elite* (Boston, MA: Little Brown, 1974), 30–31] list of the seventy most prestigious contemporary American intellectuals 1970 and that the rest of the public intellectuals were compiled from a "variety of sources," Richard A. Posner, *Public Intellectuals: A Study of Decline* (Cambridge, MA: Harvard University Press, 2001), 168–169.

99. Posner, *Public Intellectuals: A Study of Decline*, 193.

100. Posner, *Public Intellectuals: A Study of Decline*, 207 (Table 5.2).

101. Posner, *Public Intellectuals: A Study of Decline*, 169, 190–192.

102. Posner, *Public Intellectuals: A Study of Decline*, 169.

103. Posner, *Public Intellectuals: A Study of Decline*, 168, 188–190.

104. Posner, *Public Intellectuals: A Study of Decline*, 170.

105. Posner, *Public Intellectuals: A Study of Decline*, 171–172.

106. Posner, *Public Intellectuals: A Study of Decline*, 174.

107. Posner, *Public Intellectuals: A Study of Decline*, 174.

108. Posner, *Public Intellectuals: A Study of Decline*, 183, 217 (Table 5.7).

109. Posner, *Public Intellectuals: A Study of Decline*, 183, 217 (Table 5.7).

110. See, for instance, David Samuels, "Edmund Wilson and the Public Intellectuals," *Wilson Quarterly* 20 (1996): 102–112.

111. Jean Bethke Elshtain, "Why Public Intellectuals?" *Wilson Quarterly* 25, no. 4 (2001): 43.

112. While by no means a multi-volume history, Theodore Draper does provide an excellent overview of the role of intellectuals in American politics. Theodore Draper, "Intellectuals in Politics," *Encounter* 49 (1977): 47–60.

113. Carla Kaplan, "Citizen Hurst," *Los Angeles Times*, 8 August 1999, 8.

114. Tevi Troy, *Intellectuals and the American Presidency: Philosophers, Jesters, or Technicians* (New York, NY: Rowman & Littlefield, 2002), 5.

115. Troy, *Intellectuals and the American Presidency*, 6; see also Eva Etzioni-Halevy, *The Knowledge Elite and the Failure of Prophecy* (Boston, MA: George Allen & Unwin, 1985), 19.

116. Troy, *Intellectuals and the American Presidency*, 3.

117. Tevi Troy, "All the Presidents' Brains," *The Times Higher Education Supplement*, 5 July 2002, 21.

118. Other authors and their writings have been reported to shape recent American policies. For a discussion, see Michiko Kakutani, "How Books Have Shaped U.S. Policy," *Washington Post*, 5 April 2003, A15.

119. Eva Etzioni-Halevy, *The Knowledge Elite and the Failure of Prophecy* (Boston, MA: George Allen & Unwin, 1985), 19.

120. Troy, *Intellectuals and the American Presidency*, 15.

121. Benjamin R. Barber, *The Truth of Power: Intellectual Affairs in the Clinton White House* (New York, NY: W. W. Norton, 2001).

122. Kakutani, "How Books Have Shaped U.S. Policy," A23.

123. Troy, *Intellectuals and the American Presidency*, 196.

124. Personal observations of the author.

Chapter 1

WHAT ARE PUBLIC INTELLECTUALS? DEFINITION AND OVERVIEW

Public Intellectuals, Public Life, and the University*

Daniel C. Brouwer and Catherine R. Squires[1]

The figure of the public intellectual galvanizes the imagination and catalyzes social commentary. Examination of contemporary debates about public intellectuals draws our attention to competing claims about the health of public life, the conditions and resources of academe, and the relations between the academy and public life. In our analysis of popular commentary about public intellectuals we discern three major topoi: breadth, site, and legitimacy. Additionally, we explore the ways in which John Dewey imagined the relationships between schools and public life, and we argue that reference to Dewey helps to illuminate contemporary discussion about public intellectuals. We conclude with a framework for understanding and practicing public intellectualism today.

In 1999, Florida Atlantic University (FAU) commenced its "Public Intellectuals Program," an interdisciplinary, Ph.D. degree-granting program in Comparative Studies. Writing about the new program in *The Chronicle of Higher Education*, Alison Schneider remarked: "Starting a Ph.D. program for public intellectuals is a little like hanging a target on your back during hunting season" (1999). The analogy was apt, for educators, academics, activists, and lay people alike leveled potshots at the program. Some took offense at the hubris of the program and its goals, claiming that classroom instruction cannot adequately nurture public intellectuals and that, besides, public intellectuals might be nurtured but cannot be manufactured in any academic program. Others criticized the program's overly

*This article first appeared in *Argumentation and Advocacy* 39, no. 3 (2003): 201–213. Reprinted with permission.

narrow conception of "public" and its redundancy. Skepticism toward the program even took a geographical bias, as Schneider noted the perception that one is much more likely to find a palm tree than a public intellectual on a Florida campus.

This adumbration of the controversy engendered by the FAU program draws attention to the nexus of universities, public intellectuals, and public life. In this and similar controversies, participants express concern about the health of society, about the proper goals and means of education, and about the relationship of education to public life. Prominent in discussions of this nexus are voices of skepticism about the animating and ameliorative capabilities of educational institutions. From the Right, critics of educational institutions and practices decry fragmentation, the emphasis on identity and marginality, and the collapse of normative standards. From the Left, critics of education rail against capitalist principles that undergird education, corporate colonization of the university "lifeworld," and the marginalization imposed upon radical forms of scholarship. From multiple directions, folks wonder if scholarship produced in higher education can be counted on to have measurable impact on social well-being. These concerns congregate in anxieties over the lives and works of public intellectuals.

In this essay, we examine the dynamics of commentary and controversy about public intellectuals in the mainstream press from 1987 to 2002.[2] Commentary about the relationships between public intellectuals, universities, and public life has been especially robust since 1987. In that year and since, book-length treatises such as Allan Bloom's *The Closing of the American Mind* (1987), Russell Jacoby's *The Last Intellectuals* (1987), Richard Rorty's *Achieving Our Country* (1998), and Richard Posner's *Public Intellectuals* (2001) have spurred and influenced much public commentary. While not every debate about public intellectuals since 1987 draws exclusively from these authors' theories and agendas, these books demarcate a flurry of scholarly and lay activity concerning intellectuals that meshed with other widespread public controversies: the "culture wars," affirmative action, and reconstruction of the welfare state, to name a few. As such, the publication of these books and the implementation of FAU's program provide a timeline for exploring the contemporary meanings and debates surrounding the figure of the public intellectual.

Study of this widespread commentary and controversy has the potential to tell us much about "the public" and about the relationship between higher educational institutions and public life. The ways in which journalists and critics defined public intellectuals necessarily invoked particular understandings of what is "public." In turn, these variations provided competing normative models for social life. For example, definitions of public intellectuals in which they were positioned outside of the academy exposed a manifest, sometimes latent, skepticism about the social functions of universities. The comments that we unearthed generally assert that public life is in poor health, that public intellectuals are nonexistent, ineffectual, or inscrutable, and that universities are poorly equipped to affect positive change on these fronts.

In the remaining pages, we briefly chart the historical development of the notion of "public intellectual" as context for understanding the contours of the contemporary controversy over such figures. We next delineate themes, or topoi, about public intellectuals in popular publications and demonstrate how these themes are linked to narratives of the decline of universities and of the public sphere. In our third major section, we mine John Dewey's major writings for his remarks about the relationships between education, public intellectuals, and public life as a way of trying to make sense of the contemporary debate. The recent iteration of debate about public intellectuals postdates, of course, Dewey's writings, but Dewey's emphasis on "social intelligence" and associated living and his normative models for the ways in which knowledge production should assist the modern society resonate with and can speak to the contemporary debate over the roles, relevance, and existence of public intellectuals. Finally, we offer a framework for understanding—and practicing—public intellectualism in the twenty-first century.

THE ORIGINS OF "PUBLIC INTELLECTUALS"

The term "public intellectual" seems to be a modern invention. Many scholars locate its earliest iteration in late nineteenth-century France, when the term "engaged intellectual" emerged in the wake of the Dreyfus affair to describe the intellectuals who were vocal in their criticism of the state's conduct around the trial and the reaction of civil society (Sadri, 2000). Such engagement with political affairs was, apparently, new for intellectuals who were supposed to be concerned with only abstract philosophical ideas. In the United States, the term "public intellectual" has been attributed to a 1958 statement by C. Wright Mills (Jacoby, 1987), although in recent years some writers have erroneously credited Russell Jacoby with coining the term in his book, *The Last Intellectuals*. Although 1958 is the date most often cited, Mills' earlier essays showed a concern for the role of intellectuals in public life. In 1944, he wrote the essay, "The Social Role of the Intellectual," building on John Dewey's (1935/1963) pragmatic challenge to liberal and leftist intellectuals to convert their social scientific work into publicly available and useful knowledge. Although he believed in the necessity of intellectual and artistic involvement in public life, Mills was pessimistic about the institutional and political barriers faced by intellectuals. Specifically, his essay cautioned that independent artists and intellectuals were less and less in a position to access wider publics due to the growing influence of universities and commercial mass publishing on "how, when, and upon what (intellectuals) . . . will work and write" (Mills, 1944/1963, p. 297). Despite these limiting influences on intellectual expression, Mills proclaimed that it was the duty of intellectuals to become engaged and to "be aware of the sphere of strategy that is really open" to intellectual influence (p. 300).

In a later essay, "On Knowledge and Power," he outlined the role of the public intellectual as one who is "the moral conscience of his society" (Mills, 1958/1963, p. 611). One comes to occupy such a role through the deployment of individual knowledge to the benefit of society. In a tone strikingly similar to Dewey's comments on social intelligence, Mills wrote that "what knowledge does to a man [sic] (in clarifying what he is and setting it free)—that is the personal ideal of knowledge. What knowledge does to civilization (in revealing its human meaning, and setting it free)—that is the social ideal of knowledge" (p. 606). The characterization of knowledge as a means for clarifying one's subjectivity and the possibility of freedom through knowledge underscore the modern—more specifically, liberal—principles undergirding this version of public intellectualism. To occupy the grand role of moral conscience requires the grand liberal theme of the sovereign subject and the ability to imagine a broad, coherent public in the manner of John Dewey's "Great Community."

In 1987, Jacoby brought the term "public intellectual" back into general parlance. Journalists and critics took up and circulated the term in their commentary about "culture wars" and a new generation of vocal, media—friendly scholars, artists, and writers. In the academic and popular presses similar questions arose about these new public intellectuals: can university-trained specialists and/or avant-garde thinkers speak to general public issues with authority? Is academe a sufficient locus for public thought? And, finally, could the new crop of public intellectuals whose work centered on issues of identity speak to and for heterogeneous publics or only that public from which they ostensibly emerged? In the writings that we examined, responses to these questions varied, but the responses congregated around three major themes.

POPULAR COMMENTARY ON THE "PUBLIC INTELLECTUAL"

We amplify three major topoi about public intellectuals: breadth, location, and legitimacy. We confess outright that the topoi share some conceptual overlap, but we believe that our mapping of the controversy over public intellectuals elucidates the contours well. Each of these topics is accompanied by narratives about the decline of public life and universities. A consistent refrain, for example, is that today's public intellectuals pale in comparison to their early twentieth-century counterparts or at least are in need of revitalization to become as great as their predecessors. Yet inevitable decline and incorrigible malaise compete with threads of optimism about public intellectuals. Central to this optimism, for example, is a reconsideration of "authentic" modes of publicness. In the next several pages, we summarize and evaluate the details of these themes of public intellectualism.

Breadth

The topic of breadth takes several forms: the breadth of one's learning and training, the range of topics that one can address; the magnitude of the issues that one can address; the depth of knowledge about issues that one addresses; the range of "products" that one might create; and the extent of actual or possible audience members for the intellectual's work. The dominant narrative begins with the assertion that in the first half of the twentieth century, public intellectuals were in abundance. They were well-traveled and broadly educated men of letters who could speak on a myriad of topics and were listened to by important sectors of the public, thereby shaping public opinion and, in the case of some who gained access to political powerbrokers, public policy. Today, however, intellectuals are concentrated in universities that demand specialization in narrow fields of study. Thus, today's crop of intellectuals is no longer trained to do the kind of intellectual work that reaches beyond the ivory tower.

On the Left, Russell Jacoby, author of *The Last Intellectuals*, champions this narrative. As Krupnik wrote in his review of that book, Jacoby argues that "the independent non-specialist intellectuals of the 1940s and 50s who wrote for a large general public have been succeeded by professors who write for one another and tenure" (1987). On the Right, Lynne Cheney and Allan Bloom function as spokespersons for the narrative. They proffer the charge that faddish, "politically correct" theories and methodologies have stifled intellectual creativity and freedom and substituted arcane vocabularies that none but the specialists can understand, thus narrowing rather than broadening public thought. Exceptional individuals can fight these structural and political forces, however, by securing a broad education (especially one steeped in the humanities) and thus expanding the range of topics about which they might competently speak.

Public intellectuals should be able to speak about a wide range of topics, but they should also address serious or grand issues and should do so with exquisite depth of knowledge, according to another variation on the topic of breadth. Not just any topic but serious topics involving universal values or national or international (rather than local) issues should be the public intellectual's proper domain (Bawer, 1998, p. A72). From public intellectuals, we might justifiably expect a broad range of "products," from opinion to predictions, from possible solutions to public policy, from change to social justice (Samuelson, 2002; Boynton, 1991; Rosenfeld, 2001). Each intellectual might specialize in a particular type of product or outcome, or he might best work on multiple fronts simultaneously (Rosenfeld, 2001).[3]

Crucial to earning the status of public intellectual is the ability to find or cultivate a broad audience. Here, radio and televisual technologies play a significant role, serving as media through which the scholar disseminates ideas. In some cases, media access is insufficiently public, however, for the intellectual must also successfully translate heady academic idiom into accessible, plain language. Presumably, vernacular language invites wider audiences and wider audiences, in turn, predict greater social or political effectiveness (Yardley, 1987; Bawer, 1998). In this view, "public" construed as "accessible to" is more public than "public" construed as "in view or sound of."[4] In other words, public intellectuals are only truly public if they can speak about issues in a way that resonates with an imagined lay public.

Besides media access and plain language, intellectuals need to be nonpartisan and non-ideological, or at least open to other ideologies, to secure the broadest possible public. Indeed, although one might address issues that are relevant to a political community and may do so before lay audiences, his status as a public intellectual might be compromised to the extent that he is clearly aligned with a particular ideology or party. An advocate, activist, or lobbyist he might be, but not a public intellectual.

Although there are certainly contemporary scholars who are dubbed public intellectuals because of the sufficient breadth of their work, their range was often an object of discussion. Some were chastised for being too broad or trying to play to too many publics such that their message fails through dilution. Oftentimes, this critique is bound up with complaints about intellectuals who are media gadflies, expanding their book sales and public recognition by chiming in on whatever is fashionable on the public agenda. For example, in a feature on Cornel West, the author quoted a few scholars who disagree with Dr. West's populism, including Adolph Reed's declaration that "Cornel's work tends to be 1,000 miles wide and about two inches deep" (Boynton, 1991). Another article noted that "one skeptical professor described one new public intellectual journal as 'a bulletin board for fashionable academics to talk about things they know little about'" (Scott, 1994). It is possible, then, to be too broad in one's intellectual endeavors, but writers and commentators offer few explicit criteria for reining in or focusing one's work.

Site/Location

The varieties of breadth and their concomitant crises bring up a related issue: where are public intellectuals based, and where should they publish or speak their ideas to gain the eyes and ears of audiences outside academia? Responses to these questions raise issues about the sites and locations of intellectuals and their work. On this topic, some commentators repeat Russell Jacoby's famous narrative in which the explosive growth of universities, concurrent with the decay of once vibrant cities with "bohemian" neighborhoods, sent intellectuals flocking to expanding universities in order to make a living (e.g., Yardley, 1987). As smaller publications and publishing houses went under and patrons ran in short supply, the bohemian atmosphere vanished from cities, depriving intellectuals of alternative locations for their work, debate with fellow thinkers, and the ability to stay in touch with the "real world." Pressure to specialize and publish in top journals read only by scholars led to an insularity among scholars, who became more invested in the politics of tenure than in the issues of the people. Although think tanks and foundations emerged as non-university options, their partisan tendencies were seen as suspect and not conducive to fostering thought untainted by the political goals of the organizers (Wolfe, 2001; Blumenthal, 1988).

In this narrative, the university is an ambivalent site. According to some journalists and critics, the university is unable to facilitate or sustain publicly relevant work; thus, public intellectuals are primarily or exclusively to be found outside academe (Yardley, 2000; Bawer, 1998, p. A72). Here, the university is also construed as a stifling place where intellectuals who want to cultivate broad knowledge—especially conservative academics—are no longer accepted. When asked why so many conservative intellectuals worked in think tanks like the Heritage Foundation, Lynne Cheney responded that the universities' criteria for professors had changed for the worse: "the rules of what you had to do to get ahead in life were different [before in academia]," she said. "It wasn't a matter of publishing in those journals that were read by three people and your mother, but of writing in places where people might generally read what you wrote" (Scott, 1994).

According to others, the university can function as one of the multiple fronts on which scholars conduct and present their work. Many scholars are quick to debunk the idea that their university careers are antithetical to the life and goals of public intellectuals. Explaining why he chose to leave the University of Chicago for Harvard, William Julius Wilson claimed, "I made the move because I wanted to be around a community of scholars who are public intellectuals, people who are doing very, very careful work but are concerned about reaching a wide audience, people who are concerned about the direction of the country and are trying to influence public perception, public policy" (quoted in Applebome, 1996). One promising avenue for reaching outside the site of the university was noted: publishing outside of the specialist journals lampooned above in Cheney's statement. A public intellectual could remain in a professorial post and be relevant by getting work into newspapers and magazines read by larger audiences (e.g., Kershaw, 1996). Even greater evidence of a public intellectual's relevance outside the ivory tower was if, like Fannie Hurst in the first half of the 1900s, she could gain entry to sites of political and media power. About Hurst, one journalist wrote that "her writing was as likely to appear in the pages of leading newspapers as she was in the conference rooms of the White House, where her friends the Roosevelts gave her an open invitation" (Kaplan, 1999).

Finally, to some commentators, the university is fundamental to the improvement of public life. Indeed, William Damon, in an article titled "The Path to a Civil Society Goes Through the University," criticized the authors of a special report on civil society for making scant reference to universities as sites relevant to a rejuvenation of public life (1998, pp. B4–5). "On their own turf," he claims, "in the realm of ideas, intellectuals can . . . play a decisive role in redeeming civil society" (p. B5). In the forums of their classrooms, Damon argued, academics could and should inculcate principles and habits of civic virtue. Such invocations of the university as the primary means for rejuvenating public life are rare, but they merit attention here for their resonance with rhetorical training in the field of communication studies. As Ron Greene astutely observes elsewhere in this issue (*Argumentation and Advocacy*), rhetorical training historically has presumed as its goals the cultivation of the liberal, humanist subject and the improvement of civil society. In contemporary discussion about public intellectuals, this notion lingers although its force has been enervated.

Legitimacy

Variations on the topic of legitimacy focus on: the degree of one's partisanship or ideological commitments; the quality of one's training and credentials; the degree to which one speaks in her own voice; affirmation of one's work by academic elites; and affirmation of one's work by nonacademic communities. Nonpartisanship and expertise appeared earlier under the topic of breadth. There and here, these terms referred to the need to be broad-minded and broadly educated. Such breadth enhances the status of the public intellectual or, in some cases, permits the intellectual to be a public intellectual. When one is not overtly partisan or ideological, she is better able to speak in her own voice, and this bold, unique voice can serve as a legitimizing mark of the public intellectual (Wolfe, 2001;

Bawer, 1998, p. A72). Reflecting upon his experiences as a participant in and witness to a forum on public intellectuals, Alan Wolfe claimed that "it is not whether intellectuals work inside or outside the academy that is important, but whether—in either sphere—they have the courage to find their own voice" (2001).

Proving one's legitimacy is not an easy task given the critiques found in the articles. At minimum, public intellectuals should be as independent as possible: working for personal financial gain and/or fame is suspect, as in the case of Roger Scruton, a professor at the University of London who was found to have received a monthly retainer from tobacco interests (Stille, 2002). Furthermore, public intellectuals are expected to tread a fine line between having impressive academic credentials and the approval or admiration of specialists in their chosen fields and being able to reach out to wider public audiences and/or have some impact on the important debates of the day. If public intellectuals are unable to negotiate these expectations, then they are deemed unsuccessful, illegitimately taking up public attention (Rosenfeld, 2001; Wolfe, 2001).

The question of legitimacy takes on a different tone when applied to academics of color who strive to be public intellectuals. Here, the questions of to whom and for whom can they speak and whether their discipline actually encompasses "general" social issues are at stake. When discussing Black scholars in particular, who were mentioned or featured in many articles due to the ascendancy of Henry Louis Gates, Jr., and the DuBois Institute at Harvard, many writers implied or explicitly stated a belief in a fundamental distance between "the Black community" and "the Black scholar." The questions posed to Black academics who have a high public profile are whether they are "connected" to the "real" Black public sphere, and whether Black Studies can be a legitimate enterprise with or without a strong, practical, uplift-oriented relationship to non-middle class blacks (Applebome, 1996; Fulwood, 1995).

Especially haunted by an obligation to be relevant to their communities, scholars of color are sometimes each other's harshest critics. Asserting her authenticity—measured as the minimum distance between the scholar and the figure of the working-class black person—bell hooks proclaimed "there's nothing about the life of an intellectual that should separate you from other people. . . . I think a lot of black intellectuals do that. But unlike other black intellectuals, I am defined by the working-class black experience that I came from" (quoted in Applebome, 1996). According to hooks, one consequence of her commitment to authenticity has been a failure to secure a broader, White public. "The fact that ordinary black people embrace me and my work is one of the factors that keeps me from being celebrated in the same way that Skip Gates and Cornel West are celebrated by white folks," she claims (quoted in Applebome). If hooks and others (e.g., Fulwood, 1995) are correct, then scholars of color who seek the legitimating force of broad publics risk their credibility and authenticity among members of their racial, ethnic, and/or class communities.

What is interesting about these selections is that there is an overwhelming assumption that academic work by blacks is nearly always "disconnected" from "real black people." As Wahneema Lubiano (1996) points out, this assumption is set into motion by the idea that the "real" blacks are poor or working class, that these two groups outnumber all other class formations for black folks, and that they could not possibly connect with middle-class blacks. This assumption emerges from a shallow reading not only of the diversity in black communities at large, but also the complex relations across and within class that blacks experience and the role of academia in setting political trends. Furthermore, these articles reinforce the location of white scholars at the center/norm, and all other people of color at the margin, looking for a way in to the center. White intellectuals are taken to task for being overly partisan or unreadable by the common citizen, but they are not chastised for being alienated from new European immigrants, poor whites, or any white group one could name. White intellectuals' racial or ethnic identities and associations go unquestioned, even though one could answer that they are just as estranged from the average white blue-collar worker as Gates and West are alleged to be from working-class blacks. Legitimacy, then, is constituted in multiple ways, but particularly for the scholar of color it is constituted by affinity with and affirmation by members of a lay public.

DEWEY ON THE PUBLIC EDUCATION, AND PUBLIC INTELLECTUALS

We now turn our attention away from the contours of contemporary controversy about public intellectuals and toward Dewey's corpus on the public, education, and the relations between them. We begin with a claim that Dewey's corpus serves as an alternately fertile and desolate resource for diagnosis, prognosis, and amelioration of alleged contemporary crises. Fruitfully, Dewey's *optimism about schools as sites relevant to the public good and his recognition of multiple publics* prefigure yet still illuminate contemporary discussion about public intellectuals. In contrast, Dewey *fails to interrogate difference and positionality* to a degree sufficient enough for contemporary political conditions. In the paragraphs that follow, we explore each of these ways in which Dewey's work illuminates or fails to illuminate contemporary controversy.

Optimism about schools as sites relevant to the public good. Dewey's contributions to a critical social theory of his times were multiform and volu-

minous. Central to his diagnosis of social illness and his prognosis of better health were educational institutions and practices. Diagnosing the
health of his times, Dewey claimed that:

> The problem of democracy becomes the problem of that form of social or-
> ganization, extending to all the areas and ways of living, in which the pow-
> ers of individuals shall not be merely released from mechanical external con-
> straint but shall be fed, sustained, and directed (1935/1963, p. 31).

More than just a form of government, democracy was a mode of associated
living characterized by habits of individual growth and mutual obligation.
At risk, democracy needed to be reorganized—and thus revitalized—
through bold acts by liberals. "Such an organization," he continued, "demands much more of education than general schooling, which without a
renewal of the springs of purpose and desire becomes a new mode of
mechanization and formalization, as hostile to liberty as ever was government constraint" (p. 31). Educational structures and practices, then, establish conditions for the health of public life. Employing an organic
metaphor, Dewey asserts that "democracy has to be born anew every generation, and education is its midwife" (quoted in Halliburton, 1997, p. 29).
As the greater the skill of the midwife promises a greater likelihood that
the birth will proceed without complication, the greater the quality of education promises the greater health of democracy.

To salvage education's ameliorative potential, Dewey chastised both
conservative thinkers who presumed education's ameliorative impotency,
and leftist thinkers who presumed that education was incorrigibly and
ineluctably a tool of dominant classes (1940, pp. 354–355). Asserting that
technological, economic, and political changes necessitated reorganiza-
tion of educational structures and practices, Dewey insisted upon an
approach to education that recognized the school as a social institution,
wholly inter-animated with other spheres of human activity (1916,
pp. 430–431). Classrooms were to function as "embryonic [or simplified]
communities" (1916, p. 303) wherein children's different learning styles
were affirmed, where children guided their own instruction, where they
learned full and complex processes, and where they practiced various
modes of associated living. Through experience, practice, and academic
exercises in schools, young students trained their intelligences. Vigor-
ously, Dewey argued that intelligence was not an individual possession
but something that had to be integrated into the social matrix, hence his
call for us to think of "social intelligence" rather than individual intelligence. Social intelligence was necessary to confront and provide an alternative to the power "exercised by the propaganda of publicity agents and
that of organized pressure groups" (1935/1963, p. 47).

In spite of his spirited defense of the role of education in public life, he was forced to admit that:

> It is unrealistic . . . to suppose that the schools can be a main agency in producing the intellectual and moral changes, the changes in attitudes and disposition of thought and purpose, which are necessary for the creation of a new social order. Any such view ignores the constant operation of powerful forces outside the school which shape mind and character. (p. 355)

Neither autonomous nor the prime mover of social change, in Dewey's rubric education stands in organic relationship with, alternately in harmony and in discord, government, the economy, "the public," and other spheres of human activity.

Dewey's eloquent defense of schools as publicly relevant sites resonates with several of the themes that we see in contemporary discussion about public intellectuals. First, we find that a Deweyan vision of organic relations between publics motivates the criticism that academics have largely failed to embed themselves in other publics. In this view, academics are accused of being unable or unwilling to contribute their "social intelligence" for social change. Additionally, we find that Dewey represents a middle position, neither fully skeptical toward nor fully confident in schools as agents of social change. In our reading, Dewey serves as a source of generalized optimism for those who want to engage in more public work, but he is notoriously short on details for making this happen. At a general level, Rosa Eberly's (2000) description of classrooms as "protopublic spaces" (p. 169) serves as a contemporary invigoration of Dewey's notions of schools as "embryonic communities." As a companion to Dewey's recognition of "powerful forces *outside* the school" (emphasis added), Eberly recognizes the institutional constraints and power dynamics within the university classroom that compromise its status as fully public (p. 169). Yet, like Dewey and some contemporary commentators, she affirms the classroom as a type of "training ground" for participation in other publics and, in doing so, affirms the relevance of the university to wider publics.

Because Dewey focused most of his commentary on the K–12 educational system in the United States, he does not offer much guidance in accounting for universities as sites of specialized knowledge with specialized idioms. The question remains: if we affirm universities as sites of specialized knowledge, how feasible is it for university educators to cultivate organic relations with other publics? In Dewey's stead, contemporary scholar Wahneema Lubiano illustrates how visions of the academy and its brand of specialized, individual intelligence are used not only to preclude outsiders from pursuing intellectual work but also to denigrate particular types of intellectual work. Writing about Black public intellectualism, Lubiano laments the "many times [that] certain Black intellectual work has been dismissed because (a) it won't save crack babies in the ghetto, or (b) it won't reach the brother on the street corner" (1996, p. 74). Her analysis exposes the "ivory tower" metaphor as ideological and untenable just as Dewey's notion of "social intelligence" compels intellectuals to seek integration of their scholarly work with wider publics. In a different vein, Michael Warner (2002) defends academic jargons as legitimate idioms unto themselves and as means for conjuring "publics" of scholars. Untroubled by a demand to translate scholarly work into more accessible language, Warner condemns the assumption that accessible language garners more audiences and, in turn, promises greater political and social impact of one's work (see pp. 128–151).

Recognition of multiple publics. Dewey's famous account of the rise of publics via the perception of consequences that extend beyond those immediately involved merits brief reminder here. When organization of individuals is coupled with perception of social consequences, a public emerges (1927/ 1954, pp. 3–36). To this account of publics, we draw attention to Dewey's recurrent emphasis on "associated living," or habits of interaction and interdependence. Through various modes of associated living, people sustain publics. But as exigence, spirit, or both wane, publics, too, wane or pass away. Thus, Dewey recognized the existence of multiple publics under conditions of flux. In Asen's reading of *The Public and Its Problems* elsewhere in this volume (*Argumentation and Advocacy*), Dewey shows himself to be especially concerned about the quality of the relations between these multiple publics.

This concern is fundamental to the debate over public intellectuals today. About intellectuals in academe, critics ask, in a sense: how can they relate their work to other publics? Journalists and critics typically recognize multiple publics, but complications in the relations between publics arise. First, to some, academe does not constitute a public and thus its relations to "authentic" publics are strained at best. From this perspective derives views of universities as enclaved, publicly irrelevant "ivory towers" as noted above. Second, some commentators privilege a grand, general public as the most authentic public and presume that truly *publicly* intellectual work is related directly and primarily or exclusively toward this grand public. This perspective obscures or fails to recognize the ways in which scholars relate their work to smaller, more discrete publics. To both of these complications, Dewey offers conceptual optimism. On the one hand, Dewey insists that schools are types of publics—"embryonic communities," as noted above—and that schools can and must be organically related to other spheres of life. On the other hand, if we read Dewey as Asen does, then the critique of public intellectuals who do not address themselves to a grand, broad public is exposed as a straw figure. This is not to say that scholars should not worry about the Great Community; it is to say, however, that Dewey compels us to recognize multiple publics and to validate the university's relations with these varied types.

Interrogation of difference and positionality. While we affirm the riches of Dewey's corpus for our task at hand, we also recognize the limitations of his work. Most notably for the purposes of this essay, Dewey failed to interrogate difference and positionality in a manner sufficient to understand contemporary debates about public intellectuals. One form of this failure is his unproblematic assumption of a particular, liberal-humanist subject-position, as Greene astutely observes elsewhere in this issue (*Argumentation and Advocacy*).[5] A second form of this failure appears in his under theorization of deployments and inequities of power in educational institutions and policies (Seigfried, 2002, p. 9; Lagemann, 2002, pp. 33, 45). As a result, in his own time Dewey failed to anticipate the difficulties faced by a largely female instructor population in interactions with an incipient and largely male administrator population. Additionally, he failed to acknowledge fully the force of prejudice and the extensive barriers to inclusion faced by women, people of color, and others (Seigfried, 2002, pp. 49, 55). Professing faith in educational and public mechanisms that promoted the development and recognition of human subjects, Dewey was insufficiently skeptical about the effects of individual and collective acts of racism, sexism, and so forth.

This insufficiency is brought into significant relief through consideration of the legitimacy struggles of black public intellectuals. In one sense, the black public intellectual functions as a synecdoche for what allegedly ails public life and education today. This figure is especially obligated to produce relevant work that will have positive, measurable impact on her particular communities. But in fulfilling this obligation, this figure is necessarily partisan to her particular communities and thus not "public" enough. Alternatively, if this figure strives too hard to secure a broad public, she risks compromising her authenticity and relevance to her communities.

We do not deny the force of these competing assumptions, nor do we discount the unique constraints imposed upon the legitimacy of Black public intellectuals, but we argue that in a general sense the Black public intellectual can stand for the multiple possibilities of contemporary public intellectuals. The dilemma of the black intellectual reported and summarized above represents in heightened form the dilemma of all people who want to do scholarly work that has social impact. Academics must recognize their privileged positions in the academy, but they must also struggle to imagine how scholarly and pedagogical activities potentially relate to other publics. Academics must recognize their need to demonstrate competency in a narrow field of specialized knowledge, but they must also find ways to extend the breadth and circulation of their work beyond a public of academics.

TOWARD CONTEMPORARY PUBLIC INTELLECTUAL WORK

Despite the one-hundred-year period since he began publishing and the fifty-year period since his death, Dewey's writings on the relationships between education and public life remain relevant. Although political, economic, cultural, and technological changes have altered the landscape, Dewey's critical vocabulary remains relevant for contemporary discussions due in large part to both the broad scope of his writings and the persistence of the exigencies that motivated many of his writings. Current debate about the ends and means of public intellectualism iterates Dewey's insistence on the inter-animating nature of public life and educational structures and practices. Hitched together in narratives of demise, the two phenomena also hold the potential to gallop together toward progressive social change.

Should contemporary academics strive to make their work more "public"? If so, what forms might public intellectual work take? We answer the first question in the affirmative. And in the spirit of reclaiming the possibility of public intellectualism, we propose the following outline for understanding and performing public intellect. First, we advocate a particular perceptual orientation toward the university. Following Dewey, Eberly, and Mitchell (2000), we call for recognizing the university as a type of public that is inextricably bound to other spheres (such as the state and the official economy) and other publics. This perceptual orientation affirms the potential impact of the university classroom, the importance of intellectual work at the university, and the possibility of making that work relevant elsewhere. In the view of many, one specific and effective route for cultivating academic relevance to wider publics is through academic service learning (ASL). Many practitioners, scholars, and educators of service learning have drawn inspiration from Dewey; indeed, Kezar and Rhoads (2001) name Dewey as a "founding voice in the service-learning movement" (p. 150). In the field of communication, David Droge and Bren Murphy's (1999) edited volume *Voices of Strong Democracy* and the Communicating Common Ground program co-sponsored by the National Communication Association serve as exemplars of ongoing work on the front of service learning.

Second, we call for recognition of plural definitions of "public" and "publics." Often, perceptions of waning public intellectualism pivot on unduly narrow definitions of the public. Cushman (1999) argues against a "narrow delineation of the word 'public'—. . . a public consisting of middle and upper class policy makers, administrators, and professionals . . . [which] omit[s] an important site for uniting knowledge-making and political action: the local community" (p. 328). By embracing a framework of multiple publics—local and national, enduring and temporary—we can better recognize and affirm the meaningful work that scholars do for local, particular communities. In our call for greater recognition of multiple publics, we neither endorse intellectuals' self-evacuation from wide, grand, power publics nor Dewey's consternation about the proliferation of too many uncoordinated publics. Instead, we suggest a need to re-think the concept of the public and the grand progress narrative of liberalism and social action that Dewey describes. And we affirm the importance of oscillation between scholarly and wider lay audiences, the ideal result of which would be relevance through translation of knowledge across publics.

In addition to recognizing different types of publics, we also draw attention to the multiple meanings of "public." Variations of "public" range from known to all, accessible to all, relevant to all, related to the state, national in scope, and more (Asen & Brouwer, 2001, p. 1; Warner, 2002, p. 29). Clearly, not all invocations of "public"—and of public intellectual work—are the same. To prefer one particular meaning of "public" is to posit a particular criterion or limited set of criteria for what counts as authentically public work. For example, a quantitative study that uses U.S. Census data to explain the constitution of a particular neighborhood, written in an academic idiom, may not be "public" in the sense of *known to* or *accessible to* but might be profoundly public in the sense of *relevant to* the neighborhood in the form of reapportionment of municipal, state, or federal resources and reconfiguration of legislative districts.

Finally, we call for greater institutional and material recognition of these multiple forms of public intellectual work. This includes both valuing and fostering public work. For example, for those who pursue service learning, institutions might provide or require training or certification, involve all faculty in some sort of service learning, and provide release time or course load reduction for those who elaborately embed themselves in community work—as when institutions grant release time to journal editors.[6] Institutions might also do a better job of acknowledging the public relevance of writings and other creative activities that occur in nonacademic settings, the creation of nonacademic artifacts, and other ways in which academics share their expertise in local arenas. Along these lines, some grant foundations require applicants to link explicitly their academic endeavor to a discernible community and discernible public outcomes. To the extent that these funding agencies recognize a plurality of publics, they do much to promote the lives and works of contemporary public intellectuals.

NOTES

1. Daniel C. Brouwer is an Assistant Professor of Communication at Arizona State University. Catherine R. Squires is an Assistant Professor of Communication and of Afroamerican and African Studies at the University of Michigan. Portions of this manuscript were presented at the 2001 annual meeting of the National Communication Association. The authors would like to thank Robert Asen, Cara Finnegan, Ron Greene, and Michele Hammers for their helpful comments. Correspondence concerning this article should be addressed to Daniel C. Brouwer, The Hugh Downs School of Human Communication, Arizona State University, P.O. Box 871205, Tempe, AZ, 85287–1205; brouwer@asu.edu.

2. For data, we searched the *New York Times, Washington Post, Los Angeles Times,* and *Chronicle of Higher Education* for the term "public intellectual" in order to excavate discourses concerning this often chimerical figure. We retrieved over one hundred unduplicated articles, editorials, and book reviews of varying size.

3. Michael Eric Dyson makes this claim in Dobrin (1997, p. 155).

4. Michael Warner (2002), writing about styles of intellectual publics, denounces this reasoning and argues for recognition of opaque academic idiom as legitimate in itself and because it both constitutes and circulates within recognizable publics.

5. Examination of this limitation in Dewey's work is beyond the scope of this essay.

6. For a more extensive list, see Kezar & Rhoads, 2001, pp. 162–166.

REFERENCES

Addams, J. (2002). A toast to John Dewey. In C. H. Seigfried (Ed.), *Feminist interpretations of John Dewey* (pp. 25–30). University Park: Pennsylvania State University Press.

Applebome, P. (1996, November 3). Can Harvard's powerhouse alter the course of Black Studies? *New York Times Education Supplement*, p. 4. Retrieved May 1, 2002, from the LexisNexis database.

Asen, R., & Brouwer, D. C. (2001). Introduction: Reconfigurations of the public sphere. In R. Asen & D. C. Brouwer (Eds.), *Counterpublics and the state* (pp. 1–32). Albany: State University of New York Press.

Bawer, B. (1998). Public intellectuals: An endangered species? *Chronicle of Higher Education, 44*, p. A72.

Bloom, A. (1987). *The closing of the American mind*. New York: Simon and Schuster.

Blumenthal, S. (1988, April 5). Jackson and the brain trust: Jesse's team, coalescing around a common cause. *Washington Post*, p. DI. Retrieved May 1, 2002, from the LexisNexis database.

Boynton, R. (1991, September 15). Princeton's public intellectual. *New York Times Magazine*, p. 39. Retrieved May 1, 2002, from the LexisNexis database.

Cushman, E. (1999). The public intellectual, service learning, and activist research. *College English, 61*, 328336.

Damon, W. (1998). The path to a civil society goes through the university. *Chronicle of Higher Education, 45*, pp. B4–5.

Dewey, J. (1916). *Democracy and education.* New York: The Macmillan Company.

———. (1940). *Education today* (J. Ratner, Ed.). New York: G. P. Putnam's Sons.

———. (1954). *The public and its problems.* Athens, OH: Swallow Press. (Original work published in 1927)

———. (1963). *Liberalism and social action.* New York: Putnam's. (Original work published in 1935)

Dobrin, S. I. (1997). Race and the public intellectual: A conversation with Michael Eric Dyson. *JAC, 17,* 143–181.

Droge, D., & Murphy, B. O. (Eds.). (1999). *Voices of strong democracy: Concepts and models for service-learning in communication studies.* Washington, D.C.: American Association for Higher Education.

Eberly, R. A. (2000). *Citizen critics: Literary public spheres.* Urbana: University of Illinois Press.

Fulwood, III, S. (1995, April 9). An identity of their own. *Los Angeles Times Magazine,* p. 10. Retrieved May 1, 2002, from the LexisNexis database.

Halliburton, D. (1997). John Dewey: A voice that still speaks to us. *Change, 29,* 24–29.

Jacoby, R. (1987). *The last intellectuals: American culture in the age of academe.* New York: Basic Books.

Kaplan, C. (1999, August 8). Citizen Hurst. *Los Angeles Times,* p. 8. Retrieved May 1, 2002, from the LexisNexis database.

Kershaw, S. (1996, December 1). Making it work: Storm center. *New York Times,* p. 3 (sec. 13). Retrieved May 1, 2002, from the LexisNexis database.

Kezar, A., & Rhoads, R. A. (2001). The dynamic tensions of service learning in higher education. *The Journal of Higher Education, 72,* 148–171.

Krupnik, M. (1987, October 25). Today's radicals want tenure. *New York Times,* p. 44 (sec. 7). Retrieved May 1, 2002, from the LexisNexis database.

Lagemann, E. C. (2002). Experimenting with education: John Dewey and Ella Flagg Young at the University of Chicago. In C. H. Seigfried (Ed.), *Feminist interpretations of John Dewey* (pp. 31–46). University Park: Pennsylvania State University Press.

Lubiano, W. (1996). Like being mugged by a metaphor: Multiculturalism and state narratives. In A. F. Gordon & C. Newfield (Eds.), *Mapping multiculturalism* (pp. 64–75). Minneapolis: University of Minnesota Press.

Mills, C. W. (1963a). On knowledge and power. Reprinted in I. L. Horowitz (Ed.), *Power, politics and people: The collected essays of C. Wright Mills* (pp. 599–614). New York: Oxford University Press. (Original work published 1958)

———. (1963b). The social role of the intellectual. Reprinted in I. L. Horowitz (Ed.), *Power, politics and people: The collected essays of C. Wright Mills* (pp. 292–304). New York: Oxford University Press. (Original work published 1944)

Mitchell, G. R. (2000). Simulated public argument as a pedagogical play on worlds. *Argumentation and Advocacy, 36,* 134–150.

Posner, R. A. (2001). *Public intellectuals: A study of decline.* Cambridge, MA: Harvard University Press.

Rorty, R. (1998). *Achieving our country: Leftist thought in twentieth-century America.* Cambridge, MA: Harvard University Press.

Rosenfeld, M. (2001, November 6). Global thinker: Benjamin Barber's ideas on capitalism and conflict no longer seem so academic. *Washington Post*, p. Cl. Retrieved May 1, 2002, from the LexisNexis database.

Sadri, A. (Ed.). (2000). *Reason, freedom, and democracy in Islam: Essential writings of Abdolkarim Soroush* (M. Sadri, Trans.). New York: Oxford University Press.

Samuelson, R. J. (2002, April 24). United in denial: Nobody's facing the realities of an aging society. *Washington Post*, p. A29. Retrieved May 1, 2002, from Lexis-Nexis database.

Schneider, A. (1999). Florida Atlantic U. seeks to mold a different kind of public intellectual. *The Chronicle of Higher Education, 46*, p. B7. Retrieved May 7, 2002, from the EBSCOhost database.

Scott, J. (1994, August 9). Thinking out loud: The public intellectual is reborn. *New York Times*, p. B 1. Retrieved May 1, 2002, from the Lexis/Nexis database.

Seigfried, C. H. (2002a). Introduction. In C. H. Seigfried (Ed.), *Feminist interpretations of John Dewey* (pp. 1–22). University Park: Pennsylvania State University Press.

———. (2002b). John Dewey's pragmatist feminism. In C. H. Seigfried (Ed.), *Feminist interpretations of John Dewey* (pp. 47–77). University Park: Pennsylvania State University Press.

Stille, A. (2002, March 23). Think tank: Advocating tobacco, on the payroll of tobacco. *New York Times*, p. B9. Retrieved May 1, 2002, from the LexisNexis database.

Warner, M. (2002). *Publics and counterpublics*. New York: Zone Books.

Wolfe, A. (2001). The calling of the public intellectual. *Chronicle of Higher Education, 47*, p. B20. Retrieved May 7, 2002, from the EBSCOhost database.

Yardley, J. (1987, October 11). Trapped in the ivory tower. *Washington Post*, p. X3. Retrieved May 1, 2002, from the LexisNexis database.

———. (2000, August 13). American statesman. *Washington Post*, p. X01. Retrieved May 1, 2002, from the LexisNexis database.

The Future of the
Public Intellectual: A Forum*

The following debate is adapted from a forum—put together by Basic Books and held in New York City some weeks ago. Participating were: John Donatich, who moderated and is publisher of Basic Books; Russell Jacoby, who teaches at UCLA and is the author of *The End of Utopia* and *The Last Intellectuals*; Jean Bethke Elshtain, who has served as a board member of the Institute for Advanced Studies at Princeton University, is a fellow of the American Academy of Arts and Sciences, teaches at the University of Chicago and is the author of *Women and War*, *Democracy on Trial*, and a forthcoming intellectual biography of Jane Addams; Stephen Carter, the William Nelson Cromwell Professor of Law at Yale University and author of, among other works, *The Culture of Disbelief*, *Reflections of an Affirmative Action Baby*, *Integrity*, *Civility* and, most recently, *God's Name in Vain: The Wrongs and Rights of Religion in Politics*; Herbert Gans, the Robert S. Lynd Professor of Sociology at Columbia University and author of numerous works, including *Popular Culture and High Culture*, *The War Against the Poor* and *The Levittowners*; Steven Johnson, acclaimed as one of the most influential people in cyberworld by *Newsweek* and *New York Magazine*, co-founder of *Feedmag.com*, the award-winning online magazine, and author of the books *Interface Culture* and the forthcoming *Emergence*; and Christopher Hitchens, a columnist for *The Nation* and *Vanity Fair*, whose books include the bestselling *No One Left to Lie To: The Values*

*This article first appeared in *The Nation*, February 12, 2001, pp. 25–35. Reprinted with permission. For subscription information, call 1-800-333-8536. Portions of each week's *Nation* magazine can be accessed at http://www.thenation.com.

of the Worst Family and *The Missionary Position: Mother Teresa in Theory and Practice*. For Basic, he will be writing the forthcoming *On the Contrary: Letters to a Young Radical*.

John Donatich: As we try to puzzle out the future of the public intellectual, it's hard not to poke a little fun at ourselves, because the issue is that serious. The very words "future of the public intellectual" seem to have a kind of nostalgia built into them, in that we only worry over the future of something that seems endangered, something we have been privileged to live with and are terrified to bury.

In preparing for this event, I might as well admit that I've been worried about making the slip, "the future of the public ineffectual." But I think that malapropism would be central to what we'll be talking about. It seems to me that there is a central conflict regarding American intellectual work. How does it reconcile itself with the venerable tradition of American anti-intellectualism? What does a country built on headstrong individualism and the myth of self-reliance do with its people convinced that they know best? At Basic Books' fiftieth anniversary, it's a good time to look at a publishing company born in mid-century New York City, a time and place that thrived on the idea of the public intellectual. In our first decades, we published Daniel Bell, Nathan Glazer, Michael Walzer, Christopher Lasch, Herb Gans, Paul Starr, Robert Jay Lifton—and these names came fresh on the heels of Levi-Strauss, Freud, Erik Erikson, and Clifford Geertz.

What did these writers have in common except the self-defined right to worry the world and to believe that there is a symbiotic relationship between the private world of the thinker and the public world he or she wishes to address? That the age of great public intellectuals in America has passed has in fact become a cliché. There are many well-reviewed reasons for this. Scholars and thinkers have retreated to the academy. Self-doubt has become the very compass point of contemporary inquiry. Scholarship seems to start with an autobiographical or confessional orientation. The notion that every question has a noble answer or that there are reliable structures of ideology to believe in wholeheartedly has become, at best, quaint.

Some believe that the once-relied-upon audience of learned readers has disappeared, giving way to a generation desensitized to complex argumentation by television and the Internet. The movie *Dumb and Dumber* grosses dozens of millions of dollars at the box office, while what's left of bohemian culture celebrates free-market economics. Selling out has more to do with ticket grosses than the anti-materialist who stands apart from society.

How do we reconcile ambition and virtue, expertise and accessibility, multicultural sensitivity and the urge toward unified theory? Most important, how do we reconcile the fact that disagreement is a main catalyst of progress? How do we battle the gravitation toward happy consensus that paralyzes our national debate? A new generation of public intellectuals waits to be mobilized. What will it look like? That is what our distinguished panelists will discuss.

Russell Jacoby has been useful in defining the role of the public intellectual in the past half-century, especially in the context of the academy. Can you, Russell, define for us a sort of historical context for the public intellectual—what kind of talent, courage and/or political motivation it takes for someone to be of the academy but to have his or her back turned to it, ready to speak to an audience greater than one's peers?

Russell Jacoby: A book of mine that preceded *The Last Intellectuals* was on the history of psychoanalysis. And one of the things I was struck by when I wrote it was that even though psychoanalysis prospered in the United States, something was missing—that is, the sort of great refugee intellectuals, the Erik Eriksons, the Bruno Bettelheims, the Erich Fromms, were not being reproduced. As a field it prospered, but it became medicalized and professionalized. And I was struck by both the success of this field and the absence of public voices of the Eriksons and Bettelheims and Fromms. And from there I began to consider this as a sort of generational question in American history. Where were the new intellectuals? And I put the stress on public intellectuals, because obviously a kind of professional and technical intelligentsia prospered in America, but as far as I could see the public intellectuals were becoming somewhat invisible.

They were invisible because, in some ways, they had become academics, professors locked in the university. And I used a kind of generational account, looking at the 1900s, taking the Edmund Wilsons, the Lewis Mumfords. What became of them, and who were their successors? And I had a tough time finding them.

In some sense it was a story of my generation, the generation that ended up in the university and was more concerned with—well, what?—finding recommendations than with writing public interventions. And to this day, the worst thing you can say about someone in an academic meeting or when you're discussing tenure promotion is, "Oh, his work is kind of journalistic." Meaning, it's readable. It's journalistic, it's superficial. There's an equation between profundity and originality.

My argument was that, in fact, these generations of public intellectuals have diminished over time. For good reasons. The urban habitats, the cheap rents, have disappeared—as well as the jobs themselves. So the transitional generation, the New York intellectuals, ends up in the university. I mention Daniel Bell as a test case. When he was getting tenure, they turned to him and said, "What did you do your dissertation on?"

And he said, "I never did a dissertation." And they said, "Oh, we'll call that collection of essays you did a dissertation." But you couldn't do that now. Those of that generation started off as independent intellectuals writing for small magazines and ended up as professors. The next generation started off as professors, wrote differently and thought differently.

So my argument and one of the working titles of my book was, in fact, "The Decline of the Public Intellectuals." And here I am at a panel on "The Future of Public Intellectuals." Even at the time I was writing, some editors said, "Well, decline, that's a little depressing. Could you sort of make a more upbeat version?" So I said, "I have a new book called *The Rise of American Intellectuals*," and was told, "Well, that sounds much better, that's something we can sell." But I was really taking a generational approach, which in fact, is on the decline. And it caused intense controversy, mainly for my contemporaries, who always said, "What about me? I'm a public intellectual. What about my friends?" In some sense the argument is ongoing. I'm happy to be wrong, if there are new public intellectuals emerging. But I tend to think that the university and professionalization does absorb and suck away too much talent, and that there are too few who are bucking the trends.

Donatich: Maybe the term "public intellectual" begs the question, "who is the public that is being addressed by these intellectuals?" Which participant in this conversation is invisible, the public or the intellectual?

Jean Bethke Elshtain: I mused in print at one point that the problem with being a public intellectual is that as time goes on, one may become more and more public and less and less intellectual. Perhaps I should have said that a hazard of the vocation of the public intellectual lies in that direction. I didn't exactly mean less academically respectable, but rather something more or less along these lines: less reflective, less inclined to question one's own judgments, less likely to embed a conviction in its appropriate context with all the nuance intact. It is the task of the public intellectual as I understand that vocation to keep the nuances alive. A public intellectual is not a paid publicist, not a spinner, not in the pocket of a narrowly defined purpose. It is, of course the temptation, another one, of the public intellectual to cozy up to that which he or she should be evaluating critically. I think perhaps, too many White House dinners can blunt the edge of criticism.

A way I like to put it is that when you're thinking about models for this activity, you might put it this way: Sartre or Camus? An intellectual who is willing to look the other way, indeed, shamefully, explain away the existence of slave-labor camps, the gulags, in the service of a grand world-historic purpose or, by contrast, an intellectual who told the truth about such atrocities, knowing that he would be denounced, isolated, pronounced an ally of the CIA and capitalistic oppressors out to grind the faces of the poor.

There are times when a public intellectual must say "neither/nor," as did Camus. Neither the socialism of the gallows, in his memorable phrase, nor a capitalist order riddled with inequalities and shamed by the continuing existence, in his era, the era of which I speak, of legally sanctioned segregation. At the same time, this neither/nor did not create a world of moral equivalence. Camus was clear about this. In one regime, one order, one scheme of things, one could protest, one could organize to fight inequities, and in the other one wound up disappeared or dead.

Let me mention just one issue that I took on several times when I alternated a column called "Hard Questions" for *The New Republic*. I'm referring to the question of genetic engineering, genetic enhancement, the race toward a norm of human perfection to be achieved through manipulation of the very stuff of life. How do you deal with an issue like this? Here, it seems to me, the task of the public intellectual in this society at this time—because we're not fighting the issues that were fought in the mid-twentieth century—is to join others in creating a space within which such matters can be articulated publicly and debated critically.

At present, the way the issue is parsed by the media goes like this: The techno-enthusiasts announce that we're one step closer to genetic utopia. The *New York Times* calls up its three biological ethicists to comment. Perhaps one or two religious leaders are asked to wring their hands a little bit—anyone who's really a naysayer with qualms about eugenics, because that is the direction in which we are heading, is called a Luddite. Case closed, and every day we come closer to a society in which, even as we intone multiculturalism as a kind of mantra, we are narrowing the definition of what is normatively human as a biological ideal. That's happening even as we speak; that is, we're in real danger of reducing the person to his or her genotype, but if you say that, you're an alarmist—so that's what I am.

This leads me to the following question: Who has authority to pronounce on what issue, as the critical issues change from era to era? In our time and place, scientists, technology experts and dot-com millionaires seem to be the automatic authorities on everything. And everybody else is playing catch-up.

So the public intellectual needs, it seems to me, to puncture the myth-makers of any era, including his own, whether it's those who promise that utopia is just around the corner if we see the total victory of free markets worldwide, or communism worldwide or positive genetic enhancement worldwide, or mouse-maneuvering democracy worldwide, or any other run-amok enthusiasm. Public intellectuals, much of the time at least, should be party poopers. Reinhold Niebuhr was one such when he decided that he could no longer hold with his former compatriots of the Social Gospel movement, given what he took to be their dangerous naïveté about the rise of fascism in Europe. He was widely derided as a man who once thought total social transformation in the direction of world peace was possible, but who had become strangely determined to take a walk on the morbid side by reminding Americans of the existence of evil in the world. On this one, Niebuhr was clearly right.

When we're looking around for who should get the blame for the declining complexity of public debate, we tend to round up the usual suspects. Politicians usually get attacked, and the media. Certainly these usual suspects bear some responsibility for the thinning out of the public intellectual debate. But I want to lift up two other candidates here, two trends that put the role of public intellectuals and the very existence of publics in the John Dewey sense at risk. The first is the triumph of the therapeutic culture, with its celebration of a self that views the world solely through the prism of the self, and much of the time a pretty "icky" self at that. It's a quivering sentimental self that gets uncomfortable very quickly, because this self has to feel good about itself all the time. Such selves do not make arguments, they validate one another.

A second factor is the decline of our two great political parties. At one point the parties acted not just as big fundraising machines, not just as entities to mobilize voters but as real institutions of political and civic education. There are lots of reasons why the parties have been transformed and why they no longer play that role, but the results are a decline in civic education, a thinning out of political identification and depoliticization, more generally.

I'm struck by what one wag called the herd of independent minds; by the fact that what too often passes for intellectual discussion is a process of trying to suit up everybody in a team jersey so we know just who should be cheered and who booed. It seems to me that any public intellectual worth his or her salt must resist this sort of thing, even at the risk of making lots of people uncomfortable.

Donatich: Stephen, can you talk about the thinning out of political identity? Who might be responsible for either thickening or thinning the blood of political discourse? What would you say, now that we're talking about the fragmentation of separate constituencies and belief systems, is the role of religion and faith in public life?

Stephen Carter: You know that in the academy the really bad word is "popularizer"—a mere popularizer, not someone who is original, which of course means obscure, or someone who is "deeply theorized," which is the other phrase. And to be deeply theorized, you understand, in academic terms today, means to be incapable of uttering a word such as "poor." No one is poor. The word, the phrase now, as some of you may know, is "restricted access to capital markets." That's deeply theorized, you see. And some of us just say poor, and that makes us popularizers.

A few years ago someone who was really quite angry about one of my books—and I have a habit of making people angry when I write books—wrote a review in which he challenged a statement of mine asserting that the intellectual should be in pursuit of truth without regard to whether that leaves members of any particular political movement uncomfortable. He responded that this was a twelve-year-old nerd's vision of serious intellectual endeavor.

And ever since then I thought that I would like to write a book, or at least an essay, titled something like *Diary of an Intellectual Nerd*, because I like that idea of being somewhat like a twelve-year-old. A certain naïveté, not so much about great ideas and particularly not about political movements but about thought itself, about truth itself. And I think one of the reasons, if the craft of being intellectual in the sense of the scholar who speaks to a large public is in decline, is cynicism. Because there's no sense that there are truths and ideas to be pursued. There are only truths and ideas to be used and crafted and made into their most useful and appropriate form. Everyone is thought to be after something, everyone is thought to have some particular goal in mind, independent of the goal that he or she happens to articulate. And so, a person may write a book or an article and make an argument, and people wonder, they stand up in the audience and they say, "So, are you running for office, or are you looking for some high position?" There's always some thought that you must be after something else.

One of the reasons, ideally, you'd think you would find a lot of serious intellectual endeavor on university campuses is precisely because people have tenure and therefore, in theory, need not worry about trying to do something else. But on many, many campuses you have, in my judgment, relatively little serious intellectual endeavor in the sense of genuinely original thinking, because even there, people are worried about which camp they will be thought to be in.

You can scarcely read a lot of scholarship today without first having to wade through several chapters of laying out the ground in the sense of apologizing in advance to all the constituencies that may be offended, lest one be thought in the other camp. That kind of intellectual activity is not only dangerous, it's unworthy in an important sense, it's not worthy of the great traditions of intellectual thought.

There's a tendency sometimes to have an uneasy equation that there is serious intellectual activity over here, and religion over there, and these are, in some sense, at war. That people of deep faith are plainly anti-intellectual and serious intellectuals are plainly antireligious bigots—they're two very serious stereotypes held by very large numbers of people. I'm quite unembarrassed and enthusiastic about identifying myself as a Christian and also as an intellectual, and I don't think there's any necessary war between those two, although I must say, being in an academic environment, it's very easy to think that there is.

I was asked by a journalist a few years ago why was it that I was comfortable identifying myself, and often did, as a black scholar or an African-American scholar and hardly ever identified myself as a Christian scholar. And surely the reason is, there are certain prejudices on campus suggesting that is not a possible thing to be or, at least, not a particularly useful combination of labels.

And yet, I think that the tradition of the contribution to a public-intellectual life by those making explicitly religious arguments has been an important and overlooked one, and I go back for my model, well past Niebuhr, into the nineteenth century. For example, if you looked at some of the great preachers of the abolitionist movement, one thing that is quite striking about them is, of course, that they were speaking in an era when it was commonly assumed that people could be quite weighty in their theology and quite weighty in their intellectual power. And when you read many of the sermons of that era, many of the books and pamphlets, you quickly gain a sense of the intellectual power of those who were pressing their public arguments in explicitly Christian terms.

Nowadays we have a historical tendency to think, "Oh, well, it's natural they spoke that way then, because the nation was less religiously diverse and more Christian." Actually, the opposite was probably true, as historians now think—the nation is probably less religiously diverse now than it was 150, 175 years ago, when religions were being founded really quite swiftly. And most of those swiftly founded religions in the 1820s to the 1830s have died, but many of them had followers in great number before they did.

America's sense of itself as a so-called Christian nation, as they used to say in the nineteenth century, didn't really grow strong until the 1850s or 1860s. So you have to imagine the abolitionist preachers of the eighteenth and early nineteenth centuries, preaching in a world in which it could be anything but certain that those who were listening to them were necessarily co-religionists.

In this century too, we have great intellectual preachers who also spoke across religious lines. Martin Luther King is perhaps the most famous of them, even though sometimes, people try to make a straitjacket intellectual of him by insisting, with no evidence whatsoever, that he actually was simply making secular moral arguments, and that religion was kind of a smokescreen. If you study his public ministry and look at his speeches, which were really sermons, as a group, you easily discern that that's not true.

And yet, the religiosity of his language gave it part of its power, including the power to cross denominational lines, to cross the lines between one tradition and another, and to cross lines between religion and non-religion. For the religiously moved public intellectual, the fact is that there are some arguments that simply lose their power or are drained of their passion when they're translated into a merely secular mode. The greatness of King's public oratory was largely a result of its religiosity and its ability to touch that place in the human heart where we know right from wrong; it would not have been as powerful, as compelling, had it lacked that religious quality.

Now, I'm not being ahistorical, I'm not saying, "Oh, therefore the civil rights movement would not have happened or we would still have racial segregation today"—that's not the point of my argument. The point is that his religiosity did not detract from his intellectual power; rather, it enhanced it. This is not to say, of course, that everyone who makes a religious argument in public life is speaking from some powerful intellectual base. But it does suggest we should be wary of the prejudices that assume they can't be making serious arguments until they are translated into some other form that some may find more palatable. In fact, one of my great fears about the place we are in our democracy is that, religion aside, we have lost the ability to express and argue about great ideas.

Donatich: Professor Carter has made a career out of illustrating the effect and protecting the right of religious conviction in public thought. Herbert Gans, on the other hand, is a self-pronounced, enthusiastic atheist. As a social scientist who has taught several generations of students, how does a public intellectual balance the professional need for abstract theory and yet remain relevant, contribute some practical utility to the public discourse?

Herbert Gans: I'm so old that the word "discourse" hadn't been invented yet! I am struck by the pessimism of this panel. But I also notice that most of the names of past public intellectuals—and I knew some of them— were, during their lifetime, people who said, "Nobody's listening to me." Erich Fromm, for example, whom I knew only slightly and through his colleagues, was sitting in Mexico fighting with psychoanalysts who didn't think politics belonged in the dialogue. Lewis Mumford was a teacher of mine, and he certainly felt isolated from the public, except on architecture, because he worked for *The New Yorker*.

So it seems to me it's just the opposite: that the public intellectual is alive and well, though perhaps few are of the magnitude of the names mentioned. If I did a study, I'd have to define what an intellectual is, and I notice nobody on the panel has taken that one on. And I won't either. The public intellectuals that exist now may not be as famous, but in fact there are lots of them. And I think at least on my campus, public intellectuals are becoming celebrities. Some of them throw stones and get themselves in trouble for a few minutes and then it passes. But I think that really is happening, and if celebrities can exist, their numbers will increase.

One of the reasons the number is increasing is that public intellectuals are really pundits. They're the pundits of the educated classes, the pundits of the highbrow and the upper-middlebrow populations, if you will. And the moment you say they're pundits, then you can start comparing them to other pundits, of which we have lots. And there are middlebrow pundits and there are lower-brow pundits, there are serious pundits, there are not-so-serious pundits.

Some of the columnists in the newspapers and the tabloid press who are not journalists with a Ph.D. are public intellectuals. There are pundits who are satirical commentators, there are a significant number of people who get their political news from Leno and Letterman. And, of course, the pollsters don't really understand this, because what Leno and Letterman supply is a satirical take on the news.

Most public intellectuals function as quote-suppliers to legitimize the media. Two or three times a week, I get called by journalists and asked whether I will deliver myself of a sociological quote to accompany his or her article, to legitimate, in a sense, the generalizations that journalists make and have to make, because they've got two-hour deadlines. Which means that while there are few public intellectuals who are self-selected, most of us get selected anyway. You know, if no journalist calls for a quote, then I'm not a public intellectual; I just sit there writing my books and teaching classes.

I did a book on the news media and hung out at *Newsweek* and the other magazines. And at *Newsweek*, they had something they called an island, right in the main editorial room. On the island were names of people who would now be called public intellectuals, the people whom *Newsweek* quoted. And the rules were—and this is a bit like *Survivor*—every so often people would be kicked off the island. Because the editors thought, and probably rightly, that we as readers were going to get tired of this group of public intellectuals. So a new group was brought in to provide the quotes. And then *they* were kicked off.

The public intellectuals come in two types, however. First there are the ones that everyone has been talking about, the generalists, the pundits, as I think of them; and second are the disciplinary public intellectuals. The public sociologists, the public economists, the public humanists—public, plus a discipline. And these are the people who apply the ideas from their own disciplines to a general topic. And again, to some extent, this is what I do when I'm a quote-supplier, and I'm sure my fellow panelists are all functioning as quote-suppliers too.

But the disciplinary public intellectuals show that their disciplinary insights and their skills can add something original to the public debate. That, in other words, social scientists and humanists can indeed grapple with the issues and the problems of the real world. The disciplinary public intellectuals, like other public intellectuals, have to write in clear English. This is a rarity in the academy, unfortunately—which makes disciplinary public intellectuals especially useful. And they demonstrate the public usefulness of their disciplines, which is important in one sense, because we all live off public funds, directly or indirectly, and we need to be able to account every so often that we're doing something useful for taxpayers. I cannot imagine there are very many legislators in this country who would consider an article in an academic journal as proof that we're doing something useful or proof that we're entitled to some share of the public budget.

Disciplinary public intellectuals are useful in another way, too: They are beloved by their employers, because they get these employers publicity. My university has a professionally run clipping service, and every time Columbia University is mentioned, somebody clips and files the story. And so every time somebody quotes me I say, "Be sure to mention Columbia University," because I want to make my employers happy, even though I do have tenure. Because, if they get publicity, they think they're getting prestige, and if they get prestige, that may help them get students or grant money.

There are a number of hypotheses on this; I'm not sure any of them are true—whether quote-supplying provides prestige, or prestige helps to get good students, whether good students help to get grant money. There is a spiral here that may crash. But meanwhile, they think that if we're getting them publicity, we're being useful. And, of course, public social scientists and those in the humanities are, in some respects, in short supply, in part because their colleagues stigmatize them as popularizers. (They don't call them journalists, which is a dirty word in the ivory tower.)

It's also fair to say that in the newsrooms, "academic" is a dirty word. If you've ever paid attention, journalists always cite "the professor," and it doesn't matter who it is, and it doesn't even matter if they're friends of the professor. But it's always "the professor," which is a marvelous way of dehumanizing us professors. So there's this love/hate relationship between journalists and academics that's at work here. All of which means, yes, of course, it does take a bit of courage to be a public intellectual or a disciplinary public intellectual. If you turn your back on the mainstream of the academy, that's the way you get a knife in your back, at times.

Donatich: Steven Johnson has used the web and Internet energetically and metaphorically. How will the Internet change public dialogue? What are the opportunities of public conversation that this new world presents?

Steven Johnson: One of the problems with the dot-com-millionaire phenomenon—which may, in fact, be starting to fall behind us—is that it really distracted a huge amount of attention from a lot of other very interesting and maybe more laudable things that were happening online. There was kind of a news vacuum that sucked everything toward stories about the twenty-five-year-old guy who just made $50 million, and we lost sight of some of the other really progressive and important things that were happening because of the rise of the web.

I'm of a generation that came of age at precisely that point that Russell Jacoby talked about and wrote about, during the late eighties, when the academy was very much dominated by ideas from France and other places, where there was a lot of jargon and specialization, and it was the heyday of poststructuralism and deconstruction in the humanities. Which leads me to sometimes jokingly, sometimes not, describe myself as a "recovering semiotics major."

I think that I came to the web and to starting *Feed*, and to writing the book that I wrote about the Internet culture and interface culture, as a kind of a refugee from conversations like one in the academy, when I was a graduate student, in which a classmate asked the visiting Derrida a ten- or fifteen-minute, convoluted Derridean question on his work and the very possibility of even asking a question. And after a long pause, Derrida had to admit, "I'm sorry, I do not understand the question."

The web gave me an unlikely kind of home in that there were ideas and there were new critical paradigms that had been opened up to me from the academic world. But it was clear that you couldn't write about that world, you couldn't write using those tools with that kind of language and do anything useful. And it was very hard to imagine a life within the university system that was not going to inevitably push me toward conversations like that with Derrida.

So the good news, I think, is that my experience is not unique. In fact, there's been a great renaissance in the last five years of the kind of free-floating intellectual that had long been rumored to be on his or her last legs. It's a group shaped by ideas that have come out of the academy but is not limited to that. And I think in terms of publications like *Feed*—to pat myself on the back—*Hermenaut* and *Suck* are all good examples of a lively new form of public intellectualism that is not academic in tone.

The sensibility of that group is very freethinking—not particularly interested in doctrinaire political views, very eclectic in taste, very interested in the mix of high and low culture, much more conversational in tone—funny, even. Funny is an interesting component here. I mean, these new writers are funny in a way, you know, Adorno was never very funny. And they're very attentive to technology changes, maybe as interested in technology and changes in the medium as they are in intellectual fashions. If there's a role model that really stands out, it's somebody like Walter Benjamin for this generation. You know, a sense of an interest that puts together groups of things you wouldn't necessarily expect to see put together in the same essay.

How does the web figure into all of this? Why did these people show up on the web? I think one of the things that started happening—actually, this is just starting to happen—is that in addition to these new publications, you're starting to see something on the web that is very unique to it. The ability to center your intellectual life in all of its different appearances in your own "presence" online, on the home page, so that you can actually have the equivalent of an author bio. Except that it's dynamically updated all the time, and there are links to everything you're doing everywhere. I think—we've only just begun to exploit it—of combating the problem with the free-floating intellectual, which is that you're floating all over the place and you don't necessarily have a home, and your ideas are appearing in lots of different venues and speaking to lots of different audiences.

The web gives you a way of rounding all those diverse kinds of experiences and ideas—and linking to them. Because, of course, the web is finally all about linking—in a way that I think nothing has done quite as well before it. And it also involves a commitment to real engagement with your audience that perhaps public intellectuals have talked a lot about in the past, but maybe not lived up to as much as they could have.

Some of this is found in the new formats that are available online in terms of how public dialogue can happen. I'm sure many of you have read these and many of you may have actually participated in them, but I'm a great advocate for this kind of long-format, multi-participant discussion thread that goes on over two or three weeks. Not a real-time live chat, which is a disaster in terms of quality of discourse, which inevitably devolves into the "What are you wearing" kind of intellectual questions. But rather, the conversations with four or five people where each person has a day or half a day to think up their responses, and then write in 500- to 1,000-word posts. We've done those since we started at *Feed*. Slate does a wonderful job with them. And it's a fantastic forum. It's very engaged, it's very responsible, it's very dialogic and yet also lively in a conversational way. But, because of the back and forth, you actually can get to places that you sometimes couldn't get in a stand-alone 10,000-word essay.

Donatich: Professor Gans, if you had trouble with the word "discourse," I'm wondering what you'll do with "dialogic."

Johnson: I said I was recovering! That's the kind of thing that should be happening, and it seems to me that in five or ten years we'll see more and more of people who are in this kind of space, having pages that are devoted to themselves and carrying on these conversations all the time with people who are coming by and engaging with them. And I think that is certainly a force for good. The other side is just the economics of being able to publish either your own work or a small magazine. I mean, we started *Feed* with two people. We were two people for two years before we started growing a little bit. And the story that I always tell about those early days is that we put out the magazine and invited a lot of our friends and some people we just knew professionally to contribute. About three months, I guess, after *Feed* launched, *Wired* came out with a review of it. And they had this one slightly snippy line that said, "It's good to see the East Coast literary establishment finally get online." Which is very funny, to be publishing this thing out of our respective apartments. I had this moment where I was looking around my bedroom for the East Coast literary establishment—you open the closet door, and "Oh, Norman Mailer is in there. 'Hey, how's it going!'" And so there can be a kind of Potemkin Village quality online. But I think the village is thriving right now.

Donatich: Christopher Hitchens, short of taking on what a public intellectual might or might not be, will you say something about the manners or even the mannerisms of the public intellectual and why disagreement is important to our progress?

Christopher Hitchens: I've increasingly become convinced that in order to be any kind of a public-intellectual commentator or combatant, one has to be unafraid of the charges of elitism. One has to have, actually, more and more contempt for public opinion and for the way in which it's constructed and aggregated, and polled and played back and manufactured and manipulated. If only because all these processes are actually undertaken by the elite and leave us all, finally, voting in the passive voice and believing that we're using our own opinions or concepts when in fact they have been imposed upon us.

I think that "populism" has become probably the main tactical discourse, if you will, the main tactical weapon, the main vernacular of elitism. Certainly the most successful elitist in American culture now, American politics particularly, is the most successful inventor or manipulator, or leader of populism. And I think that does leave a great deal of room in the public square for intellectuals to stand up, who are not afraid to be thought of as, say, snobbish, to pick a word at random. Certainly at a time when the precious term "irony"—precious to me, at any rate—has been reduced to a form of anomie or sarcasm. A little bit of snobbery, a little bit of discrimination, to use another word that's fallen into disrepute, is very much in order. And I'm grateful to Professor Carter for this much, at least, that he drew attention to language. And particularly to be aware of euphemism. After all, this is a time when if you can be told you're a healer, you've probably won the highest cultural award the society can offer, where anything that can be said to be unifying is better than anything that can be described as divisive. Blush if you will, ladies and gentlemen, I'm sure at times you too have applauded some hack who says he's against or she's against the politics of division. As if politics wasn't division by definition.

The *New York Times*, which I'm sure some of you at least get, if you don't read, will regularly regale you in this way—check and see if you can confirm this. This will be in a news story, by the way, not a news analysis. About my hometown in Washington, for example, "recently there was an unpleasant outbreak of partisanship on Capitol Hill, but order seems to have been restored, and common sense, and bipartisanship, is again regained." I've paraphrased only slightly. Well, what is this in translation? "For a while back there it looked as if there'd be a two-party system. But, thank God, the one-party system has kicked back in."

Now, the *New York Times* would indignantly repudiate—I'm coming back to this, actually—the idea that it stood for a one-party system or mentality, but so it does. And its language reveals it. So look to the language. And that is, in fact, one of the most essential jobs of anyone describing themselves as an intellectual.

Against this, we have, of course, the special place reserved for the person who doesn't terribly want to be a part of it, doesn't feel all that bipartisan, who isn't in an inclusive mood. Look at the terms that are used for this kind of a person: gadfly, maverick and, sometimes, bad boy. Also bad girl, but quite often bad boy, for some reason. Loose cannon, contrarian, angry young man.

These are not hate words, by any means, nor are they exactly insulting, but there's no question, is there, that they are fantastically and essentially condescending. They're patronizing terms. They are telling us, affectionately enough, that pluralism, of course, is big enough, capacious enough, tolerant enough to have room for its critics.

The great consensus, after all, probably needs a few jesters here and there, and they can and should be patted upon the head, unless they become actually inconvenient or awkward or, worst of all—the accusation I have myself been most eager to avoid—humorless. One must be funny, wouldn't you say? Look to the language again. Take the emaciated and paltry manner and prose in which a very tentative challenge to the one-party system, or if you prefer, the two-party one, has been received. I'm alluding to the campaign by Ralph Nader.

The *New York Times* published two long editorials, lead editorials, very neatly inverting the usual Voltairean cliché. These editorials say: We don't particularly disagree with what Ralph Nader says, but we violently disagree with his right to say it. I've read the editorials—you can look them up. I've held them up to the light, looked at them upside down, inside out, backwards—that's what they say. This guy has no right to be running, because the electorate is entitled to a clear choice between the two people we told you were the candidates in the first place.

I find this absolutely extraordinary. When you're told you must pick one of the available ones; "We've got you some candidates, what more do you want? We got you two, so you have a choice. Each of them has got some issues. We've got some issues for you as well. You've got to pick." A few people say, "Well, I don't feel like it, and what choice did I have in the choice?" You're told, "Consider the alternatives." The first usage of that phrase, as far as I know, was by George Bernard Shaw, when asked what he felt like on his ninetieth birthday. And he said, "Considering the alternatives. . . ." You can see the relevance of it. But in this case you're being told, in effect, that it would be death to consider the alternatives.

Now, to "consider the alternatives" might be a definition of the critical mind or the alive intelligence. That's what the alive intelligence and the critical mind exist to do: to consider, tease out and find alternatives. It's a very striking fact about the current degeneration of language, that that very term, those very words are used in order to prevent, to negate, consideration of alternatives. So, be aware. Fight it every day, when you read gunk in the paper, when you hear it from your professors, from your teachers, from your pundits. Develop that kind of resistance.

The word "intellectual" is of uncertain provenance, but there's no question when it became a word in public use. It was a term of abuse used by those who thought that Capt. Alfred Dreyfus was guilty in 1898 to describe those who thought that he was probably innocent. It was a word used particularly by those who said that whether Captain Dreyfus was innocent or not, that wasn't really the point. The point was, would France remain an orderly, Christian, organic, loyal society? Compared to that, the guilt or innocence of Captain Dreyfus was irrelevant. They weren't saying he was necessarily guilty, they were saying, "Those who say he is innocent are not our friends. These are people who are rootless, who have no faith, who are unsound, in effect." I don't think it should ever probably lose that connotation. And fortunately, like a lot of other words that were originally insults—I could stipulate "Impressionist," which was originally a term of abuse, or "suffragette" or "Tory," as well as a number of other such terms—there was a tendency to adopt them in reaction to the abuse and to boast of them, and say, "Well, all right, you call me a suffragette, I'll be a suffragette. As a matter of fact, I'll be an Impressionist."

I think it would be a very sad thing if the word "intellectual" lost its sense that there was something basically malcontent, unsound and un-trustworthy about the person who was claiming the high honor of the ti-tle. In politics, the public is the agora, not the academy. The public element is the struggle for opinion. It's certainly not the party system or any other form whereby loyalty can be claimed of you or you can be conscripted.

I would propose for the moment two tasks for the public intellectual, and these, again, would involve a confrontation with our slipshod use of language. The first, I think, in direct opposition to Professor Carter, is to replace the rubbishy and discredited notions of faith with scrutiny, by looking for a new language that can bring us up to the point where we can discuss shattering new discoveries about, first, the cosmos, in the work of Stephen Hawking, and the discoveries of the Hubble telescope—the ex-ternal world—and, second, no less shattering, the discovery about our hu-man, internal nature that has begun to be revealed to us by the unravel-ing of the chains of DNA.

At last, it's at least thinkable that we might have a sense of where we are, in what I *won't* call creation. And what our real nature is. And what do we do? We have President Clinton and the other figures in the Human Genome Project appear before us on the day that the DNA string was fi-nally traced out to its end, and we're told in their voices and particularly the wonderful lip-biting voice of the President, "Now we have the dic-tionary which God used when he was inventing us." Nothing could be more pathetic than that. This is a time when one page, one paragraph, of Hawking is more awe-inspiring, to say nothing of being more instructive, than the whole of Genesis and the whole of Ezekiel. Yet we're still used to babble. For example, in the *18th Brumaire of Louis Napoleon*, Karl Marx says, quite rightly, I think, "When people are trying to learn a new lan-guage, it's natural for them to translate it back into the one they already know." Yes, that's true. But they must also transcend the one they already know.

So I think the onus is on us to find a language that moves us beyond faith, because faith is the negation of the intellect, faith supplies belief in preference to inquiry and belief, in place of skepticism, in place of the di-alectic, in favor of the disorder and anxiety and struggle that is required in order to claim that the mind has any place in these things at all.

I would say that because the intellectual has some responsibility, so to speak, for those who have no voice, that a very high task to adopt now would be to set oneself and to attempt to set others, utterly and contemp-tuously and critically and furiously, against the now almost daily practice in the United States of human sacrifice. By which I mean, the sacrifice, the immolation of men and women on death row in the system of capital punishment. Something that has become an international as well as a national disgrace. Something that shames and besmirches the entire United States, something that is performed by the professionalized elite in the name of an assumed public opinion. In other words, something that melds the worst of elitism and the absolute foulest of populism.

People used to say, until quite recently, using the words of Jimmy Porter in *Look Back in Anger*, the play that gave us the patronizing term "angry young man"—well, "there are no good, brave causes anymore." There's nothing really worth witnessing or worth fighting for, or getting angry, or being boring, or being humorless about. I disagree and am quite ready to be angry and boring and humorless. These are exactly the sacrifices that I think ought to be exacted from oneself. Let nobody say there are no great tasks and high issues to be confronted. The real question will be whether we can spread the word so that arguments and debates like this need not be held just in settings like these but would be the common property of anyone with an inquiring mind. And then, we would be able to look at each other and ourselves and say, "Well, then perhaps the intellectual is no longer an elitist."

Chapter 2

ROLES OF
PUBLIC INTELLECTUALS

Intellectuals, Dissent, and Bureaucrats

Irving Howe*

O f definitions of intellectuals there is no end. One major approach places intellectuals according to their social position or occupational role; this has at least the value of reducing our tendency to excessive pride, for it analyzes us in terms no different from those employed for the bourgeoisie, the lumpen proletariat, and other questionable types. A second approach places intellectuals according to their declared ideals, thereby buoying our morale by invoking a tradition of courage and independence. Intellectuals, says Edward Shils, "employ symbols of general scope and abstract reference, concerning man, society, nature and the cosmos." They form, says Karl Mannheim, "an unanchored, *relatively* classless stratum" floating more or less freely within the spectrum of classes. But Mannheim acknowledges the limitations of this sociological approach: it "might describe correctly certain . . . determinants and components of this unattached social body, but never the essential quality of the whole." Whether the sociological approach can ever describe "the essential quality" of anything is an interesting question.

History seems to work a little better here. Many historians have seen the intellectuals as distant offspring of priestly orders, still caught up with visions of the sacred, though now in secular guise. Albert Salomon ties the modern intelligentsia to the bohemians of the eighteenth-century coffeehouse, proposing as our archetypal ancestor Denis Diderot: "He lived for a time on the margins of bohemia, in debt to his grocer, engaged in a fantastic charade with monks from whom he received money on the strength

---

*This article first appeared in *Dissent* 31, no. 3 (1984): 303–306. Reprinted with permission.

of spurious promises to join their orders. He wrote sermons for lazy and incompetent priests and earned his living tutoring on subjects with which he was not acquainted." All of which sounds uncomfortably familiar, except perhaps the ghosting of sermons.

Normative definitions may be more useful; they are certainly more solacing. Ralf Dahrendorf sees the intellectual as the modern "fool" whispering unwelcome truths to the king, barking his unwanted dissent at state, party, class. Sometimes he alone, this poor forlorn "fool," cares about or speaks for freedom. Lewis Coser sees intellectuals as "the men who never seem satisfied with things as they are. . . . They question the truth of the moment in terms of higher truth; they counter appeals to factuality by invoking the 'impractical ought.' They consider themselves special custodians of abstract ideas like reason and justice. . . ."

Inheriting the roles of priest, jester, and prophet, we stand—presumably (some of us)—as critics of the given, devotees of speculation, irritants, gadflies who find our models in Tolstoy's "I Cannot Remain Silent," Zola's "J'accuse," Melville's "No, in Thunder."

From all this we may conclude that there is never likely to be easy accord on how to define intellectuals, though in practice we have little difficulty in recognizing them (nor do the various secret police); that for intellectuals the struggle for definition takes on, at times, an aggressive and compensatory function; and, given the irony that must sooner or later be recognized as an occupational trait, this struggle for definition can also become a mode of "black humor."

DISSENT, POWER, AND PUBLIC LIFE

What should be the role of the intellectual in the public life of a democratic society? The relation between intellectuals and state power? Two sharply divergent traditions have been at work here, that of detachment and that of commitment, and both have their dignity, truth, and limitations.

In his *Treason of the Intellectuals* Julien Benda put forth some decades ago a classical argument for intellectuals as "a priestly-secular" order:

> They are all those whose activity essentially is not the pursuit of practical aims, all those who seek their joy in the practice of an art or a science or a metaphysical speculation . . . and hence in a certain manner say, "My kingdom is not of this world."

Though rigid in his commitment, Benda was not so rigid as to propose a complete withdrawal from history. Intellectuals, he says, should speak up for innocent victims like Dreyfus, since in doing so they serve as "the officiants of abstract justice and [are] sullied with no passion for a worldly object." What Benda deplored was entering the political arena for "the triumphs of a realist passion, whether of class, race, or nation." This position is clear: do all you can to help a Sakharov, but do not become an adviser to government or propagandist for a party.

I doubt that there has ever been a serious intellectual who has failed to respond, if only inwardly, to this vision of a life devoted to disinterested philosophical and intellectual contemplation; and I say this as one who, a good part of the time, has chosen another path. If, nevertheless, we often feel that we cannot accept the way that Benda urges, we do so—or so we tell ourselves—because there are imperatives of conscience not to be denied. Suppose we must defend not only a great figure like Sakharov but an entire martyred nation like Poland? The world's agony cries out, and there are times when Benda's vision must seem morally pinched.

This clash between detachment and commitment has been an obsessive concern, sometimes a source of torment, for generations of intellectuals, and by its very nature it cannot ever be fully resolved. But if not resolved it has been dissolved in the brilliant pages of Joseph Schumpeter, who sees intellectuals as inescapably caught up in the struggles and confusions of modern society:

> Unlike any other type of society, capitalism . . . inevitably creates, educates, and subsidizes a vested interest in social unrest. . . . On the one hand, freedom of public discussion involving freedom to nibble at the foundations of capitalism is inevitable. On the other hand, the intellectual group cannot help nibbling, since it lives on criticism and its whole position depends on criticism that stings; and criticism of persons and of current events will, in a situation in which nothing is sacrosanct, fatally issue in criticism of classes and institutions.

In providing this mordant description Schumpeter hardly meant to praise intellectuals, though at least until a few decades ago many of them would have accepted his description as both truth and tribute, perhaps mumbling to themselves: Nibblers of the world, unite; you have nothing to lose but your bite.

A central difficulty with Schumpeter's analysis is that it is not sufficiently historical, that is, it fails to account for the ways in which the roles of intellectuals may change, as of course they have, within capitalist society.

THE HISTORIC MYTH OF THE AVANT-GARDE

There can be no doubt that for at least the early period of capitalism Schumpeter's portrait of the intellectual as a nibbler at accepted values has its large truth. Indeed, the encompassing myth—by which I mean more than fact and other than lie—of the nineteenth- and early twentieth-century intelligentsia, in Europe and to a lesser extent the United States, has been that of a proudly independent critical group submitting all doctrines and values to critical inspection, asserting the legitimacy of the free mind. It is a myth I inherited when I began writing some thirty-five years ago, and for a time it was accepted as a "given" among those writers we have come to call the New York intellectuals.

It seemed at the time as if the intellectual life—free-wheeling, wide-ranging, speculative—could be regarded as a "permanent revolution" in consciousness, a ceaseless dynamic of change. Neither rest nor retreat! Influenced by figures as diverse as Valery and Trotsky, Eliot and Edmund Wilson, the New York intellectuals of thirty-five years ago proposed to link a defense of modernist culture with a politics of anti-Stalinist radicalism. An attractive idea, this linkage helped to energize a good many writers; but it lacked durability and it has long since come to an end.

In Europe this union of *the advanced*—of critical consciousness and political conscience—had flourished only briefly, perhaps in Paris during the late nineteenth century, perhaps in Berlin during the 1920s. And even there, one ought to stress the "perhaps." The very nature of this alliance, insofar as it existed, made probable its rapid collapse, for in its cultural style the European left, usually middlebrow, was often hostile to the avant-garde, while the avant-garde was often apolitical when not reactionary. The two wanted to express disdain for bourgeois liberalism, but for opposite reasons and, as soon became clear, in opposite directions. No, the union between cultural modernism and independent radicalism was neither proper marriage nor secure liaison; it was a meeting between parties hurrying past one another, brief, hectic, messy.

In that meeting, nevertheless, a few of us were conceived. I have, in my own fashion, remained faithful to both parents, though by now they no longer speak to each other, have for some time not been feeling well, and are reported to take no pride in their offspring.

Clearly then, we have passed the moment when a vital dissent might be expected in our culture from the encounter between literary modernism and political radicalism. Nor is there much reason to suppose that such a moment will recur.

THE BURIED SCANDAL OF CULTURAL MODERNISM

In the decades between the Paris Commune and World War II—the decades when bourgeois liberalism in Europe suffered its most severe tests—both right- and left-wing intellectuals (also writers, artists, composers) were gravely mistaken in their easy dismissal of liberalism. More than mistaken: morally at fault. That bourgeois society required scathing criticism I do not doubt. But the writers of those decades failed to estimate the limits of what was historically possible, just as they failed to consider the consequences of their contempt of liberalism.

It is a matter of the greatest urgency to ask ourselves: What was it that drove some of the major writers of our century to one or another form of authoritarianism? The reactionaries, as we may conveniently call them, hoped that an authoritarian state would restore an earlier cultural grandeur, real or imaginary. They knew little about fascism and its costs, any more than the left-wing writers knew about Stalinism and its costs. They were guilty of fecklessness, dilettantism, arrogance.

Bourgeois society in Europe was overripe for social change, and the writers who were repelled by its hypocrisy and corruption were by no means mistaken. But the assumption that change required a trampling of liberal values in the name of "hierarchical order" and/or "proletarian dictatorship" proved a disaster beyond reckoning. I am not saying that the writers of Europe were responsible for the rise of modern totalitarianism; writers never have that degree of power. What I am saying is that they contributed—some a little more, some a little less—to an atmosphere in which the discrediting of bourgeois society became indistinguishable from a contempt for liberal values.

In the joyful brutality of their verbal violence, some of our greatest writers simply failed to realize how large a stake they had in preserving the norms of liberalism. They felt free to sneer at it because they remained within its psychological orbit. Taking for granted its shelter, they could not really imagine its destruction. Dreaming of natural aristocrats and high aristocratic cultures, or a "temporary" dictatorship of a historically ordained "vanguard," they helped, in a small way, to ready the path for manic *lumpen* and brutal *apparatchiks*. Here "dissent" degenerated into a mode of fecklessness, and in our century the price of fecklessness runs high.

INTELLECTUALS IN A BUREAUCRATIC SOCIETY

As if the effort to cope with the rise of the totalitarian movements was not difficult enough, intellectuals in the postwar era began to find that their traditional stance of independence—the proud assertion that their place was on the margin of society so as, all the better, to be its critics— was now endangered by new social developments that neither Marxist nor liberal thought had foreseen. Schumpeter's portrait of the intellectual as the agent of ceaseless unrest, the obsessive "nibbler," turned out to be comically outmoded. Schumpeter had failed to take into account— he who had kept insisting that capitalism "not only never is but never can be stationary"—that in its new bureaucratic stage capitalism would find honored roles and high status for intellectuals. Few intellectuals still thought of themselves as a "permanent opposition" to the world of power; few writers could still say with Flaubert, "bohemia is the fatherland of my breed." Philip Rahv called this a process of *embourgeoisement*, but I suspect it would be more accurate to speak, in an equally inelegant phrase, of the bureaucratic institutionalization of intellectuals.

The kind of society now emerging in the West turned out to need intellectuals—far more so than earlier capitalism ever had. Ideology began to play an unprecedented part. In 1954 I noted, "As social relations become more abstract and elusive, the human object is bound to the state with ideological slogans and abstractions—and for this chore intellectuals are indispensable." But with a crucial proviso: that while the institutional world of government, corporation, and mass culture needs intellectuals *because* they are intellectuals, it does not want them *as* intellectuals. It needs them for their skills, knowledge, inclinations, even passions; without these, they would be of no use whatever; but it does not look kindly upon, indeed it does all that it can to curb, their traditional role of free-wheeling critics.

This once-admired vision of the proudly independent intellectual—I still admire it—drew in America at least as much upon native Emersonian sensibility as upon social radicalism; but by the '50s it was being pronounced outmoded, naïve, irresponsible. What followed was the absorption of large numbers of intellectuals into the academy, government bureaucracies, and the industries of pseudoculture—a few decades later also into the corporations, as ideologues, speech-writers, and sloganeers.

In one sense, the intellectuals did gain power: they were now advisers and spokesmen for major institutions; C. Wright Mills's once-famous description of them as "powerless people" now had to be severely qualified. Yet insofar as they still remained, or wished to remain, thinkers and critics, they *lost* power—the only kind of power they had ever really had, which was to assail the insolence of office, to criticize stale ideas, and to keep venturing into new thought. And this power had been possible only, in fact, when they were "powerless people."

A parallel—though far more harsh—version of this process could be observed in the Communist countries. Western liberals and socialists, moved by outbreaks of dissent in those countries, were inclined to focus their attention on the intellectuals who dared to speak out against totalitarian or authoritarian power; but the truth had also to be recognized that many of the *apparatchiks* were intellectuals, or at least semi-intellectuals, people skillful at manipulating ideas and using words.

The bureaucratization of mind was a process apparently inseparable from modernization, and for that reason, among others, the right to dissent, even when confined to small powerless groups, remained especially precious for those of us living in democratic countries. We might be disturbed by the process of bureaucratic erosion; we might sadly observe the extent to which younger academics and writers preferred their comfortable specializations and institutional comforts, as against the free intellectual's role of the critic; but we knew that the margin of freedom that was ours made all the difference in the world.

DISSENT AT HOME, THE TOTAL STATE ABROAD

All I have been saying thus far has for its tacit premise that Western society could be regarded as more or less self-contained. But for some decades that has of course not been true, and a crucial variable—in the judgment of some, *the* crucial variable—has been the presence and pressure of totalitarian states. A turning point in intellectual history occurred when we recognized that there is more than one enemy of progress and that this enemy can be located by looking in almost any direction. Decades of bitter struggle, exhaustion of whole generations, the spilling of quantities of blood: all were required to learn that tyranny can come from right and left, and that the dissenter who cares about freedom must become agile in facing both ways. Still more, this dissenter must now take into account not only how his behavior will affect the life of the country in which he functions, but also how it may affect the fate of that country in relation to its external adversaries.

How hard it has been, during my lifetime, to adjust between competing enemies, to maneuver among bloody opponents! We who wanted to oppose Stalinism at a time when that was extremely unpopular in the American intellectual world also wanted not to become apologists for the status quo. A two-sided politics may be clear enough in principle, but it is often confusing in practice. And sometimes it disables the sophisticated.

All through the last several decades it was no longer enough, even while it remained necessary, to declare oneself a critic of American society. We had to recognize that, together with the wrongs within the gates, there were evils without. To deny that this sometimes inhibited or damaged our dissent would be foolish. When that happened, the enemy beyond the gates really triumphed.

DISSENT EAST, DISSENT WEST

We come to one of the most difficult problems in contemporary intellectual life—the necessary divergence of outlook and the frequent misunderstandings between Western intellectuals and the Soviet dissidents who have chosen or been driven into exile.

Soviet dissidents often feel something like this:

- Western intellectuals are hopelessly innocent about the deadly pur-
posiveness of the Russian party-state dictatorship; some Western intellectuals still share the illusions of earlier decades. It is hard for all
but a few in the West to realize they are facing an imperialistic, dic-
tatorial state quite as ruthless and in some ways more formidable
than that of Nazism. The West is slack in its responses. And Western
intellectuals still play games, holding to an outmoded stance of opposition within societies that suffer mostly from an excess of tolerance, softness, and ease. The single most important task in the world
today is to resist Communist power.

Western intellectuals may respond something like this:

- For people like Solzhenitsyn to write as if all or most Western intellectuals had been fellow-travelers in past decades is a piece of ignorance or impudence. Some of us were fighting Stalinism at a time
when he was still a faithful admirer of the Beloved Leader. A certain
degree of historical scruple is necessary if there is to be any serious
exchange between us.

In any case, simply to issue grand declamations of opposition to communism is not yet to answer the difficult problems we face in the West.

For example: how is it that the mere accumulation of Western military
power seems to be of so little help? How are we to develop a politics that
might simultaneously enable resistance to Communist power and minimize the danger of a nuclear war? Does not the frequent support by the
United States of right-wing authoritarianism in underdeveloped countries rebound to the advantage of the Communists? And are we not
morally obliged to speak out against injustices at home even though these
do not add up to anything so dreadful as the totalitarian state? What is the
point of cheering the right of dissent in the Western democracies if we do
not use it forcefully and responsibly?

HALF-IN, HALF-OUT, AND ALL THE WAY OUT

For intellectuals who want to combine serious criticism of their society
with defense of its democratic structure, there are two major courses of action. Let us call them Fabian and free-lance, or social democratic and anarchist. In practice, most of us combine the two, but there's a value in iso-
lating the "pure types."

The Fabian attaches himself to a movement of social reform, though he
is likely to feel he serves it best as historical mentor. He provides it with

intellectual rationale; he ennobles it with claims to historical value; he gives it ideology. If his movement achieves office he may become its leader, like Léon Blum in France, or its spokesman, like Richard Crossman in England. Once he takes on these roles, he ceases, in some strict sense, to be an intellectual, for now he cannot act out of a dispassionate search for truth but must write propaganda, which sooner or later means telling lies. If he is clever, and his party liberal enough to give him some living space, he can try to perform a dual function, as Crossman did: that of being at once an agent of politics, and an intellectual who keeps a distance between his movement and himself. Crossman, while a member of a British Labour cabinet, kept a scandalously frank journal—he intrigued at least as much as his colleagues, he maligned them, he stepped back to see them and himself with some critical objectivity, and he was clearly planning to publish this journal, so as to make the passage from politics to history.

The free-lance or anarchist intellectual will have none of this. All political entanglements he sees as inherently debasing: They prevent him from expressing himself; they force him into a role for which he is ill-equipped, indeed, into a self-violation that easily becomes a pitiable dependence on power. The free-lance offers one product: criticism, and he offers it unceasingly, for it is always needed, though by no means always wanted. He cares not for power but for influence, and less for influence within the larger society than among the community of fellow intellectuals.

I think of two recent examples, both brilliant writers, the late Harold Rosenberg and the late Paul Goodman. Rosenberg was some sort of Luxemburgist Marxist, Goodman some sort of Kropotkinish anarchist. Both despised the constraints of ideological systems and the shabbiness of pragmatic politics. Where did this leave them? With the persuasion that no government is likely to be very good, or good for very long; that the greatest service an intellectual can do a democratic government is to irritate and needle it, keep crying that the king has no clothes, the president only a few. It is a deeply American tradition, this crying of "No, in Thunder."

Criticism, however, has its own exhaustions, sterilities, and self-delusions. It may settle into its own familiar, even comfortable rut. It may become quite as conventional as the celebration of conventions. Still, as Harold Rosenberg once memorably put it, "The weapon of criticism is undoubtedly inadequate. Who on that account would choose to surrender it?"

And the paradox of it all is that the very intellectual who eschews power hungers for influence—he is, after all, human. Influence concentrated and focused soon becomes a kind of power. Rosenberg had spent years as a one-man guerrilla band within the intellectual world, and then, almost to his own surprise, became the spokesman for a major art movement, "abstract expressionism." He now had power, limited but real.

Goodman may have been against all states, but in 1960 he wrote an influential book, *Growing Up Absurd*, which not only describes how a frivolous commercial society wastes the resources of its youth but also offers some concrete suggestions for social amelioration. Perhaps to his own surprise, he became a guru of the youth rebellion of the '60s in its earlier, fraternal phase. Once he saw that the movement was turning mindless and authoritarian, he had the courage to criticize it publicly and see his influence disappear overnight. He was unhappy about this, but he accepted it. He wanted to be true to himself.

Your Fabian runs the risk of accommodation, slyness, a curling deceit of voice; your free-lance of righteousness, isolation, sterility. It is just when the Fabian's movement starts winning that it needs the free-lance to criticize, and just when the anarchist's ideas take on cogency that he needs the pragmatic skills of the Fabian.

Why Public Intellectuals?

Jean Bethke Elshtain*

Some time ago I spent a year at the Institute for Advanced Study in Princeton, New Jersey, where one of the pleasures is the opportunity to exchange ideas with scholars from other countries. One evening, a particularly animated member of an informal discussion group I had joined began to lament the sorry state of public intellectualism in the United States—this by contrast to her native France, and particularly Paris, with its dizzying clash of opinions. I remember being somewhat stung by her comments, and joined the others in shaking my head at the lackluster state of our public intellectual life. Why couldn't Americans be more like Parisians?

The moment passed rather quickly, at least in my case. I recalled just how thoroughly the French intellectual class—except for the rare dissenters, such as the estimable, brave, and lonely Albert Camus—had capitulated to the seductions of totalitarian logic, opposing fascism only to become apologists for what Camus called "the socialism of the gallows."

French political life would have been much healthier had France embraced Camus and his few compatriots rather than Jean-Paul Sartre and the many others of his kind who wore the mantle of the public intellectual. When Camus spoke in a political voice, he spoke as a citizen who understood politics to be a process that involves debate and compromise, not as an ideologue seeking to make politics conform to an overarching vision. In the end, Camus insisted, the ideologue's vision effectively destroys politics.

*This chapter first appeared in *Wilson Quarterly* 25, no. 4 (2002): 43–50. Reprinted with permission.

Perhaps, I reflected, America's peculiar blend of rough-and-ready pragmatism and a tendency to fret about the moral dimensions of public life—unsystematic and, from the viewpoint of lofty ideology, unsophisticated as this combination might be—was a better guarantor of constitutionalism and a healthy civil society than were intellectuals of the sort my French interlocutor favored. Historically, public intellectuals in America were, in fact, members of a wider public. They shared with other Americans access to religious and civic idioms that pressed the moral questions embedded in political debate; they were prepared to live, at least most of the time, with the give-and-take of political life, and they favored practical results over systems.

The American temperament invites wariness toward intellectuals. Because they are generally better at living in their heads than at keeping their feet on the ground, intellectuals are more vulnerable than others to the seductions of power that come with possessing a worldview whose logic promises to explain everything, and perhaps, in some glorious future, control and manage everything. The twentieth century is littered with the disastrous consequences of such seductions, many of them spearheaded and defined by intellectuals who found themselves superseded, or even destroyed, by ruthless men of action once they were no longer needed as apologists, provocateurs, and publicists. The definitive crackup since 1989 of the political utopianism that enthralled so many twentieth-century public intellectuals in the West prompts several important questions: Who, exactly, are the public intellectuals in contemporary America? Do we need them? And if we do, what should be their job description?

Let us not understand these questions too narrowly. Every country's history is different. Many critics who bemoan the paucity of public intellectuals in America today have a constricted view of them—as a group of independent thinkers who, nonetheless, seem to think remarkably alike. In most accounts, they are left-wing, seek the overthrow of bourgeois convention, and spend endless hours (or at least did so once-upon-a-time) talking late into the night in smoke-filled cafés and Greenwich Village lofts. We owe this vision not only to the self-promotion of members of the group but to films such as Warren Beatty's *Reds*. But such accounts distort our understanding of American intellectual life. There was a life of the mind west of the Hudson River, too, as Louis Menand shows in his recent book, *The Metaphysical Club*. American intellectuals have come in a number of modes and have embraced a variety of approaches.

But even Menand pays too little attention to an important part of the American ferment. American public intellectual life is unintelligible if one ignores the extraordinary role once played by the Protestant clergy and similar thinkers, from Jonathan Edwards in the eighteenth century through Reinhold Niebuhr in the twentieth. The entire Social Gospel movement, from its late-nineteenth century origins through its heyday about the time of World War I, was an attempt by the intellectuals in America's clergy and seminaries to define an American civil religion and to bring a vision of something akin to the Peaceable Kingdom to fruition on earth, or at least in North America.

As universities became prominent homes for intellectual life, university-based intellectuals entered this already-established public discourse. They did so as generalists rather than as spokesmen for a discipline. In the minds of thinkers such as William James, George Herbert Mead, and John Dewey, there was no way to separate intellectual and political issues from larger moral concerns. Outside the university proper during the last decades of the nineteenth century and early decades of the twentieth, there arose extraordinary figures such as Jane Addams and Randolph Bourne. These thinkers and social activists combined moral urgency and political engagement in their work. None trafficked in a totalizing ideology on the Marxist model of so many European intellectuals.

Addams, for example, insisted that the settlement house movement she pioneered in Chicago remain open, flexible, and experimental— a communal home for what might be called organic intellectual life. Responding to the clash of the social classes that dominated the public life of her day, she spoke of the need for the classes to engage in "mutual interpretation," and for this to be done person to person. Addams stoutly resisted the lure of ideology—she told droll stories about the utopianism that was sometimes voiced in the Working Man's Social Science Club at Hull-House.

Addams saw in Nathaniel Hawthorne's short story "Ethan Brand" an object lesson for intellectuals. Ethan Brand is a lime burner who leaves his village to search for the "Unpardonable Sin." And he finds it: an "intellect that triumphed over the sense of brotherhood with man and reverence for God, and sacrificed everything to its mighty claims!" This pride of intellect, operating in public life, tries to force life to conform to an abstract model. Addams used the lesson of Ethan Brand in replying to the socialists who claimed that she refused to convert to their point of view because she was "caught in the coils of capitalism." In responding to her critics, Addams once described an exchange in one of the weekly Hull-House drawing room discussions. An ardent socialist proclaimed "socialism will cure the toothache." A second fellow upped the ante by insisting that when every child's teeth were systematically cared for from birth, toothaches would disappear from the face of the earth. Addams, of course, knew that we would always have toothaches.

Addams, James, Dewey, and, later, Niebuhr shared a strong sense of living in a distinctly Protestant civic culture. That culture was assumed,

whether one was a religious believer or not, and from the days of aboli-
tionism through the struggle for women's suffrage and down to the civil
rights movement of the 1960s, public intellectuals could appeal to its values. But Protestant civic culture thinned out with the rise of groups that
had been excluded from the consensus (Catholics, Jews, Evangelical
Christians), with the triumph of a generally secular, consumerist worldview, and with mainline Protestantism's abandonment of much of its own
intellectual tradition in favor of a therapeutic ethos.

The consequence, for better and for worse, is that there is no longer a unified intellectual culture to address—or to rebel against. Pundits of one
sort or another often attempt to recreate such a culture rhetorically and to
stoke old fears, as if we were fighting theocrats in the Massachusetts Bay
Colony all over again. Raising the stakes in this way promotes a sense of
self-importance by exaggerating what one is ostensibly up against. During the Clinton-Lewinsky scandal, for example, those who were critical of
the president's dubious use of the Oval Office were often accused of trying to resurrect the morality of Old Salem. A simple click of your television remote gives the lie to all such talk of a Puritan restoration: The
screen is crowded with popular soft-core pornography packaged as confessional talk shows or self-help programs.

The specter of Old Salem is invoked in part because it provides, at least
temporarily, a clear target for counterargument and gives television's
talking heads an issue that seems to justify their existence. But the truth is
that there are no grand, clear-cut issues around which public intellectuals,
whether self-described media hounds or scholars yearning to break out of
university-defined disciplinary boundaries, now rally. The overriding issues of three or four decades ago on which an unambiguous position was
possible—above all, segregation and war—have given way to matters
that are complex and murky. We now see in shades of gray rather than
black and white. It is difficult to build a grand intellectual argument
around how best to reform welfare, structure a tax cut, or protect the environment. Even many of our broader civic problems do not lend themselves to the sorts of thematic and cultural generalizations that have historically been the stuff of most public intellectual discourse.

My point is not that the issues Americans now face raise no major ethical or conceptual concerns; rather, these concerns are so complex, and the
arguments from all sides often so compelling, that each side seems to
have some part of the truth. That is why those who treat every issue as if
it fit within the narrative of moral goodness on one side and venality and
inequity on the other become so wearying. Most of us, whether or not we
are part of what one wag rather uncharitably dubbed "the chattering

classes," realize that matters are not so simple. That is one reason we often turn to expert researchers, who do not fit the historical profile of the public intellectual as omnicompetent generalist.

For example, well before today's mountains of empirical evidence came in, a number of intellectuals were writing about what appeared to be Americans' powerful disaffection from public life and from the work of civil society. Political theorists like me could speak to widespread discontents, but it was finally the empirical evidence presented by, among others, political scientist Robert Putman in his famous 1995 "Bowling Alone" essay that won these concerns a broad public hearing. In this instance, one finds disciplinary expertise put to the service of a public intellectual enterprise. That cuts against the grain of the culturally enshrined view of the public intellectual as a bold, lone intellect. Empirical researchers work in teams. They often have hordes of assistants. Their data are complex and must be translated for public consumption. Their work is very much the task of universities and think tanks, not of the public intellectual as heroic dissenter.

Yet it would be a mistake simply to let the experts take over. A case in point is the current debate over stem cell research and embryonic cloning for the purpose of "harvesting" stem cells. Anyone aware of the history of technological advance and the power of an insatiable desire for profit understands that such harvesting is a first step toward cloning, and that irresponsible individuals and companies are already moving in that direction. But because the debate is conducted in highly technical terms, it is very difficult for the generalist, or any non-specialist, to find a point of entry. If you are not prepared to state an authoritative view on whether adult stem cells have the "pluripotent" potential of embryonic stem cells, you may as well keep your mouth shut. The technical debate excludes most citizens and limits the involvement of nonscientists who think about the long-range political implications of projects that bear a distinct eugenics cast.

Genetic "enhancement," as it is euphemistically called, will eventually become a eugenics project, meant to perfect the genetic composition of the human race. But our public life is so dominated by short-term considerations that someone who brings to the current genetic debate such a *historical* understanding sounds merely alarmist. This kind of understanding does not sit well with the can-do, upbeat American temperament. Americans are generally relieved to have moral and political urgency swamped by technicalities. This is hardly new. During the Cold War, debators who had at their fingertips the latest data on missile throw-weights could trump the person who was not *that* sort of expert—but who wasn't a naif either, who had read her Thucydides, and who thought there were alternatives to mutually assured destruction.

Americans prefer cheerleaders to naysayers. We tend to concentrate on the positive side of the ledger and refuse to conjure with the negative features—whether actual or potential—of social reform or technological innovation. Americans notoriously lack a sense of tragedy, or even, as Reinhold Niebuhr insisted, a recognition of the ironies of our own history. By naysayers I do not refer to those who, at the drop of a hat, issue a prefabricated condemnation of more-or-less anything going on in American politics and popular culture. I mean those who recognize that there are *always* losers when there are winners, and that it has never been the case in the history of any society that the benefits of a change or innovation fall evenly on all groups.

Whenever I heard the wonders of the "information superhighway" extolled during America's years of high-tech infatuation, my mind turned to the people who would inevitably be found sitting in antiquated jalopies in the breakdown lane. It isn't easy to get Americans to think about such things. One evening, on a nightly news show, I debated a dot.com millionaire who proclaimed that the enormous wealth and expertise being amassed by rich techno-whiz kids would soon allow us to realize a cure for cancer, the end of urban gridlock, and world peace. World peace would follow naturally from market globalization. Having the right designer label on your jeans would be the glue that held people together, from here to Beijing. When I suggested that this was pretty thin civic glue, the gentleman in question looked at me as if I were a member of some extinct species. It was clear that he found such opinions not only retrograde but nearly unintelligible.

The dot.com millionaire's attitude exemplified a larger American problem: the dangers of an excess of pride, not just for individuals but for the culture as a whole. It isn't easy in our public intellectual life, or in our church life, for that matter, to get Americans to think about anything to do with sin, the focus of much public intellectual discourse in America from Edwards to Niebuhr. We are comfortable with "syndromes." The word has a soothing, therapeutic sound. But the sin of pride, in the form of a triumphalist stance that recognizes no limits to human striving, is another matter.

The moral voices—the Jane Addamses and Reinhold Niebuhrs—that once had real public clout and that warned us against our tendency toward cultural pride and triumphalism seem no longer to exist, or at least to claim an audience anywhere near the size they once did. There are a few such voices in our era, but they tend not to be American. I think of President Vaclav Havel of the Czech Republic, who has written unabashedly against what happens when human beings, in his words, forget that they are not God or godlike. Here is Havel, in a lecture reprinted in the journal *First Things* (March 1995):

> The relativization of all moral norms, the crisis of authority, the reduction of life to the pursuit of immediate material gain without regard for its general consequences—the very things Western democracy is most criticized for—do not originate in democracy but in that which modern man has lost: his transcendental anchor, and along with it the only genuine source of his responsibility and self-respect. Given its fatal incorrigibility, humanity probably will have to go through many more Rwandas and Chernobyls before it understands how unbelievably shortsighted a human being can be who has forgotten that he is not God.

Our era is one of forgetting. If there is a role for the public intellectual, it is to insist that we *remember*, and that remembering is a moral act requiring the greatest intellectual and moral clarity. In learning to remember the Holocaust, we have achieved a significant (and lonely) success. Yet to the extent that we now see genocide as a historical anomaly unique to a particular regime or people, or, alternatively, as a historical commonplace that allows us to brand every instance of political killing a holocaust, we have failed to achieve clarity. The truth lies somewhere between.

Where techno-enthusiasm and utopia are concerned, we are far gone on the path of forgetting. One already sees newspaper ads offering huge financial rewards to young egg donors *if* they have SAT scores of at least 1400 or above, stand at least 5'10" tall, and are athletic. The "designer genes" of the future are talked about in matter-of-fact tones. Runaway technological utopianism, because it presents itself to us with the imprimatur of science, has an automatic authority in American culture that ethical thinkers, intellectual generalists, the clergy, and those with a sense of historic irony and tragedy no longer enjoy. The lay Catholic magazine *Commonweal* may editorialize against our newfangled modes of trading in human flesh—against what amounts to a "world where persons carry a price tag, and where the cash value of some persons is far greater than that of others." But the arguments seem to reach only those who are already persuaded. Critics on the environmental left and the social-conservative right who question techno-triumphalism fare no better. Instead of being seen as an early warning system—speaking unwelcome truths and reminding us what happens when people are equated with their genetic potential—the doubters are dismissed as a rear guard standing in the way of progress.

So this is our situation. Many of our pressing contemporary issues—issues that are not often construed as intrinsically political but on which politics has great bearing—raise daunting moral concerns. The concerns cannot be dealt with adequately without a strong ethical framework, a historical sensibility, and an awareness of human limits and tragedies. But such qualities are in short supply in an era of specialization and techno-logical triumphalism. Those who seize the microphone and can bring the almost automatic authority of science to their side are mostly apologists for the coming new order. Those who warn about this new order's possi-ble baneful effects and consequences can be marginalized as people who refuse, stubbornly, to march in time, or who illegitimately seek to import to the public arena concerns that derive from religion.

We are so easily dazzled. We are so proud. If we *can* do it, we *must* do it. We must be first in all things—and if we become serious about bring-ing ethical restraint to bear on certain technologies, we may fall behind country X or country Y. And that seems un-American. The role for public intellectuals under such circumstances is to step back and issue thought-ful warnings. But where is the venue for this kind of discourse? Where is the training ground for what political theorist Michael Walzer calls "con-nected critics," thinkers who identify strongly with their culture, who do not traffic in facile denunciations of the sort we hear every night on tele-vision (along with equally facile cheerleading), but who speak to politics in a moral voice that is not narrowly moralizing?

That question underlies much of the debate about the state of civil so-ciety that occurred during the past decade. The writers and thinkers who warned about the decline of American civil society were concerned about finding not just more effective ways to reach desirable ends in public pol-icy but about finding ways to stem the rushing tide of consumerism, of privatization and civic withdrawal, of public apathy and disengagement. We will not stem that tide without social structures and institutions that promote a fuller public conversation about the questions that confront us.

Whenever I speak about the quality of our public life before civic groups, I find a real hunger for public places like Hull-House. Americans yearn for forums where they can engage and interpret the public questions of our time, and where a life of the mind can emerge and grow communally, free of the fetters of overspecialization. Without an engaged public, there can be no true public conversations, and no true public intellectuals. At Hull-House, Jane Addams spoke in a civic and ethical idiom shaped and shared by her fellow citizens. The voices of the Hull-House public served as a check on narrow, specialized, and monolithic points of view. It was from this rich venue that Addams launched herself into the public debates of her time. Where are the institutions for such discussion today? How might we create them? It is one of the many ironies of their vocation that contemporary public intellectuals can no longer presume a public.

Intellectuals and others who speak in a public moral voice do not carry a card that says "Have Ideology, Will Talk." Instead, they embrace Hannah Arendt's description of the task of the political theorist as one who helps us to think about what we are doing. In a culture that is always doing, the responsibility to think is too often evaded. Things move much too fast. The role for public intellectuals today is to bestir the quiet voice of ethically engaged reason.

The Calling of the Public Intellectual

Alan Wolfe*

These days, the proposition that the university has stunted intellectual life in the United States has reached near dogma. In 1987, Russell Jacoby's book *The Last Intellectuals* created a stir by suggesting that the absorption of public intellectuals into the university in the 1950s and 1960s had produced a generation more preoccupied with methodological correctness and academic careerism than with the kind of fearless criticism once associated with nonacademic intellectuals like Edmund Wilson, Mary McCarthy, and Dwight Macdonald. The full implications of that thesis are still being debated: Witness two much-publicized forums on the fate of public intellectuals—one sponsored by Basic Books, the other by Lingua Franca and New York University—this past winter.

I spoke at one of the forums, and what struck me was that we tend to approach the issue in the wrong way. It is not whether intellectuals work inside or outside the academy that is important, but whether—in either sphere—they have the courage to find their own voice.

There were reasons to both like and dislike the public intellectuals who clustered in New York after World War II: They were brilliant stylists throbbing with intellectual energy, but they also led irresponsible lives and made questionable political judgments. But love them or leave them—they certainly loved and left each other—what made the whole thing tick was the tension between their conservative views on culture and their radical views on politics. Politically, they all had qualms about

*This article first appeared in the *Chronicle of Higher Education*, May 25, 2001, 20. Reprinted with permission.

capitalism—even Irving Kristol gave it only two cheers. But instead of just urging political reforms that would spread the benefits of capitalism more equitably, they considered other options, led by their culturally conservative views: Hannah Arendt advocated returning to the Greek polls for ideas about participatory democracy, while the University of Chicago's Committee on Social Thought called for the study of great books.

Because their views on culture clashed with their views on politics, the New York intellectuals were forced to make their judgments one by one, especially when, as happens so often, it was impossible to tell where culture left off and politics began. That is why their views could be so unpredictable. Dwight Macdonald, something of a mandarin in his cultural views, was radicalized by the Vietnam War and marched on the Pentagon. Daniel Patrick Moynihan did not, as a senator, endorse all the positions he had supported as an intellectual, and not for reasons of political cowardice.

One found the same unpredictable attitude toward the institution with which Jacoby was concerned: the university. The New York intellectuals never wrote about academic life with the apology for professionalism of a Marjorie Garber; nor did they denounce it in the scathing words of a Roger Kimball. When the university was under attack by student radicals at Berkeley and Columbia, the New York intellectuals rushed to its defense. When the university became a home for postmodernism and affirmative action, they found much they disliked. In both cases, they saw the university in nuanced terms, as sandwiched between its links to the high culture of the past and the democratic pressures of the contemporary world.

How the New York intellectuals understood their world was also shaped by their anti-Stalinism; if you considered yourself on the left but were a fervent enemy of communism, you had to explain yourself frequently, and at some length. It was that constant need to draw distinctions—yes, I support socialism, one can still hear Irving Howe saying, but no, I do not support Cuba—that helped give the New York intellectuals a predisposition to judge events one by one. Such a stance is harder to find today, if for no other reason than, outside of Cuba, socialism barely exists. The global triumph of capitalism is good for people who want to share the joys of consumption, but not for nurturing the questions of intellectuals, who thrive on opposition to what everyone else takes for granted.

I wish Jacoby had been right about the university's absorbing American intellectuals; the problem is that, if public intellectuals were willing to settle for academic jobs in the 1950s and 1960s, we do not see that happening much today. Daniel Bell and Nathan Glazer used to teach sociology at Harvard, but the current department has only one person—Orlando Patterson—who can be called a public intellectual, someone who brings academic expertise to bear on important topics of the day in a language that can be understood by the public. What Jacoby saw as a significant trend turned into something of a blip.

That does not mean, however, that big thinkers, no longer seduced by the comforts of academe, are launching a slew of latter-day *Partisan Reviews*. The United States has more than its share of opinion magazines, think tanks, advocacy journalists, and television commentators. But most of the time, those who are conservative in their cultural views are also conservative in their politics—and vice versa. On the right, a distrust of democracy informs commentary on both culture and elections, skeptical of a country capable of electing Bill Clinton and of considering Robert Mapplethorpe a serious artist. On the left, populism in politics and culture flows seamlessly together in opposition to those in power in either arena.

The trouble with such elitism and populism is that it is reflexive: You want either to strengthen or to weaken authority. Yet neither in politics nor in culture does such a reflexive response work. Since so much of high culture was once low culture, including such staples of authoritative taste as Italian opera, critical cultural judgments cannot be made by reviewing the popularity of any particular cultural event, or its source of funds.

Much the same is true of politics. At the very moment conservatives discover that America has a moral majority, Americans refuse to force Bill Clinton out of office. Yet when conservatives say that Americans have no morality at all, those same people vote George W. Bush into office. Democracy is like that. If you start with the assumption that everything the people do is wrong, you will be wrong about half the time—just about the same as if you begin with the proposition that the people are always right.

I do not know whether a new generation of think tanks or magazines will arise to support intellectuals who wish to think for themselves. If it happens, however, it is likely to occur outside the ideologically charged atmosphere of Washington. Nor do I know whether American universities, ever faddish, will once again discover a taste for independently minded intellectuals. Academic departments, as Jacoby pointed out, tend not to appreciate intellectual independence, but provosts and presidents, ever on the lookout for name recognition, tend to sympathize with those who pursue ideas in unorthodox fashion. Professional schools still look more favorably upon thinkers with broad interests than academics in the arts and sciences generally do. For reasons particular to their traditions, specific kinds of institutions, including liberal-arts colleges and religiously affiliated universities, like the prestige of having public intellectuals around. But if and when we do see the emergence of a new generation of intellectuals in the academy, they will then have to answer the question raised by Jacoby in 1987: Can they retain their critical voices while teaching students, serving on committees, and being mentors to graduate students?

I believe they can. But whether they work inside or outside the academy, they will have to have the confidence to find their own voice.

Intellectuals speak with authority, but what gives them the authority to speak? No one designated me an intellectual. I took on the role myself, found some people willing to publish me, and presumably drew some others willing to read me. If I have any authority, I developed it in the course of what I do. I am not saying that, on the matters of the day on which I have weighed in, I have always been right. But I have tried to convey that, when you get an opinion from me, it is my own. My authority for being an intellectual comes only from me, and to be true to that authority, I have to be true to myself.

I became an intellectual the day I decided that no one was looking over my shoulder as I sat down to write. Before that moment, I considered myself part of a political movement. My causes in the 1960s were the causes of the left: racial justice, opposition to capitalism, protest against the Vietnam War. Good causes all, but adherence to their demands was deadly. When I wrote opinion articles, I understood my role to be providing moral support to those on the side of all that was presumed good and true. Now, when I look back on my writings from that period, I do not see the fearless critic of the United States that I thought I had been at the time. Instead, I see someone simplifying the world's complexity to fit the formula for understanding the world developed by the Left.

A few of the '60s radicals in my circle, like David Horowitz, chastened by the violence and hypocrisy of the movements they once supported, shifted their political views quite drastically to the right. I reaffirmed my status as an intellectual, when, having second thoughts of my own about the Left, I opted not to join them. Reading those born-again conservatives, I feel as if I am reading ideology, stretched this way or that to fit whatever topic is under discussion. Their efforts, today, to prove how good things are under American capitalism strike me as remarkably similar to their efforts, yesterday, to emphasize how bad they were. I get the feeling that pleasing a movement (or a financial sponsor) explains much of what they write.

Because the role of public intellectual resembles so much what Max Weber called a vocation—you have to have a calling for it, and it has to come from within—institutions like universities, magazines, and think tanks are capable of putting pressure on intellectuals that can undermine their authority to speak: the need to obtain tenure and satisfy colleagues, the need to boost circulation, the need to win the support of politicians. Resisting those pressures requires an odd combination of self-confidence and humility, the former required to have something valuable to say, the latter necessary to steer clear of dogmatism.

There can be no guidebook on how to become a public intellectual. There can be only the desire to make sense out of the world one issue at a time.

Forum

Frances Ferguson*

Since the time Kant forcefully established the claim of the intellect with his critical idealism, reason has looked—in both serious philosophical work and popular usage—like something of an antonym to sensation, experience, and action. From Marx's attacks on the abstraction of the young Hegelians to the attitudes of mid-twentieth-century American society, as described by Richard Hofstadter, anti-intellectualism has seemed to be supported by good reasons. Apparently preferring theory over practice and committed to rationalizing rather than emotional response, intellectuals have seemed not just skeptics but obstructionists as well. Urged to "just do it," intellectuals want to know just what is to be done.

It would be a mistake to defend the intellectual too quickly against the charge of being simply a scold, a glorified hall monitor. For the intellectual does not possess clearly superior knowledge about issues that people would prefer not to be challenged on. Nor does the intellectual's unpopularity come from saying things that are uncomfortably true. Rather, intellectuals have a special role in modern society and in the information age because they do *not* have a pre-established body of knowledge, set of facts, or specific constituency (in the way that a pundit like Rush Limbaugh speaks for a sector of public opinion).

That is, the intellectual has historically been imperfectly professionalized. The intellectual offers a special approach to a problem or a series of problems but cannot claim to be a perfect specialist—someone who can

*Reprinted by permission of the Modern Language Association of America from *PMLA* 112, no. 5 (1997): 1125–1126.

assume responsibility for a particular activity, acting on behalf of others so that they cease to need to act themselves. Unlike the tailor, the carpenter, and the lawyer, who sew, build, and sue for their clients, intellectuals claim only to say something, and thus they may affect, for example, the political conduct, views on the economy, or literary understanding of others but will never vote, hold opinions, or read for them.

The situation of intellectuals as imperfect representatives has marked the university and the social structures that it contributes to. In *The Conflict of the Faculties*, Kant analyzes the various claims of the faculties in the university, beginning with the professions—law, medicine, and theology— to which individuals cede their authority out of a plausible commitment to their legal rights, physical health, and spiritual well-being. Then, as now, those professions were underwritten by their considerable utility, which gave them the practical mandate to continue without rethinking their discourse or questioning their basic presuppositions. They were professions of the book, by virtue of their role in assimilating particular cases to modes of preexistent practices, statutes, and maxims; but, Kant argued, these professions should not be able to choose their books and claim that their professional expertise could incorporate everything. The basic task of restraining the professions that were powerful on account of their immediate usefulness, he thought, had to fall to the philosophy faculty (the precursor of present-day departments in the humanities and social sciences). The philosophy faculty would be able, for instance, to argue specifically against the theology faculty's requiring religious conversion as part of its program.

Retracing Kant's position to provide a historical model of the rise of critical studies in the humanities, Ian Hunter argues against the notion that humanists should feel authorized to challenge others' professions ("The Regimen of Reason: Kant's Defense of the Arts Faculty," John Hinkley Memorial Lecture, Johns Hopkins Univ., spring 1995). He faults the humanities today for continuing to act as if its professional approval mattered and ought to matter to those professions. In his view, the witty remarks that literature professors make about what they take to be the biases and follies of statistical sociologists, census takers, and scientists are licensed by a genealogical accident. Hunter proposes a philological perspective that, marking the difference between the university in the eighteenth century and now, will chasten the intellectual's sense of self-importance as censor.

My position involves both greater modesty and greater ambition for intellectuals and the intellectual professions. The modesty appears in the view that there is no methodological position that can help intellectuals to tell what terrain they ought to cede to other fields. The ambition lies in the view that literary criticism and other intellectual professions are, at least potentially, committed to a project that is political in the most basic sense—scrutinizing texts in such a way as to enable one to recognize views that one doesn't hold. This is, I take it, the importance of the formalist legacy in literary criticism. Texts like Propp's *Morphology of the Folktale* ask readers to make sense of tales whose anonymous and collective authorship requires that analysts not begin by visualizing an author with an agenda; texts like Freud's case studies argue that there is significant sense even to the apparent nonsense of Dr. Schreiber and the Wolf Man.

The most important contribution that the intellectual has to make to the society of the new millennium is, it seems to me, to demonstrate that texts needn't all be recruited for consensus, that they can instead enable society to acknowledge the existence of views that it does not—and may never—endorse.

Chapter 3

THE DIVIDE: ACADEMIC VS. FREE-STANDING PUBLIC INTELLECTUALS

The Public Intellectual, Service Learning, and Activist Research

Ellen Cushman*

While I support the good intentions of those who have recently proposed definitions of the public intellectual, I find these definitions problematic in their narrow delineation of the word "public"—they focus on a "public" consisting of middle and upper class policy makers, administrators, and professionals, and, in doing so, omit an important site for uniting knowledge-making and political action: the local community. Canvassing the letters submitted to the October 1997 PMLA forum on intellectual work in the twenty-first century, one notices numerous tensions regarding the larger public role of the intellectual:

> New and old intellectuals in the twenty-first century need to try to answer such questions as: "What do people(s) want?" and "What is the meaning of the political?" (Alina Clej; Forum 1123)

> In the next century, the intellectual must be willing to take more risks by choosing exile from confining institutional, theoretical, and discursive formations. (Lawrence Kritzman 1124)

> American intellectuals appear to have entered a period of non-engagement, cherishing their autonomy over engagement and retreating into the ivory tower. (Patrick Saveau 1127)

---

*This article first appeared in *College English* 61, no. 3 (1999): 328–336. Copyright 1999 by the National Council of Teachers of English. Reprinted with permission.

If there is a task ahead for the kind of intellectual I have in mind, it lies in the attempt to forge a more secure link between the love of art and human decency. (Steven Greenblatt 1131)

[The modern intellectual's] goal would be to enact in one's research an informed concern with specific questions of public value and policy. (Dominick Lacapra 1134)

A postoccidental intellectual [is] able to think at the intersection of the colonial languages of scholarship and the myriad languages subaltemized and banned from cultures of scholarship through five hundred years of colonialism. (Walter Mignolo 1140)

Taken together, these statements indicate a growing pressure for intellectuals to make knowledge that speaks directly to political issues outside of academe's safety zones. This urgency comes in part from administrators and legislators who demand accountability, but it also comes from academics who have grown weary of isolation and specialization and who hope their work might have import for audiences beyond the initiated few. They wonder if knowledge-making can take risks while both cultivating aesthetics and leading to political action. Above all, these quotations reveal the nagging suspicion that academics have yet to realize their full potential in contributing to a more just social order. I believe public intellectuals can indeed contribute to a more just social order, but to do so they have to understand "public" in the broadest sense of the word.

The kind of public intellectuals I have in mind combine their research, teaching, and service efforts in order to address social issues important to community members in under-served neighborhoods. You know these neighborhoods: they're the ones often located close by universities, just beyond the walls and gates, or down the hill, or over the bridge, or past the tracks. The public in these communities isn't usually the one scholars have in mind when they try to define the roles of "public" intellectuals. For example, Pierre Bourdieu recognizes that the intellectual has dual and dueling agendas: "on the one hand, he [sic] must belong to an autonomous intellectual world; . . . on the other hand, he must invest the competence and authority he has acquired in the intellectual field in a political action" ("Fourth Lecture" 656). Yet Bourdieu advocates only one kind of political action: "the first objective of intellectuals should be to work collectively in defense of their specific interests and of the means necessary for protecting their own autonomy" (660). Granted, academics must have the secure position that autonomy (typically gained through tenure) provides if the knowledge they make is to be protected from censorship. Yes, academics need to defend their positions, particularly in this socio-economic climate where big business ethics of accountability, total quality management, downsizing, and overuse of part-time labor conspire to erode academics' security within the university. However, the fight for our own autonomy is a limited and self-serving form of political action addressed only to an elite "public" of decision-makers.

Another type of public intellectual, in the limited sense of the word *public*, believes in protecting scholarly autonomy through popularizing intellectual work. Here's Michael Berube on this kind of public intellectual: "the future of our ability to produce new knowledges for and about ordinary people—and the availability of education *to* ordinary people—may well depend on how effectively we can . . . make our work intelligible to nonacademics—who then, we hope, will be able to recognize far-right rant about academe for what it is" (176). Going public, turning to mass media, dressing our work in plain garb may help preserve autonomy, may even get intellectuals a moment or two in the media spotlight, but how will this help individuals who have no home, not enough food, or no access to good education? Popularizing scholarship may help solve problems on academe's front lines, but such action does not seem to do democracy any great favors. Popularizing suggests that public intellectuals simply translate their thinking into less specialized terms, then publish in the *New Yorker* or *Academe*. Yet publishing to a greater number of elite audiences works more to bolster our own positions in academe than it does to widen the scope of our civic duties as intellectuals.

Bourdieu and Berube belong to the modern ranks of public intellectuals, among whom I might include such currently prominent figures as Henry Louis Gates, Jr., and Stanley Fish. They all share an implied goal of affecting policy and decision-making, and they reach this goal by using their positions of prestige as well as multiple forms of media (newspapers, radio, and television) in order to influence a public beyond the academy, though this public will usually be limited to the educated upper echelons of society. In their dealings with this public, moreover, they typically remain scholars and teachers, offering their superior knowledge to the unenlightened.

When public intellectuals not only reach outside the university, but actually *interact* with the public beyond its walls, they overcome the ivory tower isolation that marks so much current intellectual work. They create knowledge with those whom the knowledge serves. Dovetailing the traditionally separate duties of research, teaching, and service, public intellectuals can use the privilege of their positions to forward the goals of both students and local community members. In doing so, they extend access to the university to a wider community. Academics can reach these goals in two ways: service learning and activist research.

SERVICE LEARNING

To enact citizenship in the larger sense, and to unify the locations of research, teaching, and service, the public intellectual can begin by developing service learning or outreach courses. Service learning asks students
(both graduate and undergraduate) to test the merit of what they learn in
the university classroom against their experiences as volunteers at local
sites such as philanthropic agencies, primary and secondary schools,
churches, old-age homes, half-way houses, and shelters. When students
enter communities as participant observers, they "begin not as teachers,
but as learners in a community setting where the goals and purposes of a
'service' effort are not established beforehand" (Schutz and Gere 145).
Students enter the community in a sincere effort to both engage in and observe language use that helps address the topics that are important to
community members. When activist fieldwork is a cornerstone of the
course, students and community residents can develop reciprocal and dialogic relations with each other; their relationship is a mutually beneficial
give-and-take one.

As participant observers, students take field notes that reflect on
their experiences with community members and how these experiences
relate to the set of readings chosen by the professor. These field notes
serve a twofold purpose. First, they offer students a ready supply of examples to analyze in their essays, and second, they become potential
source material for the professor. The professors' own notes, video and
audio tape recordings, evaluations from the public service organization
or area residents, and other literacy artifacts constitute a rich set of materials for knowledge-making. Since the professors also volunteer,
teach, and administer the service learning course, they have firsthand
familiarity with the important social issues and programmatic needs at
the local level, and they tailor the curriculum to fit these. Thus, when
activist methods are employed, knowledge-making in outreach courses
happens *with* the individuals served. The course must respond to the
immediate concerns and long-standing problems of the area in order to
remain viable.

In their most limited sense, service learning courses unite in a single
mission the traditionally separate duties of research, teaching, and service.
The research contributes

   to teaching by informing a curriculum that responds to both students'
      and community members' needs, and
   to service by indicating emerging problems in the community which
      the students and curriculum address.

The teaching contributes

to research by generating fieldnotes, papers, taped interactions and other materials, and

to service by facilitating the community organization's programmatic goals with the volunteer work.

The service contributes

to research by addressing political and social issues salient in everyday lived struggles, and

to teaching by offering students and professors avenues for testing the utility of previous scholarship in light of community members' daily lives and cultural values.

Because service learning includes an outreach component, the knowledge generated together by the area residents, students, and the professor is exoteric (as opposed to esoteric) and is made in interaction (as opposed to isolation).

Among composition and rhetoric scholars, Bruce Herzberg, Linda Flower, and Aaron Schutz and Anne Ruggles Gere, to name a few, have created community literacy projects which include service learning. Joan Schine has recently discussed elementary and secondary programs in service learning, and Barbara Jacoby addresses the practical and political aspects of developing outreach courses at the university level. Although scholars have begun to develop these outreach initiatives, few have offered a methodology that integrates the civic-minded mission of service learning with the politics of research in local settings.

ACTIVIST RESEARCH

One limitation of service learning courses can be students' perception of themselves as imparting to the poor and undereducated their greater knowledge and skills. Instructors in the service learning course that Anne Ruggles Gere and her colleagues developed noted that "their students often entered seeing themselves as 'liberal saviors,' and that the structure of tutoring had the potential to enhance the students' vision of this 'savior' role" (Schutz and Gere 133). Indeed, if the university representatives understand themselves as coming to the rescue of community residents, students will enact this missionary ideology in their tutoring. Service learning courses can avoid this liberal do-gooder stance when they employ activist research methodologies.

Activist research combines postmodern ethnographic techniques with notions of reciprocity and dialogue to insure reciprocal and mutually beneficial relations among scholars and those with whom knowledge is made. Since a central goal of outreach courses is to make knowledge *with* individuals, scholars need a methodology that avoids the traditional top-down approaches to ethnographic research: "The Bororos of Brazil sink slowly into their collective death, and Levi-Strauss takes his seat in the French Academy. Even if this injustice disturbs him, the facts remain unchanged. This story is ours as much as his. In this one respect, . . . the intellectuals are still borne on the backs of the common people" (de Certeau 25). Traditional forms of ethnographic fieldwork yield more gains for the intellectual than the community residents. On the other hand, activist ethnographic research insures that, at every level of the ethnographic enterprise—from data collection through interpretation to write-up—the researcher and participants engage in openly negotiated, reciprocal, mutually beneficial relations.

Theories of praxis can be united with notions of emancipatory pedagogy in an effort to create a theoretical framework for activist methodology. Scholars who advocate praxis research find the traditional anthropological method of participant observation unsatisfactory because it has the potential to reproduce an oppressive relationship between the researcher and those studied (Oakley; Lather; Bleich; Porter and Sullivan). Instead of emphasizing observation, research as praxis demands that we actively participate in the community under study (Johannsen; for a thoughtful exploration of the connections between critical ethnography and critical pedagogy, see Lu and Horner). Applied anthropology provides theoretical models for how praxis—loosely definable as ethical action to facilitate social change—enters into the research paradigm, but many scholars still need to do the work of intervention, particularly at the community level.

Praxis research can take emancipatory pedagogy as its model for methods of intervention, since notions of emancipatory pedagogy work with the same types of theoretical underpinnings. Paulo Freire's *Pedagogy of the Oppressed* exemplifies the pragmatic concerns of politically involved teaching aimed at emancipating students. His work teaching illiterate peasants in Latin America has been adapted to American educational needs in schooling institutions (Apple and Weis; Giroux; Luke and Gore; Lankshear and McLaren). Emancipatory teaching can only go so far in instantiating activist research, though, because teachers often apply liberating teaching only in the classroom, and they are hard-pressed to create solidarity and dialogue within the institutionalized social structure of American schools. In order to adapt Freire's pedagogy to the United States, we must also practice it outside the academy, where we can often more easily create solidarity. In a conversation with Donaldo Macedo, Freire says: "it is impossible to export pedagogical practices without re-inventing them. Please, tell your fellow American educators not to import me. Ask them to recreate and rewrite my ideas" (Macedo xiv). Our revisions of his pedagogy can be more fully expanded if we move out of the institutionalized setting of classrooms and into our communities. In this way, liberatory teaching can be brought together with praxis research to create the activist research useful to service learning.

Although I have conducted a three-and-a-half-year-long ethnography of literacy in an inner city (Cushman), Spring 1998 offered me the first opportunity to bridge activist research and service learning through a course called "Social Issues of Literacy." The course links Berkeley undergraduates with the Coronado YMCA in Richmond, a place residents of the East Bay call "the forgotten inner city." Undergraduates read scholarship on literacy, volunteer at the YMCA, write field notes, and then integrate theory and data in case studies. The course has met with initial success in three ways.

First, students immediately saw the tight integration of literacy theory and practice. Their essays revealed careful attention to the scholarship and some rigor in challenging the limitations of these readings against their own observations. One student's paper noted that Scribner and Cole's famous work on Vai literacy showed their limited access to Vai females' literacy practices. Her paper then illustrated two interactions where she noticed how girls were excluded by the boys during storytelling, playing, and writing. She considered methods of participant observation that might invite more of the girls to engage in these activities. At the same time, she conducted informal interviews with the YMCA members in order to understand better how their values for oral and literate language shifted along gender lines. She did this with an eye toward filling gaps in knowledge that she saw in the scholarship on literacy that we read in class.

Second, the outreach course has filled a very real need for the YMCA staff. While this particular YMCA had numerous programs, including African dance, sports, teen pregnancy prevention, and scouting, they needed adults to engage youths in language use that would promote their reading and writing—without reproducing a school atmosphere. As one supervisor told me, "if the undergraduates come in here with too much school-like structure, they could turn the kids off to the reading and writing that they'll need to get ahead in school. So let's create a flexible structure for activities." Her point was subtle; area children hold schoolwork in low esteem, but the adults value the reading and writing needed to succeed in education.

With the supervisor's goals in mind, the undergraduates and I ask the YMCA members what kinds of activities they would like to do and offer a broad range of reading, writing, and artistic events in which they can engage. One ongoing literacy event centers around the creation of personal journals. Shawn, a nine-year-old, told me he wanted his "own journal here [at the YMCA] where I can keep all my stories and things." Together with the undergraduates, the children have produced journals with decorated covers bound with staples or yarn. Inside the journals, they keep their stories, math homework, spelling words, drawings, and letters to the undergraduates and myself. Leafing through a set of completed journals, the YMCA supervisor noted that the children "don't even realize that all the art, math, and writing they're doing in these journals will help them with their schoolwork." At the intersection where university representatives and community members meet, these journals offer a brief illustration of the way in which public intellectuals and community members can work together to identify and ameliorate local-level social issues. In this case, we together found ways to engage in reading and writing that would bridge a problematic split in generational values attached to literacy.

Finally, "Social Issues of Literacy" has met with some success in terms of research: the course has generated numerous literacy artifacts and events that could potentially serve as data for an extended study of community literacy. In exchange for the hours I have invested in curriculum development, site coordination, grant writing, and local research, I have the immediate reward of writing this paper. Thus, at least the initial results indicate that everyone seems to benefit from the service learning and activist research in this project.

However, even with examples of outreach and activist research like this, literary scholars may be hard-pressed to see their intellectual work as amenable to service learning courses. To put a finer point on it, can outreach courses help forge a more secure link "between the love of art and human decency" (as Greenblatt put it in the *PMLA* forum), between intellectual work which cultivates aesthetics and work which speaks to common, lived conditions of struggle in the face of vast and deepening social inequalities? If public intellectuals hope to find and generate overlaps between aesthetics and politics, they need to first understand that what they count as art or political choices does not necessarily match what community members count as art or political choices. Because university representatives tend to esteem their own brand of knowledge more than popular forms of knowledge, they deepen the schism between universities and communities. Bourdieu described well the production of legitimate (read specialized, publishable, esoteric, academic) language, which gains material, cultural and symbolic capital by implicitly devaluing nonstandard (read colloquial, vernacular, common, vulgar) language. The educational system, particularly higher education, "contributes significantly to constituting the dominated uses of language as such by consecrating the dominant use as the only legitimate one" through "the devaluation of the common language which results from the very existence of a literary language" (*Language* 60–61). How can public intellectuals link the love of art and human decency if we continue to value university-based knowledge and language more than community-based knowledge and language? Unless the love of art and human decency, as they manifest themselves in university culture, justify themselves against local cultural value systems, academic knowledge-making will remain esoteric, seemingly inapplicable, remote, and elitist.

Public intellectuals challenge the value system of academe by starting with the assumption that all language use and ways of knowing are valuable and worthy of respect. To enact this principle, service learning offers meeting places for community and university values, language, and knowledge to become mutually informative and sustaining, places where greater numbers of people have a say in how knowledge is made, places where area residents, students, and faculty explore works of art, literature, and film to find ways in which these works still resonate with meaning and inform everyday lived struggles. Service learning "mak[es] rhetoric into a social praxis . . . assigning students to effective agency in the ongoing struggle of history" (France 608). Public intellectuals can use service learning as a means to collapse harmful dichotomies that traditional university knowledge espouses: literary/vernacular; high culture/low culture; literature/literacy; objective/subjective; expert/novice. Because these dualities place faculty members in a presumably higher social position, they distance academics from those they hope their knowledge serves—from those their knowledge must serve.

Public intellectuals can use their service, teaching, and research for the benefit of those inside and outside the university. Their knowledge, created with students and community members, can have political implications in contexts beyond the university. Their positions as faculty members can have readily apparent accountability, and their intellectual work can have highly visible impact. In the end, public intellectuals can enact the kind of civic-minded knowledge-making that engages broad audiences in pressing social issues.

WORKS CITED

Apple, Michael, and Lois Weis, eds. *Ideology and Practice in Schooling*. Philadelphia: Temple University Press, 1983.

Bérubé, Michael. *Public Access: Literary Theory and American Cultural Politics*. London: Verso, 1994.

Bleich, David. "Ethnography and the Study of Literacy: Prospects for Socially Generous Research." *Into the Field: Sites of Composition Studies*. Ed. Anne Ruggles Gere. New York: MLA,1993, 176–92.

Bourdieu, Pierre. "Fourth Lecture. Universal Corporatism: The Role of Intellectuals in the Modern World." *Poetics Today* 12.4 (1991): 655–69.

———. *Language and Symbolic Power*. Cambridge, MA: Harvard University Press, 1991.

Cushman, Ellen. *The Struggle and the Tools: Oral and Literate Strategies in an Inner City Community*. Albany: SUNY Press, 1998.

de Certeau, Michel. *The Practice of Everyday Life*. Berkeley: University of California Press, 1984.

Flower, Linda. *The Construction of Negotiated Meaning*. Carbondale: Southern Illinois University Press, 1994.

Forum. *PMLA* 112.5 (October 1997): 1121–41.

France, Alan. "Assigning Places: The Function of Introductory Composition as a Cultural Discourse." *College English* 55.6 (1993): 593–609.

Giroux, Henry. *Ideology, Culture, and the Process of Schooling*. Philadelphia: Temple University Press, 1981.

Herzberg, Bruce. "Community Service and Critical Teaching." *College Composition and Communication* 45.3 (Oct. 1994): 307–19.

Jacoby, Barbara. *Service-Learning in Higher Education*. San Francisco: Jossey-Bass, 1996.

Johannsen, Agneta. "Applied Anthropology and Post Modernist Ethnography." *Human Organization*. 50.1 (1992): 71–81.

Lankshear, Colin, and Peter McLaren, eds. *Critical Literacy: Politics, Praxis, and the Postmodern*. Albany: SUNY Press, 1993.

Lather, Patti. "Research as Praxis." *Harvard Education Review*. 56 (1992): 257–77.

Lu, Min–Zhan, and Bruce Horner. "The Problematic of Experience: Redefining Critical Work in Ethnography and Pedagogy." *College English* 60.3 (March 1998): 257–77.

Luke, Carmen, and Jennifer Gore. *Feminism and Critical Pedagogy*. New York: Routledge, 1992.

Macedo, Donaldo. *Literacies of Power: What Americans Are Not Allowed to Know*. Boulder: Westview Press, 1994.

Oakley, Annie. "Interviewing Women: A Contradiction in Terms." *Doing Feminist Research*. London: Routledge, 1981, 30–62.

Schine, Joan. *Service Learning*. Chicago: NSSE/U of Chicago Press, 1997.

Schutz, Aaron, and Anne Ruggles Gere. "Service Learning and English Studies: Rethinking 'Public' Service." *College English* 60.2 (1998): 129–49.

Sullivan, Pat, and James Porter. *Opening Spaces: Writing Technologies and Critical Research Practices*. Greenwich, CT: Ablex, 1997.

Race and the Public Intellectual: A Conversation with Michael Eric Dyson

Sidney I. Dobrin*

Recently, conversations regarding what role universities play in larger communities have become prolific. Some scholars have argued that the walls that divide academics from the "real world" are false and that the university is as much the real world as any other entity. Yet others have adamantly sought ways to maintain and strengthen the protective walls of the ivory tower insisting that what gets done in the academy is somehow more virtuous because it is cerebral. Michael Eric Dyson, the self-proclaimed "Hip-Hop Public Intellectual," has emerged as a vocal radical who seeks to bring the intellectual work of the academy to popular/mass culture in ways that not only encourage political action in world communities, but that retain academic integrity at the same time. For Dyson, doing this involves getting one's hands dirty and taking one's work to sites outside the academy. He says, "A kind of geography of destiny is linked to whether you occupy the terrain of the academy, specifically and particularly as an academic, you ought to stay there. We love to talk about transgressions intellectually, academically, but we don't want to do it physically or epistemologically. We don't want to actually do it."

Dyson is by trade a preacher and a teacher. His books and articles appear in scholarly forum, religious forum, and popular press and address issues that range from critique of rap music to critical readings of Malcolm X to cultural theory to examining religious values. His voice is heard by many in the academy and many more outside its walls. It is to this end

*This article first appeared in *JAC: A Journal of Composition Theory* 17, no. 2 (1997): 143–181. Reprinted with permission.

that Dyson works. He is clear: "I want to speak to the academy in very powerful and interesting ways, but I don't want to be limited to the academy." For Dyson, what goes on outside of the academy is of tremendous consequence, and in the conversation that follows, he is adamant about our need to talk about how matters of race and discussions of race affect people on both sides of the academic wall.

What many will find interesting about Dyson's relational view of the university and the outside world is that he sees a great importance in the kinds of theoretical work that get done in the university. For Dyson, theory becomes the avenue by which important questions get asked; yet, he contends that those questions do not need to be asked in ways that deny non-academics access to the answers. At the forefront of Dyson's agenda is a push for academic and mass-cultural discussions to better inform one another. This gets done, he argues, through public intellectualism. For Dyson, the job of the public intellectual—the black public intellectual, in particular—is to be a "paid pest" whose function is to "disrupt and intervene upon conversations in ways that are disturbing, that in their very disturbance force people to ask why they frame the questions in the way that they did or they make the analysis they do."

For Dyson, disrupting notions of race and multiculturalism provide access to understanding how issues of race, gender, class, and culture get constructed. Dyson is critical of the market multiculturalism that inhabits American universities. He contends that the rough edges of multiculturalism are smoothed over in the versions universities promote; they lack the raw vitality and danger that should be associated with issues of conflict. However, he makes plain that the ways in which multiculturalism and issues of race are safely broached in classrooms are critically important. Dyson is clear that he would rather see conflicts of race break out in safe contestations in classrooms than not be discussed at all and that he would much rather see classroom approaches to race and multiculturalism than many of the violent ways in which race gets "debated" in the street. When he talks of the conflict of race and culture, his metaphors reflect this violence and his wish for race to break out in classrooms so it "wounds our most cherished expectations" of the safety of classroom multiculturalism.

What compositionists will notice immediately about Dyson is his acute awareness of how language comes to the fore in matters of race. He is self-conscious of the language he uses and the ways in which he addresses different audiences. But he is also cognizant of how theoretical approaches to understanding discourse and writing affect the epistemological ways in which race, gender, class, ideology get constructed. Dyson identifies this intellectual engagement with language as having powerful implications in redefining the relationship between the work that gets done in the academy and lives of people who live outside of its borders. Dyson seeks to make available the intellectual projects of the academy to the masses in accessible ways in order to enact change and re-envision how the world views race, class, gender, and the other constructs that shape our thinking about difference.

Q: In *Reflecting Black* you write: "The desire for literacy has character-ized the culture of African-Americans since their arrival here under the myriad brutalities of slavery. Although reading and writing were legally prohibited, black folk developed a resourceful oral tradition that had cul-tural precedence in African societies. . . . Black folk generated an oral tra-dition that expressed and reinforced their cultural values, social norms, and religious beliefs. . . . Even with the subsequent development of liter-ate intellectual traditions, resonant orality continues to shape and influ-ence cultural expression." You are a prolific writer; your work appears in scholarly forums, major newspapers, popular magazines, religious fo-rums, and so on. How important has writing become in the tradition of black story telling, in shaping and influencing black cultural expression? How do you think of writing in the larger scopes of black narrative?

A: I think that writing has become extraordinarily important in terms of black storytelling and shaping and influencing black cultural expres-sion, especially because of the centrality of narrative. The narrativity of black experience—the ways in which stories shape self-understanding and mediate self-revelation racially—is enormously powerful in narra-tive forms, especially autobiographical narratives, which constitute the attempt of the race both to state and then to move forward to its goals as revealed in stories of "overcoming odds," "up from slavery," "out of the ghetto." Narrativity is an extraordinarily important component of self-understanding and the way in which African-American peoples consti-tute their own identities, especially in this postmodern world. I think that writing per se—the capacity of people to reflect critically upon their experiences and then filter those experiences through the lens of their own written work—certainly shapes and changes self-expression in a way different from, say, oral expression. In other words, as Ali Masri, the Africanist, says, there is something extraordinarily conservative about the oral form because the oral form only preserves that which people re-member and that which people deem necessary to integrate into the fab-ric of their collective memory. Whereas the written form contests certain narrow limitations of the oral form because it situates the writer and the reader in a transhistorical moment that allows the articulation of an ex-traordinary convergence of contested identities and conflicting identities. So for instance, when we're writing, and we have a body of writing to ap-peal to and a body of writing against which we can contrast our own self-understanding, our own self-revelation, our own self-invention against what Foucault said, against what Ellison said, against what Baldwin said, against what slave narratives have been talking about for the last century and as we've recuperated them, it's an extraordinarily different moment, because the narrative community there constitutes a wedge of interpretation that is provided by the writing, the very physical act of having the paper to refer to.

In regard to the creation of the self through narrative, it is much different when you have an oral community where people are relying upon memory, upon the texture of their memory, and to mediate their own self-understanding. So orality provides a different lens than it seems writing does as the very textured, embodied, in what, I guess, Haraway calls *material density*. The physical reality of the writing itself has a kind of phenomenological and epistemological *weight* levied against this memory because you can refer *to* the text. Whereas in the oral traditions, they certainly have a kind of genealogical effect: one passes one thing on from another, as opposed to a kind of Nietzschian or Foucauldian sense of geneality. The oral reference provides a kind of artifice of invented memory that in one sense is *not* the same as in written work.

So I think that writing is very important, and it's very important in terms of the transition of African peoples from modernist to post-modernist forms. Writing is enormously important to try to figure out what the past is about, what the present is about in relationship to that past, and how the writing itself becomes a bridge of communication and connection between previous cultures and contemporary ones, *and* a way, of course, of reinventing the very character and texture of experience in light of one's own writing. Writing is as much about revelation as it's about invention. When one is writing, one is literally *writing into* and *writing from*, and I think that those poles of writing into and writing from—inscribing and re-inscribing—situates us in a kind of interpretive and performative moment that allows us to be the mediator, that is, "the writer," to mediate between these two different poles of invention. I think that especially for African-American people who are preoccupied with this literacy, who are preoccupied with the articulation of a self through the narrative, writing becomes a most important avenue of both revealing and inventing the future of the race.

Writing becomes, in relationship to other narrative forms, a crucial aspect of connecting ourselves to an old debate about black intelligence, but it also becomes a way of unleashing and constituting different forms of self-understanding that are necessary if we're to move beyond the *mere* fixation on the oral and the *mere* fixation on the cinematic talk about the legitimate concern of literate expression. I think black people have been torn in two directions here. On the one hand, we've said, "well, that's about white folk and what they do, that's about mainstream society and

WESTMINSTER BOOKSHOP
8 ARTILLERY ROW
LONDON SW1P 1RZ

Tel: 020 7802 0018
Thu 25 May 2006   03:57PM

1 X 0742542556   PUBLIC INTELLECTUALS
         Unit £ 14.99 Total: £ 14.99

    TOTAL DUE   £   14.99

PAID: CASH   £ 20.00

CHANGE: £ 5.01

SHOP ONLINE AT
WWW.WESTMINSTERBOOKSHOP.CO.UK
----

culture, black folks' abilities to articulate self-identity and revelation and culture is about orality." So, writing is not a central part of our own project. On the other hand, people have said, "no, *only* when we begin to write with a certain level of mastery with those narrative patriarchal codes in place, will we be able to exemplify our own specific form of mastery and intelligence, and therefore we will be, in one sense, entering the modern world and able to, in a very powerful way, show that we are worthy of participation in this American project of democracy and that we're worthy bearers of culture." What's interesting to me, then, is not to discard writing as a central project of African and African-American peoples. There have been all kinds of writings embedded in black culture from the get-go. And that one of the things we have to see is that it's a deeply racist moment, to suggest to people that writing is about an external tradition to African-American culture, as opposed to orality. And I think that it's necessary for us as *writers*. I see myself as a writer first and foremost in that sense: an articulator of speech, an articulator of ideals, and the way in which ideals are not only mediated through speech but constituted in very powerful ways through the very act of writing, the physical weight of writing, the intellectual and ontological self-revelation that is expressed in writing, as well as the constituting of narrative communities that weigh against racist arguments, against black identity and black intelligence and black culture—that stuff is very important.

We have to then figure out a way to link writing to a very powerful articulation of black culture, and this is where, for me, questions of authenticity come in. It's not authentic for black folk to write at a certain level; it's authentic for them to speak. It's not authentic for them to engage in intellectual performances; it's about the articulation of the self through the body. So all of these other narrative forms (cinema and forms of musical culture) have precedence in African-American culture because as Hortense Spillers points out, these are the forms that were demanded during slavery. Slave masters didn't say, "Come and perform a trope for us; come and perform a metaphoric allegory." Rather, "come and perform a song for us, and come engage in physical activity." We have to refocus activity upon black intellectual expression through narrative forms that become a way of black people extending a tradition and investigating a tradition that we have neglected. The best of black cultural scholars, of course, and literary scholars, have begun to force us to re-think these issues in light of notions of not only multiple literacy but the way in which most multiple literacies are connected to certain forms of cultural expression within black society.

So, I think that writing is central. As we move into this hyper-text and cyber-world, and the way in which the forms of expression are mediated not through people's physical writing but through exchange of information systems, I think that the recovery of writing becomes a kind of both nostalgic project—already ironically at the end of the twentieth century—but also an articulation of the necessity of still having a mediating agent. That is, the *writer* standing in, not only for a larger narrative community, but for intervening with his or her own viewpoints about what constitutes authentic real legitimate powerful black identity.

Q: You've begun to discuss technology, and recently, in contemporary composition scholarship there has been a lot of conversation regarding how technology affects writers. But there hasn't been much written about how technology specifically affects African-American writers. There are some who see cyber-writing and publishing as closer to oral communication, than traditional writing and publication. Do you see this as a potential advantage for blacks and others? That is, how do you see the role of technology and writing being affected by or affecting matters of language and race?

A: There certainly are advantages to new technologies in terms of cultural expressivity for black people. There is the argument that black people are scared off by scientific technology and that the fears are deserved primarily because these new technologies are controlled by a bunch of white elites who have no interest in investing the requisite economy in black communities to expand the super-information highway into the black ghetto or into black communities to make sure it has an off-ramp into the inner city. On the other hand, we need to examine whether or not these technical elites are reproducing narratives of technical proficiency that already stigmatize black people because of their ostensible exclusion from the regime of intelligence that they represent. There are two things going on here: first of all, that new technologies can primarily increase the capacity for black people to become part of this larger "global" world— *global* with scare quotes there because part of globalization is about the reproduction of narratives with mastery that allow the expansion of information in ways that I think are very problematic. In the sense of a global village, that international perspective that black people are talking about, this allows us to tap into that flow of information—here again, knowledge is mobility. There's only good for African-American peoples to be involved in, and communities to be involved in, this new technology.

One of the ongoing ironies and paradoxes of black life is that when we were still in our pre-modern world, America entered the modern world. African-American communities are in a modernist mode precisely as America moves into a postmodernist mode. Now, God knows, as black people enter into a postmodernist mode what mode that means the rest of American society is involved in, some post-post-modernist, which could be modernism. I've written that post-modernism may turn out to be modernism in drag. So what happens, then, is that for black people the attempt somehow to see ourselves related to technology is a historically specific one: the ways in which those technologies have been deployed against black bodies, against black intelligences. We see this breaking out everywhere. The O. J. Simpson trial was an example of black people's resistance to certain forms of medical technology, feeling that this stuff had been used against us. The reason why so many people were willing to believe that O. J. was perhaps innocent—or at least not guilty—is because of the Tuskegee experiment where black folk had all kinds of medical/technological surveillance on their bodies. There's a kind of inbred hostility toward certain technologies not because of their inherent capacity to do ill or good, but simply because of their social uses on black bodies. What we have to do is to uncouple or de-couple the relationship between technological advance and racial repression, because there's a very strong tradition of that. Once we find ways to intervene upon those kinds of historically unjust and corrupt manifestations of technology, then what black people have to do is to seize the day if we're going to be part and parcel of a new world where technology has not only shaped the nature of writing, but it's also shaped the capacity of people to interact with one another.

In a larger theoretical and philosophical sense, if we say oral communication is closer to technology than traditional writing and publication, there are some arguments to be made on both sides. In one sense, absolutely right because people have a kind of spontaneity about oral communication. If you're on-line and you're responding to a question being pressed to you, there's a kind of textured dense immediacy that one has responding spontaneously to a question. Whereas writing is about re-writing. Writing is about re-invention. It's about taking an ideal in certain linear forms and expressing a logic of inevitability that one either agrees with or disagrees with, that one is able to revise in light of a rejection of that sentiment. Because if you're in a semiconscious state, as many writers are while they're writing, and then find out "Oh, I really don't believe what I just wrote," you can revise that. Whereas in oral communication that is mediated through this new technology of being on-line, the possibility of that spontaneity is greater, but the capacity to revise, of course, once one has committed oneself to a statement, is limited when the other person immediately responds. Whereas in a written situation, there's a prefabricated consciousness that allows one to write, rewrite, revise, and then come at a multiple sense of understandings before one delivers what the definitive statement is that one believes. Now, in one sense, that's being interrupted by new technologies where one commits oneself with more immediacy. That's closer to an oral communication where orality is seen as the kind of spontaneous articulation of beliefs. But there's a different sense of orality that I think is much more profound: the way in which the oral tradition itself has already weeded out alternative visions of a particular story to become that oral tradition. When we talk about oral tradition versus orality, oral tradition says, there's a much more conservative estimation of what can survive transmission from one generation to another. New technologies explode that kind of oral tradition. New technologies explode the capacity of a thousand people to reflect on a particular instance of articulation. For instance, if I make a statement on-line that I think Michael Jackson's hyperbaric chamber was a way of preserving what has already disappeared: his race as a signifier for his own identity. If you're on-line, you've got a hundred people who are going to just argue with you, reaffirm that, give you alternative readings of that particular reality. That's a very powerful moment where indeed there's a communal sense of creating an ideal. The very act of creativity is predicated upon a kind of Lone Ranger metaphor or trope for self-understanding and invention of the text. At least on-line there's a capacity of interaction with a whole range of narrative communicants who are able to shape, re-shape, revise, or at least argue with you about what you think, and therefore it's not simply what you think; it's about the interaction between that artificial community. In *that* sense, this new form bodes extraordinarily well for a range of black people to get involved in this. In terms of language and race, this technology has the capacity to expand the boundaries of the American democratic experience into hyper-space in ways that are very positive. So that it's all for the good that black people are involved in getting on-line, e-mail, getting hooked up and wired, because that expands our capacity to talk about issues of mobility, of democracy, of arguing about the welfare reform, of getting tapped into resources that can help us re-think how we can get connected around the globe, or even around this country. That's very powerful.

On the other hand, to the degree to which African-American people are excluded from that process, there will be the re-articulation of this notion that technology and African-American identity are somehow not simply juxtaposed but contradictory. And that black people, with their refusal to, or inability to, get wired in this so-called technological world, will be a kind of reassertion of a horrible, horrible tradition in the western world—especially in American culture—where scientific and techno-scientific processes have excluded black people and their lives have become the object of that techno-scientific culture and not the object. One of the powerful things about this new technology is that it allows black people to extend their capacity for agency, to become subjects of that techno-scientific culture and not merely as objects. So, I think that it shouldn't be just an uncritical celebration; it should be some kind of cautionary note about the ethical limits imposed upon techno-scientific culture.

Q: You mentioned access, briefly. Could you speak to how class intersects matters of race when we talk about technology?

A: Yes. Well, there's no question that the folk who are getting wired and who are getting on-line more or less are middle-class black folk or black folk who have access to traditional forms of literacy through traditional forms of education through college and so on. There have been many attempts to try to get some of this technology into the inner-city, and we're just now getting people to use computers in the inner-city in ways that people were doing twenty years ago in suburban America throughout this country. So I think that class intervenes powerfully in race in terms of techno-scientific culture precisely because those African-American people who get hooked up, who get wired, are those who already understand the nature of the game, and the nature of the game is about manipulation of information. It's about reproduction of identity through techno-scientific narratives that allow people not only to control and dominate information, but allow that information to allow them to accumulate capital. Because the connection between capital and technology is being obfuscated by this ostensible notion of the democratic exchange of information among participants, and we know that's not the case. What is really the case is that a kind of specific class of people have had access to this technology. So I think that in that sense, class and race work against many black folk, and many brown folk, who really could take greater advantage of what's being offered on-line.

Q:You're very conscious of language. You seem to enjoy words; you play with them when you write: You refer to your "color commentary" on BET about the O.J .case; you pun with phrases like "Crossing over Jordan" in reference to Michael Jordan and "what a difference a Dre makes." You even use racial tension in the sounds of words when you play with alliterations like the "charm and chutzpa" of your son. You've also written that it is clear that "language is crucial to understanding, perhaps solving, though at other times even intensifying, the quandaries of identity that vex most blacks." You argue that, "Black culture lives and dies by language." It's a big question to ask about the relationship between race and language—an inquiry which your work regularly explores in depth. But could you talk about how language affects your own coming to terms with race?

A: Yes, well, that's a very powerful question. You know, that old Bible passage, somewhere in the Psalms: "I was conceived in sin and born in iniquity." I feel like I was born in language; I feel that there's a verbal womb, the rhetorical womb, that I was nurtured in. My mother, who was a highly intelligent black woman, appreciated literacy but was prevented because of being a female and the youngest of a family of five children born to a farmer in Alabama. I feel that from the very beginning, I was bathed in the ethos of linguistic appreciation. My mother talked to us and read to us. And then I went to church; the church is a very important narrative community for me, very powerful, not only in terms of the norms it mediates in regard to the stances one should take politically and spiritually, but simply because of the resplendent resonances that were there in terms of language. Hearing the power for articulations of black preachers, hearing the linguistic innovations of black singers, hearing the rhetorical dexterity of a revivalist who came to town to try to paint for us the picture of God dying on a cross and the differences that the death on that cross made, not simply telling us about a theology of atonement, not simply talking to us (in dry, arcane, academized, theological language) about the dispensation of God, talking about these deep theological concepts. They wanted to paint the picture; they wanted us to feel it. They wanted us to feel the kind of existential and ontological density of linguistic specificity. What I mean by "linguistic specificity" is that the language itself had a performative capacity, and the performative in the most enlarging and very powerful sense of that word. They not only were performing The Word from God, but they themselves, the words, were performing a kind of oracular and wisdom-tradition intervention upon our lives. That was extraordinarily important to me, because I got a sense of the rhythms, of the passions, and of the almost physical texture of language, of feeling the very visceral dimensions of verbal articulation.

In elementary school, my fifth-grade teacher Mrs. James (about whom I've written) had an extraordinary capacity to make black history come alive off the page, and she did so through teaching us painting and poetry. The poetry, especially, and writing our own stories was very important. Mrs. James encouraged us to see that there was a direct connection between the capacities for invention and self-revelation from prior black generations to our own. She made the capacity to be a linguistic animal a very real one for us and a very appealing one for us. Mrs. James taught us that if we're going to really be powerful black people, we're going to be intelligent black people, then we've got to be black people who did what other powerful, intelligent black people did—they wrote, they thought, they created.

As you say, I try to integrate a variety of perspectives about language in my own work now. Because I think that we should take note of what Derrida does with language and how he challenges straightforward traditional literary conceptions of language such as logocentrism. We've got to de-mythologize that through a kind of deconstructive practice that asks not simply, "What does it mean?" but, "How does it signify?" Multiple valences and multiple convergence of meanings which contest in a linguistic space for logic have to be acknowledged as both an index of the political economy of expressive culture, but also, its situatedness and embodiedness and embeddedness in a real political context where words make a difference about who we are and what we understand and what uses those words will be put to. I saw that operating in the black church in terms of spiritual and moral differences, and I've now taken that lesson seriously in the so-called secular arena. I think we have to take Derrida seriously; we have to take Foucault seriously when he talks about the insurrection of subjugating knowledges and the ways in which those knowledges make possible different articulative moments within African-American expressive culture and writing. Also, I think we've got to baptize them, as I've tried to argue. I think that the baptism of Derrida or Foucault or Guattari or Baudrillard or Deleuze doesn't mean that we have a narrow nation-state articulation of the logic of American democracy or nationalism, that is, make them show passports because we Americans demand that foreigners genuflect before the altar of American identity. No; it simply means that we have to take the lesson of shading and of creating a discursive frame that allows the particularities and resonances of this soil, of the American and, in my case, the African-American soil, to dirty the language, to dirty the theory, to make more gritty the realities that so smoothly travel from European culture to American theory, especially as they are applied to African-American culture. I think that language is in itself a metaphor of the extraordinary capacity of identities to be shaped and reshaped, of the incredible convergences of different and simultaneous meanings of life that in some senses claim space within both our intellectual and moral worlds and the ways in which those of us who are writers, artists, intellectuals have to appreciate the extraordinary power that language continues to have especially in minority communities and in oppressed communities where language becomes an index of one's own status. It becomes an index of one's own attempt to create oneself against the world and to say to the world, "I *do* exist." And that's why, for me, instances of certain hip-hop culture have been incredibly important in mediating that reality, especially for young black men and women who have been marginalized, not only within the larger white society and mainstream culture, but who have been marginalized even within African-American culture. Those linguistic divisions in black society continue to index deeper class divisions that we have not paid sufficient attention to.

Q: In the preface to *Between God and Gangsta Rap*, you write: "The recycling of tired debates about racial and cultural authenticity abounds. These debates have taken many forms in many different forums, but they all come down to the same question: how can we define the Real Black Person?" Obviously, there is also no Real Black Writer, but do institutional, mass-read texts—such as multicultural readers—that depict particular black experience attempt to construct a "Real Black Person" and a "Real Black Writer" in the name of diversity and tolerance?

A: I think yes, to answer that, and no [laughter]. Yes, in the sense that, you're absolutely right, one of the hidden logics of multiculturalism is an attempt somehow to elide or distort or at least obfuscate the incredible heterogeneity and the raucous diversity that is contained in black identity—or any minority identity. Multiculturalism is a concession to the need to package black identity for a larger world, to mainstream the particularity and specificity of black identity for a larger world, to be consumed. So in this case, multiculturalism is indivisible from the commodity fetishism and the consumptive realities of the American intellectual scene.

Q: Something like the Epcot version of culture.

A: There it is; that's exactly right! Multiculturalism at that level indexes the necessity to, or need to, or desire to cross over black culture in acceptable mainstream forms under the guise of accepting this reality that other voices must be heard. What's interesting about multiculturalism, however, is that there's a leveling effect in the sense that it says that there are interchangeable others that are being mobilized within the multicultural discourse. In other words, multiculturalism suggests that we have a relative equality of articulation within the space of American intellectual culture and that what we have to do is pay attention to equally objective and informative ways of understanding the world. I don't know if that's what was meant by all those struggles from Frederick Douglass to DuBois down from Sojourner Truth down to Angela Davis. That was meant in terms of appealing to certain literate and oral traditions within African-American culture to situate black life against the injustice and the economic inequality that was being perpetrated. I think that multiculturalism doesn't pay attention to the need to argue that these things are not all the same, that we're not all participating equally at the table. This is the problem of course, and as important as it is in my own understanding of the intellectual project of a person like Richard Rorty talking about conversation as if we all had equal access to the table, that there were no filters, in terms of class or race or gender as to who got to the table, who could get to the table to converse about differences. There's an enormous advance in saying that philosophy is no longer the tribunal of pure reason before which other disciplines must now genuflect in acknowledgment of philosophy's technical superiority or that philosophy is itself value-laden and theory-laden, that it's narrative-laden, that it is, as Rorty borrows from Derrida, a form of writing. It doesn't constitute a kind of disciplinary territory against which we must barricade other epistemological interventions, that is, philosophy is different from theology, theology is radically different from sociology, and so on. But they don't have their epistemological barriers reared that other outsiders must show intellectual passports in order to gain access through genuflection before their disciplinary terrorism.

On the other hand, to use that metaphor of conversation that Rorty got from Michael Oakeshott is to suggest that there is no political/economic analysis of who gets to get at that table, who gets to participate in that dialogue about determining what is real and what's not real, what's important and what's not important, what's moral and what's immoral. I feel the same about multiculturalism that argues that there is a kind of implicit equality of means by which people have access to the debate about what gets to constitute real knowledge. And the reality is that it's radically unequal, it has tremendous marks of inequality, and those marks of inequality are marked in the very appropriation of marginalized minority discourses for the purposes of reproducing a hegemonic conception of what is real and authentic by using the name and the color of blackness to repress other dissident forms of blackness that challenge that narrow market multiculturalism that has been prevalent. In that sense, the Real Black Person is being put forth. Here is the authentic African-American being put forth, not only for the consumptive desires of a market multiculturalism that demands the Real Black, but it's the ability of this market multiculturalism to exclude the capacity of other legitimate, powerful black voices to challenge that narrow hegemony and also to suggest that there are alternative versions of even that conception that need to be taken seriously. In that sense, I'm suspicious. I think it's a dubious project to have this kind of corporate multiculturalism, this market multiculturalism that doesn't pay attention to the radical particularity and the specific heterogeneities that are being produced on the African-American terrain.

The institutionalization of black identity through multiculturalism is at least as problematic to me as those people who are critical of gangsta rap and the way in which gangsta rap presents this authentic black person to the narrative as black-as-thug or the ghetto as only about thugerian thanatopsies and not about black school teachers working against the odds, young black ghetto residents trying to master their algebra through a hail of bullets. I think that the reduction to the Real Black person, the tropes of authenticity and the narrow conceptions of what reality is about, this template of ontological essentialism that really obscures the radical complexity and heterogeneity of black identity, is deeply problematic. Market multiculturalism and corporate multi-centrism are really deeply problematic.

Q: Many people argue that the jargon-rich language of the academy is more obfuscating than illuminating for those outside of the specialized area of academic work. Yet, you write in *Between God and Gangsta Rap* that "The language of the academy is crucial because it allows me to communicate within a community of scholars whose work contributes to the intellectual strength of our culture. . . . The language of the academy is most important to me because it provides a critical vocabulary to explore the complex features of American and African-American life. The language of the academy should never divorce itself from the politics of crisis, social problems, cultural circumstances, moral dilemmas, or intellectual questions of the world in which we live." You continue, "As a public intellectual, I am motivated to translate my religious, academic, and political ideas into a language that is accessible without being simplistic." How do you seque the transition between academic discourse and more public discourses affecting your work? And, are there problems of translation when moving between discourses?

A: I see the transition from the academic to the public as a self-conscious decision to intervene on debates and conversations that happen in public spheres—a different public sphere from the academy because I consider the academy a public sphere—that have enormous consequence on everyday peoples' lives that I want to have a part of. The transition, however, is not smooth; the demands for rigorous debate within the academy are much different from those demands in the public sphere. Within academic, linguistic practices, there are enormous debates going on right now that are being prosecuted within the academy in the larger intellectual scene about the function of academized language. I'm not one of these people who—for obvious reasons, self-interest being the primary one [laughter]—jumps on academics because they don't speak for a public audience or that they cannot speak in ways that are clear and articulate, because those are loaded terms: clarity, articulate. As many other scholars—Henry Giroux, Donna Haraway—have all reminded us that language has multiple functions even within a limited context. To understand that is to acknowledge that there are a variety of fronts upon which we must launch our linguistic and rhetorical resistances against political destruction, against moral misery, and against narrow conceptions of what language does and how it functions. Being reared in a black church, being reared in a so-called minority linguistic community that had rich resources that were concealed and obscured for a variety of reasons, I think that I'm sensitive to the claim against academics and probably understand their defensiveness when they say, "We're writing for a specific audience." That's fine. I think that if you write an article that will be read by a thousand people, and that those thousand people gained something from it, there's an exchange of information, there's an exchange of ideas, there's a sharpening of the debate, there's a deepening of the basis upon which we understand a particular intellectual subject. There's no reason to be apologetic for that because that's a very specific function within a larger academic enterprise that needs to be prosecuted. If, for instance, somebody writes an essay upon a specific aspect of Foucault's conception or appropriation of Benthamite conceptions of the prison and they make clear the relationship between not only Bentham and Foucault, they also rearticulate our conceptions of the panopticon and how surveillance operates as it's extended into the black ghetto. That's all for the better and good—even if only a thousand people understand the language in which it's deployed and if only they get it. That means that some advance and understanding and exchange of information has gone on, and that's a legitimate enterprise. The problem I have is we don't have a problem with brain surgeons who speak languages that only twelve people can understand. If the man or woman can save your life, speak the jargon; do what you've got to do; operate! We haven't got any problem with that. So, I don't have a problem with the similar kind of precise, rigorous uses of language that happen in academic circles. The problem arises when the hostility is directed against those who are able to take the information, to take the knowledge, to take the profound rigor that is often suggested in such exercises and make them available to a broader audience. Now, necessarily giving up something in terms of depth for breadth is inevitable. I've written for *Cultural Studies* and *Cultural Critique* and journals that four or five thousand people may read, and I've written in audiences where a million and a half and two million people have read them. We have to respect the genre. We, as academics, have a deep hostility to those who are public; those who are public intellectuals are viewed necessarily as sell-outs. We have our own version of the authentic academic and the authentic intellectual. Authenticity is quite interestingly debated, not only within African-American circles, but it's debated within academic circles where people have their narrow conception of what the authentic intellectual is. And interestingly enough, from the late '80s with Russell Jacoby's book on the last intellectual, this debate has been fiercely prosecuted and interestingly enough around the black public intellectual. I think some of that hostility may be racially coded, but a lot of that hostility is coded in terms of these rigid territorial disputes. A kind of geography of destiny is linked to whether you occupy the terrain of the academy, specifically and particularly as an academic, you ought to stay there. We love to talk about transgressions intellectually, academically, but we don't want to do it physically or epistemologically. We don't want to actually do it.

Q: We resist the critique of being put in the ivory tower, but then we're the ones who insist on putting us in the ivory tower.

A: That's exactly right; it can't be better stated than that. We want to attack the ivory tower from the ivory tower. And what's interesting is that these bullets are boomeranging. We celebrate transgression, we celebrate this hybrid, we celebrate all of this migration and mobility, but when people actually do it there's a curiously incredible resentment against that kind of movement.

Q: In his recent book *Political Correctness*, Stanley Fish questions "the possibility of transforming literary study so that it is more immediately engaged with the political issues that are today so urgent: issues of oppression, racism, terrorism, violence against women and homosexuals,

cultural imperialism, and so on. It is not so much that literary theory critics have nothing to say about these issues, but that so long as they say it
as literary critics no one but a few of their friends will be listening, and,
conversely if they say it in ways unrelated to the practices of literary criticism, and thereby manage to give it political effectiveness, they will no
longer be literary critics, although they will be something and we may regard the something as more valuable." In *Race Rules*, you write that "the
university isn't all it's cracked up to be: an artificial environment removed
from the lives of real people." But you also write in *Between God and
Gangsta Rap* that "although the university has come under attack for its
practiced irrelevance to the larger society, and its intrinsic elitism, it is a
wonderful place to be in the world." You go on to say, "The vocation of in-
dulging the life of the mind is just as important as the ingenious accomplishments of basketball heroes and superstar singers, talk show hosts
and movie stars." Fish's critique of public intellectualism insists on disciplinary discreteness. That is, that disciplines are defined against other disciplines: "we do this; you do that." Fish argues that as university intellectuals we cannot be public intellectuals and as public intellectuals we give
up our roles as university scholars. In essence, Fish argues that Michael
Eric Dyson cannot be an academic and a public intellectual. Your critique
of university sees the academy as inseparable from the "real world" and
that our roles in the university are as important as any other vocation outside of the academy. How do you respond to Fish's critique? And, as the
university becomes more interdisciplinary, do you see, as Fish does, that
inter-disciplinarity is a threat to universities or do you see it as having a
greater potential to intervene in public policy and the larger culture?

A: Well, I think that Stanley Fish is a real smart guy. I always listen carefully to what he says. I think that some of his criticisms are right on target. But I think that, at this point, I dissent. Because I think that he's actually right to force us, to challenge us, to re-think the relationship
between what we do and what we say. He's also forcing us, even more
poignantly, to take seriously that serving on a committee in the academy
where you deploy Marxist language to demythologize class relationships
is not the same as being involved in a labor dispute in the local AFL-CIO
or talking about the interests of black workers on the line in Detroit. No
question that he's absolutely right. But that doesn't mean, therefore, that
the function of the intellectual deploying Marxist language to demythologize class relations is not, therefore, important. It's a different kind
of importance. As a black person in the academy, I don't have the luxury
of saying who's more real than the next person. I don't have the luxury of
saying, "this is good and this is not good," precisely because we just got
here in terms of the so-called mainstream academy. I think the real point
is that there are multiple sites for intervention on behalf of political inter-

ests, and in this Fishian universe and cosmology there's this radical bifurcation between the *real* world in which people operate with political interests at hand, deploying languages to defend those interests and those who are operating in the academy who are being segregated in a different sphere of knowledge-production and consumption that has a difference in political interests. They both have a set of interests that need to be taken seriously. The academy is a public sphere; it is a deep and broad public sphere where interesting, important debates are happening. That's from the perspective of African-American people, or at least this particular black intellectual, who have been closed out from that debate for so long. Knowing that we were closed out from that debate for so long means that we understood that what was going on there was important, because Charles Murray and Richard Herrnstein (although dealing with simple scientific theories that have been deconstructed by people back to 20 years ago who were dealing with theories about genetic inheritance of race) sold 400,000 copies of a book. Now in one sense, we know most people didn't read that book; the very existence of that book was a phenomenological weight to justify cultural prejudices about African-American intelligence. But what that also suggests is that black people understand that those debates have enormous consequence and significance upon African-American material interests. We already see the connection between the academy and the "real world," because the real world looks to the academy to justify its prejudices, to dress them up in scientific discourse that allows them to gain legitimacy and power. We have understood all along that even though twelve people may be reading that book, one of the twelve people reading that book ends up being a congressman; one of the other twelve people reading that book could end up being a policy maker; one of the other twelve people reading that book could end up being the director of an institute that has ability to determine resources for a whole lot of black people. We have to deconstruct and demythologize this radical bifurcation between the academy and the real world. Both of them are real worlds constituted equally by narratives of political interest that are being deployed to defend certain perspectives of the world. Truth and politics are deeply united in ways that, I think, Fish is not paying sufficient attention to.

What's important about inter-disciplinarity is that it certainly threatens those people who have narrowly political interests about maintaining and preserving their bailiwick. And I think what's interesting is that Fish gives eloquent, but I think quite problematic, articulation to a narrower vision of the life of the mind than I would like. He gives us caution about thinking that those of us who indeed make Marxist or progressive analyses of forms of oppression as substituting for real work. It is itself real work. It performs an intellectual function that is both daring given the narrow

hegemony of a conservative vision of the academy that prevails, and in itself intellectually important to the concrete interests of people outside of
the academy. Before I came into the academy, I worked in two factories,
and I was a teen father working and hustling at two different jobs. People
in Detroit University and Wayne State University who were trying to
think about the relationship between labor and commodity and wage and
alienation and intellectual projects were very powerful and important to
making substantive political interventions on behalf of those people and
forcing those of us in that real movement to take seriously the life of the
mind to defend our interests and to be conscious of the fact that we had
interests to be defended.

Inter-disciplinarity is really an index of this postmodern moment where
we take the multiplicity not only of ideals and knowledges, but where we
get to ask questions about who gets to control knowledge, for what purposes is it being deployed, and then finally, whose interests are being protected by a narrow conception of the life of the mind that is rooted in academic disciplines that pay no attention to what other people in other
disciplines are doing and other people in other intellectual enterprises are
doing. What's important is that it is the most powerfully artificial conception of the life of the mind to segregate knowledge in terms of academic disciplines. It argues against the best, most powerful traditions of
Western intellectual enterprise that we have available.

Q: In *Race Rules* you write: "The anointing of a few voices to represent
The Race is an old, abiding problem. For much of our history, blacks have
had to rely on spokespersons to express our views and air our grievances
to a white majority that controlled access to everything from education to
employment. For the most part, powerful whites only wanted to see and
hear from a few blacks at a time, forcing us to choose a leader—when we
could. Often a leader was selected for us by white elites. Predictably,
blacks often disagreed with those selections, but since the white elites had
the power and resources, their opinions counted." You continue in *Race
Rules* to discuss "who gets to be a black public intellectual, who chooses
them," and why black public intellectuals currently receive the attention
they do. However, in contemporary America there really are very few
black intellectuals, and those that achieve recognition seem to be split into
tiers of importance with the top tier consisting of you, bell hooks, Henry
Louis Gates, Houston Baker, and Cornel West, and then a second tier with
a host of scholars such as Patricia Williams, William Strickland, Jerry
Ward, Robin Kelly, Stephen Carter, David Levering Lewis to name a few.
This suggests that the intellectual/academic world—which is still made
up primarily of middle-class Anglo males—have constructed particular
methods of gatekeeping (for example, graduate school entrance requirements, hiring practices, tenure, publication, speaking engagements) that

"select" particular leaders to serve as "the representative" voice. More exact, having only a few black intellectuals is a product of the kind of oppressive strategies of management and containment maintained by the
academy. What does this say about the small numbers of black public intellectuals and the possibility of the "radicalness" of public intellectuals
such as yourself, hooks, West, and the others? Can you really be radical
and affect change from the inside, when the institution has, in fact, sanctioned your radicalness? After all, you are a high-profile, well-paid member of the academy.

A: Exactly right. No question about it. No doubt about it. It's very difficult. And I think that it's necessary to acknowledge not only the accuracy of the critique, but furthermore, to extend the political efficacy of that
accuracy by being self-critical. There's always a dimension of hubris in
self-criticism because then you're pointing to how self-critical I can be and
look how critically engaging I can be about my own position even as I
consolidate my interest as a high-profile, well-paid black intellectual. I
face that problem head on. It is very difficult. And you're absolutely right
in terms of the sanctioning of the radicalism that we express: it is being
deployed within a larger narrative of co-optation by the American Academy that we criticize and from whose base we articulate our own conceptions of the world. So there's no doubt that it's very difficult, but I
think it's the inevitable condition that we live in right now, inevitable in
the sense that this is the present condition under which we live as we fight
for change from within and certainly from without. There's no question
that we have to begin to raise larger questions and to really provoke a
more profound analysis not only of our own subject positions but our
own professional positions within the hierarchy of privilege and visibility
that we presently enjoy. What's very difficult is to figure out how we both
criticize our own participation in the Academy, in this regime of black intellectuals who have been anointed, and at the same time maintain
enough visibility and influence to have our voices make a difference. In
that one sense, it is a very difficult project. Another way we can make sure
that we undermine is to ask questions about whom we refer to in our
work. What is interesting to me is when we read interviews with some of
these high-profile black intellectuals you have mentioned, we get the
same old names. In other words, there's a kind of narrative reinscription
of fame and a hierarchy of privilege established within the linguistic practices of black intellectuals. So that if we keep hearing about the same novelist, the same intellectual, even though they are deserving of enormous
mention and enormous merit, what happens is that we feel they are the
only important voices out there. And I think one of the most powerful
things we can do as black intellectuals, especially those of us who are
highly visible, is to talk about those intellectuals whose work not only is

different from ours and whose work may challenge ours, and whose voices would not ordinarily be heard if we did not mention them.

Q: You're leading into my next question: You write that "We don't speak for The Race. We speak as representatives of the ideological strands of blackness, and for those kinships we possess outside of black communities, that we think most healthy . . . we ain't messiahs." At the same time, though, you also write: "Equally worrisome, too many black public intellectuals hog the ball and refuse to pass it to others on their team. Many times I've been invited on a television program, a prestigious panel, or a national radio program because a white critic or intellectual recommended me. Later I often discover that another prominent black intellectual, when consulted, had conveniently forgotten to mention my name or that of other qualified black intellectuals. Ugly indeed." Do you think perhaps this is because those black public intellectuals who now have the spotlight actually do want to be anointed as spokesperson "to represent The Race"? And, how do you—if, indeed, you, do at all—think the cult of celebrity, the protection of position as black public intellectual, works against a sort of "hand up for someone on the rung below" attitude? Do you see this "hand" as a moral imperative? That is, is it the moral imperative of those who have achieved the status of black public intellectual to help others into the same position?

A: There is no question that many of us black intellectuals do want to be the "head nigger in charge." We do want to be the most visible, or as I say in my book, the "hottest Negro in the country." There's no question that to attain a certain form of visibility in American culture as an intellectual is itself dizzying, and there is a kind of narcotic effect. When people like Oprah or Charlie Rose or Montel Williams call you up, or when you are invited to write op-eds for the *Washington Post* or the *New York Times*, or when you're referred to as one of the leading voices of your generation, or in my case as the leading young, black, Hip-Hop intellectual, that is very seductive. It's very powerfully entrapping. First of all, it invites us to read our own press. Secondly, it invites us to believe our own press, and then thirdly it invites us to reproduce our own press—even if we consciously, through the rhetoric of humility, defer that to others or assign it to other onlookers or other sycophants who believe in the absolute integrity of our intellectual vision. I think there is no doubt that the temptation among any intellectual—especially among black intellectuals given the small numbers of us who are able to survive and thrive to be *the person*, as Zora Neale Hurston said, "the Pet Negro." We have to constantly resist that temptation by constantly making forays into, and interventions into, and excursions into those base communities that we say we represent or at least ostensibly speak for.

There is no question that one of the most dispiriting things that I've seen among black public intellectuals is the kind of vicious, cruel snipping, the rhetorical attacks that I see being lobbied and the kind of pettiness behind the scenes. Now this is not endemic to black culture. This is where I think Henry Kissinger is absolutely right, that the politics of the Academy are so vicious because there is so little at stake. So we are fighting for this small land. The topography of black intellectual space in the Academy is so constrained and so constricted that we are indeed fighting over a narrow terrain. The vicious consequence of those kinds of contestations is that they do not produce good benefits for the people that (A) we claim we represent, or (B) we were put in place to represent or speak for. The inevitability of representation and the politics of representation are something we have to contend with. So, yes, not only are there many who want to be and who have a secret desire to be *the One*, we also prevent, by virtue of our fame and visibility, the kind of moral imperative that used to be "each one teach one, each one reach one" or lifting as we climb. There ain't much lifting as we climb, except lifting our own mobility, lifting our own stakes, lifting our own visibility. We are not lifting others, carrying those on our rhetorical, intellectual backs. The consequence is that it creates this hierarchy, this two- or three- or four-tiered system.

Q: You're very critically conscious of your role as black public intellectual. In *Race Rules* you offer a critical series of awards you call the "Envys." Your purpose in these awards is both to critique black public intellectuals and to answer critiques leveled by black public intellectuals. Though many of these critiques are unrelenting in their criticism, you don't leave yourself out of your own attack, and you award yourself "The Spike Lee/Terry McMillan Award for Shameless Self Promotion" for your lobbying for publicity for your work. Nonetheless, you are critical of how other black public intellectuals use the role of public intellectual and what they promote in that role. In light of your other comments regarding the "lone black leader," and the "ugliness" of not nurturing other black intellectuals' careers, is such criticism helpful?

A: It can be construed as a kind of self-congratulatory self-flagellation in public that only reinforces the very visibility that I claim has unequally been cast on some intellectuals, including myself. I think I'm caught in a kind of endless night of the soul in being preoccupied with those levels of unfairness that prevent other worthy black intellectuals from coming to the fore. In that sense, my criticism can be construed in a negative way. The positive way in which that criticism can be construed is in the ability of black intellectuals to take this tongue-in-cheek. Partly what I'm saying is "lighten up." This is not something that is going to ultimately change the world if we ourselves participate or do not participate in it.

What I was trying to say in tongue-in-cheek awards is that we talk about being critical, but let's bring some of that critical light upon ourselves. Let's cast that critical acumen upon ourselves and by doing so, let's raise questions about the nature of our work, about the real limits that our work has, and the ways in which we are able to make interventions. We can be at least more conscious about the need to include others and to open up that space. The positive nature of my work can be that it will create a larger discourse space where people can say, "That was really funny, but . . ." or they can say, "That wasn't so funny because these charges are on target because . . ." or thirdly they can say, "Well, even though Dyson is trying to promote himself *yet again*, what's important about his critique is that it does raise very powerful issues about the nature of the kind of work where we give the voice of the Negro to a very few black people, while the masses of intellectuals and academicians have no access." That can be helpful if it produces a material effect of having people interrogate their own practices, of having people ask why is there a need to salute and anoint a few voices, and finally what the function of a gatekeeper is. What I want to raise out of this, if nothing else, is why is it that a few black people are anointed to determine what other black people receive. The very purpose of those of us who are so-called "radical black intellectuals" was to raise questions about gate-keepers, about the intellectual Booker T. Washingtons who were able to dole out punishment or reward based upon their understanding of the political efficacy of a particular work or a particular career. That is the kind of thing we have to relentlessly interrogate if we are to at least raise the possibility of other voices emerging.

Q: In April of 1996, *Harper's* published a conversation on race between Jorge Klor De Alva, Earl Shorris, and Cornel West. In this discussion, West argues that "when we talk about identity, it's really important to define it. Identity has to do with protection, association, and recognition. People protect their bodies, their labor, their communities, their way of life; in order to be associated with people who ascribe value to them, who take them seriously, who respect them; and for purposes of recognition, to be acknowledged, to feel as if one actually belongs to a group over time and space, we have to be very specific about what the credible options are for them at any given moment." De Alva later says, "All identities are up for grabs. But black intellectuals in the United States, unlike Latino intellectuals in the United States, have an enormous media space within which to shape the politics of naming and to affect the symbols and meanings associated with certain terms. Thus, practically overnight, they convinced the media that they were an ethnic group and shifted over to the model of African-American, hyphenated American, as opposed to being named by color. Knowing what we know about the negative aspects of naming, it would be better for all of us, regardless of color, if those who consider themselves, and are seen as, black intellectuals were to stop participating in the insidious one-drop-rule game of identifying themselves as black." You've written quite a bit about identity politics. How do you respond to this exchange between West and De Alva?

A: West is absolutely right in terms of protection, association, and recognition, especially as those three modes of response to the formation of identity have played themselves out within historically constituted black communities. It is an implicit reproval of and rebuttal against Paul Gilroy's notion that any notion of ethnic solidarity is itself to buy into a backwards view of black identity. Gilroy has been especially critical of black American intellectuals for what he considers to be their essentialist identities. Interestingly enough, those very black intellectuals in America have written powerfully about hybridity and about identity and about the need to talk about the transgressive potentials of black identity, of pulling into view what Stuart Hall calls postmodern identity. It's a very complex navigation of a variety of possibilities and subject positions within a narrative of recognition. So West's notion that it's protective, associative, and recognition is about rooting it in a very specific context of how African-Americans have contested the erosion of their identities, the attack of their identities, and how identity politics at a certain level is a response to narrow, vicious stereotypes imposed on us from the outside.

Jorge' s response about seeing black Americans in the public considering themselves black as a kind of surrender to this "one drop rule" misses the point of history and the context of culture. History suggests that these are objective criteria—objective in the sense that they were socially constructed as the norm by which black people were judged. So even if black identity is up for grabs, it has a limit. It certainly is up for grabs as I've argued in my work about the fluidity of these boundaries of black identity, but it has real historical and cultural and racial limitations. Jorge is expressing the bitter edge and a misled conception of this postmodern vision of black identity. Saying black identity is much more fluid, it has much more movable boundaries, that black identity is a moveable feast of self reinvention is not to say that there are no bottom lines. As Elizabeth Alexander says, "Listen, I believe in de-essentialized, racialized politics. But there's got to be a bottom line." And the bottom line is what are the material effects of the historically constituted notions of blackness both within African-American culture and outside of black culture. As the old saying goes, you can tell the policeman that race is a trope, but if he's beating your head and you're saying, "Listen, this is a historically constituted, socially constructed reality that has no basis beyond our agreement and consensus in American culture," that's cool, but your head is still being beat. So the material consequences of the association of race with black identity with black skin has to be acknowledged as a serious consequence against which we must articulate our understanding.

In this exchange between West and Jorge, what West understands is the need to ground the politics of black identity in cultural specificity and in racial particularities that acknowledge the function of geography and of biology, even if we want to overcome and transgress against them. Whereas Jorge appeals to a language that is much more inviting in terms of interrogating blackness as a historically constituted and socially constructed reality, but he does not pay sufficient attention to how blackness signifies in multiple ways in the public sphere. One of the most powerful ways it signifies is as a descriptive term to name people of color who have historically been constituted as black, and therefore their identities are both invested in protecting that boundary of blackness and also raising questions about its limitations at the same time. So, I would agree with West about the historical constitution of it and the social rooting of it, and Jorge about the need to raise questions about those boundaries but to link them politically.

Q: Composition, like many intellectual disciplines, has been engaged in its own version of the "theory wars." You are very careful in your writing to acknowledge the importance of academic theories—particularly postmodernisms and poststructuralisms. You write "At its best, theory should help us unmask the barbarous practices associated with some traditions of eloquent expression. But like a good sermon or a well-tailored suit, theory shouldn't show its seams." You also write in *Between God and Gangsta Rap* "with some adjustments, I think theory may help to explain black culture." What role do you see theory playing in race issues? And, could you describe the "seamless" theory?

A: [laughter] Hey man, I just write about these things; I didn't expect to get asked about them. Well, the role of theory in black culture is a multiple one. First of all, I think theory should help us clarify what we take to be concrete experience, the relationship between so-called theory and practice. I think all practices are theorized and all theories are practiced at a certain level, not necessarily in a particular logical or linear order. The first function of theory is to make us understand that practices have components of intellectual aspiration that are sometimes obfuscated and often concealed.

Second, theory, in regard to black culture, forces us to understand that black culture is much more difficult, much more complex, much more multi-layered, and much more combative, even within its own boundaries than people have given voice to. The need for theory is to name the different aspects and components of that contested terrain. For instance, say that Gates is trying to talk about the way in which signifying practices name certain rhetorical devices that have been deployed within black culture from Blues culture down to other literary expressions; that is very important. But also what is important is that theory trying to help us understand the difference between signifying practices in Blues culture and signifying practices in Hip-Hop culture. So what is important is that the theorization of black culture helps us comprehend elements that we historically have neglected, elements that have always been there that we have not sufficiently paid attention to, and the ways in which our own understandings of black culture are already theory laden. That is, we never begin in a pre-theoretical density in terms of interpreting black culture. We are already theorizing even if we do not have the official language of the academic proles to express that theory. People who interpret black culture are already working with a theoretical base. What theory does is ask that to become explicit. Theory asks this pre-theoretical density, that is really an illusion and a mythology, to come out of the closet and to admit that it is already theoretical. I'm not suggesting that pre-theoretical poses that people take in response in terms of consciousness to culture. I'm saying that theory is always operating in terms of how people understand themselves in relationship to black culture.

For me a seamless theory is a theory that does not have to display the most rampant forms of jargon-ridden discourse to make its point. To intervene on that debate, of course, is not simply to say that there is no room for jargon. There is. So to me a seamless theory is the ability to express very powerfully, very intelligently, and very articulately an ideal that is very complex but in ways that broader people beyond your discipline have access to. That, to me, is a theory that may have some jargon involved, but mostly does not rely upon the old habits of thought that jargon signifies and forces us to break new ground in saying it in ways that a geologist who is educated may understand as well as a literary theorist who has training in the field. The importance of that is that a person like myself who has written for these different audiences gives up something when you do either one. What that kind of writing has forced me to see is that if I'm going to write for an audience beyond even my discipline, beyond my particular so-called training, beyond the people who speak a similar language to me, I then have to write in ways that appeal broadly to people who are intelligent, who are intellectual, but people who have some capacity for understanding language and who have the capacity not only to understand the language but to use it in ways that I may never have the opportunity to do. I want to reach them. The best, most politically efficacious use of theory is its capacity to show people things they did not know before in ways that they understand. That to me is a seamless theory, at least in terms of its linguistic practice.

Q: For many theorists of race, class, gender and culture, notions of disruption become critical in the critique of traditional power structures. For

instance, feminist linguists such as Hélène Cixous look to create awareness through the disruption of phallogocentric language. You write of
black public intellectuals that they are "leaders of a particular kind. We
stir up trouble in broad day light so that the pieties by which we live and
the principles for which we die, both as a people and a nation, are subject
to critical conversation." However, in many of your discussions of black
political figures and movements you are also critical of how disruption
gets used. For instance you clearly juxtapose the militant disruptiveness
of Malcolm X and the assimilative, non-disruptiveness of Colin Powell.
Would you speak to the idea of disruption in the role of racial matters?

A: I think that disruption is a primary prerogative of those of us who are
paid pests. I consider cultural critics and black intellectuals paid pests. We
are trying to point to the emperor not only having no clothes, but the imperialism that has a whole bunch of clothes and what it is dressed up in. I
think our function is to disrupt and intervene upon conversations in ways
that are disturbing, that in their very disturbance force people to ask why
they frame the questions in the way that they did or they make the analysis they do. Disruption is not simply a kind of orgasm for its own sake, a
kind of intellectual anarchy that has no political efficacy. Disruption has a
political goal, and that political goal is to force us to interrogate practices
through a different lens or to see them differently in the same lens. For instance, race may be the lens that people use, but if they begin to see different aspects of race differently because of the questions we raise, that is
a very important function. We do not always have to do away with the
very lens through which people see, although that metaphor itself gives us
a kind of ideological purchase that is very narrowly conservative. In some
instances we have to shatter the whole lens. Not only do we have to shatter the lens, but we have to shatter the paradigm of the lens, the ocular-
centrism by which we understand knowledge. As Martin James has written about it in *Downcast Eyes*, this ocular-centric metaphor misses the way
in which the other metaphors of knowledge can operate. We have to talk
about hearing; we have to talk about feeling. Partly what we do then as a
black intellectual is to disrupt that ocular-centric metaphor whereby vision or blindness operates and the lens is important to talk about how we
experience visceral realities phenomenologically that have been downplayed through, say, anti-feminist discourse. What we have to do is create
a string of metaphors that give us a different interventional possibility
onto the terrain of knowledge, and politics and culture.

That kind of disruption is very important in terms of race because of the
way in which historically constituted black communities have had to argue with, not simply intellectual paradigms of injustice, but the ways in
which they have struggled against them in terms of their own bodies and
movements that have gone on. So that Marcus Garvey's movement, so

that Martin Luther King, Jr.'s civil rights movement, so that A. Philip Randolph's movement are very important sites and terrains of contestation that imagine a different space than an intellectual argument with inequality. It is putting forth a very powerful rejection and rebuttal of both stereotype and inequality through the embodied articulation of black resistance.

But intellectually the disruption, too, is important in terms of racial matters where those of us who are called upon to think critically about race have to not only disrupt dominant paradigms, but we also have to disrupt the ways in which we settle into our own resistant paradigms that themselves become new orthodoxies. Disruption is quite unsettling precisely because we can never be settled finally in a position from which we would defend certain visions or attack certain versions of black life for the rest of our intellectual lives. The kind of perennial, migratory possibilities, the kind of endless mobility, is what disruption is about. That is why it can never be settled in the hands of one set of intellectuals to talk about what black culture is about. That is why the very nature of disruption is a critical necessity for interrogating black practices and racial matters and has to always be changing hands. And it is not that we cannot have a long career in disruption, or a long career in interrogating race. It means that we have to have other voices that challenge us, even in our disruptive practices about what the function of our disruption is and the political absorption of that disruption into a larger trajectory.

Q: There's a photocopied poster on a colleague's door in my department; it is of a photograph of an old, wooden sign that reads "We Serve Whites Only. No Spanish or Mexicans." The sign was posted in 1949 to enforce the Jim Crow laws in San Antonio, Texas. On the copy, someone has written, "History is not just black and white." Though you certainly make an effort to discuss race—particularly when you discuss issues of violence—in terms of Latinos/as, Koreans, Asians, and so on, your work on race deals mostly—as most work in race does—with issues of black and white. Could you discuss the black and white depictions of race in America, and perhaps speak to the (fewer than black) "other" race intellectuals?

A: I think that if we are asking what it means if the narrative frame is black and white, it certainly buys into a very narrow conception, although a very real one, for Africans in the diasporate America. The black/white disjunction was one that curtailed our own economic and social mobility, one that contained the potentiality for the destruction of our material interest and one in which we have had to exist in a kind of symbiotic relationship. This is why the work by theorists like James Scott, who talks about infra-politics and everyday forms of resistance and how it gets played out in African-American culture through the theorized relationship between the black and the white, is so important. How symbiotically have black people had to exist in relationship to white people? As Ralph

Ellison said, we can't even imagine America without black Americans, although white Americans have not always taken that seriously. The black/white, disjunction is a reflection of the existential and economic and political realities that obtain for Africans in the Diaspora and their relationship to the mainstream. That is why James Scott's work is very important because you figure out how to situate yourself as a degraded subject in relationship to the overarching object of both your interests and the need for survival, that is the white majority, the white mainstream. And so much of black culture has been developed in response to maintaining, preserving, and surviving *vis-à-vis* this dominant, hegemonic Other and the survival techniques that had to be marshaled in the face of that. This is how these infra-politics are talked about by people like Robin Kelly who in his book *Race Rebels* talks about black people on the bus in Birmingham and how, even though they were not involved explicitly in terms of racial politics, they were involved nonetheless in very powerful ways by refusing on that space of the bus certain racial meanings that were ascribed to them.

All this means is that the black/white bifurcation has been one of necessity and survival for African-American people in this country. The depictions of black/white among black and white people have been about overcoming barriers to get to know one another. But really that white people must know more about black people because one of the necessities and strategies for survival is that black folk had to know white folk. You have to know your enemy; you have to know whom you are dealing with. Was it Fanny Lou Hamer who said that the mistake that white folk made is that they put black people behind them and not in front of them? Because if they put black people in front of them, they could have surveilled them in a certain way. But since they put black people behind them, black people learned all the secrets and strategies of white folk and how to please them and how to "get over" on them. So all that means that the black/white bifurcation has been about *knowing* white people; there is a kind of epistemology of friendship. If you know white people, you will know better how to get along with them.

One of the real liabilities of simply seeing race in black and white is that we begin to miss how race is being constructed and, has been constructed around a number of axes that go beyond the black/white divide. Even certain debates within black culture and white culture are geographical. For instance, the black/Jewish conflict is a geographical one at a certain level. It is going to be happening much more powerfully in New York than in California. Whereas in California the black/white divide is challenged by the black/brown divide or the black/Korean divide, not only in terms of black/Korean and black/Latino but Latinos and whites and Latinos who are white, Hispanic as white and Hispanic as non-white,

Hispanic as black and non-black. What it begins to introduce is that there is a racial millennialism that does not simply follow the axis of black/white, but follows many more axes that force us—should force us—to rethink how we understand the black/white divide. It does not mean that the black/white divide is not important or that it has not been crucial even as an analogy or metaphor for other minorities who have fought for inclusion in the larger circle of American identity and privilege. What it does suggest to us is that the black/white divide misses how we try to impose upon other minorities substitute black status as a minority.

Q: In the *Harper's* interview that I mentioned earlier, Klor De Alva claims that "with the exception of black-white relations, the racial perspective is not the critical one for most folks. The cultural perspective was, at one time, very sharply drawn, including the religious line between Catholics and Protestants, Jews and Protestants, Jews and Catholics, Jews and Christians. But in the course of the twentieth century, we have seen in the United States a phenomenon that we do not see anyplace else in the world—the capacity to blur the differences between these cultural groups, to construct them in such way that they become insignificant and to fuse them into a new group called whites, which didn't exist before." If this is true, why has "difference" in America been reduced, at least publicly, to matters of color?

A: It's been reduced to matters of color, but it's more or less what's called "pigmentocracy." I talk about the difference between pigmentosis and pigmentification. Pigmentification means that you get adapted within the larger pigmentocracy, the regime of color that's associated with white skin. Within pigmentosis you get excluded from that regime of color. Color is so important because color was never a reference to itself. Color was a politically invested category that revealed our own prejudices and biases and the ways in which we distributed political and economic resources. Jorge is right that whiteness became a blurred distinction in America. Whiteness in America became a self-sufficient, or all-sufficient, category that wiped out certain distinctions: German, Polish, Irish. But they did survive in terms of ethnic and religious practices within American culture; I don't think he's right there. But the function of the racialization in America is predicated by pigmentocracy, that is the way in which goods are distributed according to one's own relationship to an ideal of color.

But color never was simply about skin tone. It was about the intellectual, ideological, and political dimensions of American culture that revealed our conflicts over issues of African versus European and American identity. I think that if we are literalist about this color thing, we missed the way in which a pigmentocracy was predicated upon a whole range of conflicted political and economic and social meanings that were themselves being mediated through this notion of skin and pigment. Skin and pigment become the more visible index of a regime and hierarchy of privilege and status that was associated with a different understanding of species. What I think Jorge is overlooking here is that there was what some people call pseudo-speciation, the attempt to divide and divorce black people from the quality and character of what it meant to be a human being. What didn't happen with all those other different ethnic groups that came over to America is that they did not get pseudo-speciated. They did not get written out of the dominant narrative text of humanity that included all white ethnics even if there was a hierarchy of visibility, influence and privilege. Whereas with black people there was an attempt to rule them out of the race.

Q: In the Preface to *Making Malcolm*, you discuss an uncomfortable incident that occurred in one of your classes when tension between students about racial divisions erupted. Where does race belong in the classroom?

A: Everywhere and nowhere, I guess. Race and the classroom is an inevitable feature; it is the ineluctable product of the racialization of American society. To expect that the classroom will somehow be exempt from the racialized meanings that are just exploding in our culture is to have a sort of pedagogical naivete that is not only insular but is also destructive. Race belongs in the classroom where race belongs in society. I think about race in the sense that Foucault thinks about power. It's not simply about, as Weber conceives it, these structures of domination, these hierarchies in which we have power associated with certain positions. Power breaks out everywhere, Foucault reminds us, even among and between people who are themselves oppressed or marginalized. Race is a kind of fusion of these Weberian and Foucauldian perspectives. There certainly is a hierarchy of race where power is associated with white Americans and power is associated with being white and not black, being white and not brown, being white and not red. These are objective conditions of race that we would do well to heed.

On the other hand, race breaks out in all kinds of interesting and unfastidious ways. It breaks out in uncomfortable and disruptive ways, just as we talked about earlier in terms of disruption. I think that race has the possibility to always surprise us. Like a camel on the loose, it has the capacity to do greater injury when we attempt to coop it up as opposed to when we let it run free. A classroom is an artificial cage for the animal of race, and race breaks out everywhere. That is powerful and productive because it wounds our most cherished expectations of what we called earlier "market multiculturalism." In African-American studies classes like mine at Brown, race breaks out in the most uncomfortable, but I think highly instructive, ways. In the conflict between this set of black men who thought they knew Malcolm and had earned their right and privilege to define Malcolm for the rest of us, and to cage Malcolm up, not only did race break out but I think Malcolm did, too. The place of race in the classroom is precisely at the center of our conversations about a whole range of not only disciplines and professions but a range of issues and subject matters. It does not simply belong in a class on ethnic studies or African-American culture. Race belongs in a class on Aristotelian conceptions of inequality. Race belongs in classrooms that deal with Neo-Platonic philosophy. Race belongs in every American classroom and in every American subject matter precisely because it is like what they call in logic the suppressed premise of so many syllogisms of American democracy. Race is part and parcel of the very fabric of the American intellectual project and also at the heart of the American project of democracy and self-discovery. We would be well-served by being more explicit about it, and therefore taking it into account, rather than allowing it to inform our debates from a distance. By informing our debates from a distance, we do not get a chance to theorize race, we do not get a chance to explore race, and we do not get a chance to deconstruct or demythologize racist power to hurt and harm us precisely because it is excluded from our explicit articulations. That is where I think it belongs.

Q: A few running themes have started to evolve in your answers and I'd like to follow along with those, but I'd also like to change your metaphor of the wild animal in the classroom a little and ask, have we made race safe? Have universities done to race what may have been done to some feminisms by saying that we can talk about these discourses in universities, so long as this is what we discuss, and this isn't? Have multicultural readers that address race taken the thorns out of race matters by offering "here is an example of a discussion of race, feel free to touch it without getting stuck or tangled in it"?

A: Yes, there is no question about it. But that is the risk we run for the kind of progress we want. And the kind of progress we want is that we would rather people talk about it in denuded contexts that deprive race of its real vigor, of its real fierceness, of its rhetorical ferocity. We would rather have that than fights in the streets. We would rather have that than the riots in 1992. We would rather have that than the situations where black or white or other people lose their lives contesting terrain that has become deeply racialized but not theorized around race. Yes, there are trade-offs. But with the kind of conscientious objection to the war of multiculturalism that is fought with rubber bullets rather than real ones, we certainly want to introduce (excuse this violent metaphor) sharper distinctions between where the blood is really being spilled on the outside of these debates. There is an advantage to that. There is no doubt about the articulation of the real divisions that race brings, the real conflicts that it introduces. And they have to be touched on in our debates in ways that make us uncomfortable with our ability to so smoothly dismiss the differences that race introduces without paying the consequences. We do not often pay the consequences in our own classrooms, in our faculty meetings, in the Academy in general. That is why when we have racial representation by proxy that is one thing. But when real gays and lesbians show up, when real black folks show up, when real Latinos show up, and they are not as nice and they are not as observant of the traditions of racial discourse as white liberals who set out twenty years ago, that creates real tension. I do not think we should gainsay those kinds of tensions. Those kinds of tensions are real, and they are instructive politically about the limits to which we are able to go in dealing with racial discourse, and more important, not only racial discourse, but racial transformation. So, yes, we have done that, but at the same time I'd rather have that kind of discourse against which we must fight and that we have to deploy in service of defending a more radical, a more powerful, a more disruptive conception of multiculturalism than one in which the debates are handled in the street where bloodshed and violence are its only consequences.

Q: How do public intellectuals play into that then?

A: Partly we either play the good role or the bad role. We play into it in the sense that we extend the capacity for people to feel safe by saying, "Well, I've listened to Michael Eric Dyson or Cornel West or bell hooks and now I feel that I've gotten my multicultural booster; I've got the multicultural vaccination that protects me, that gives me a vaccination against any form of racism." And that is obviously not the case. So we get used as these vaccinations and people feel that they are immune now to racist ideology and become much more problematic than those who have not been vaccinated, who do not give a damn about being vaccinated, and who resist it and who in their own honest expression of their feelings, talk quite frankly in ways that lead to more racial progress than those who feel that they have nothing to learn. We can end up perpetuating that by being used against our own will that way, but we can also disrupt that as public intellectuals by going on these shows and disagreeing with the common market version of multiculturalism by saying that it is much more complex, it is much more deep, and it is much more profound than that.

Q: What do you do then to keep race from being safe? What kinds of work—both public and academic—do you advocate in the face of such safety?

A: What I do is I preach. One thing I do, I stay in contact with people whose anger is much more meated and raw. When I visit prison—I have a brother who is serving life in prison for second-degree murder who's converted to the Moorish Temple of Muslim Experience—and listen to him on the phone, and we talk about race rules, race realities, race differences, race matters, racial issues, and he gives me a hell of an interesting perspective: both of us coming out of the ghetto of Detroit and now living the proverbial difference of the professor and the prisoner. That reality of feeling the sharp edges of his own critique of people like me, and me specifically, delivers me from a kind of anesthetized, romanticized sphere where I'm somehow exempt from the very passions that I claim I want to represent in my work, and that I certainly do and hope to do.

Also, by trying to get involved with union movements and trying to get involved with black churches, especially where black people are concerned on the front line about issues of race and how their anger and their conspiracy theories come together and how even if intellectually I want to avoid some of the conspiracy theories that they have or the resentments that they nurture, I understand and feel what drives that. It reminds me of where I was as a poor black kid in Detroit or as a teen father who was hustling, who was thought of as one of these pathologized, nihilistic black kids. I try to bring that into the classroom by means of some of the subject matters that I deal with and some of the issues of race that I try to confront.

Q: There is an interesting division that gets played out in discussions of race and discussions of postcolonial theories. Jenny Sharpe, in her essay "Is the United States Postcolonial? Transnationalism, Immigration, and Race," argues that "when used as a descriptive term for the United States, *postcolonial* does not name its past as a white settler colony or its emergence as a neocolonial power; rather, it designates the presence of racial minorities and Third World immigrants." She goes on to argue that "an understanding of 'the postcolonial condition' as racial exclusion offers an explanation for the past history of 'internal colonies' but not the present status of the United States as a neocolonial power." With the noted exception of bell hooks, who looks at African-American writers, Gloria Anzaldúa who works with Latina/Chicana literature and cultural experience, and a few scholars of indigenous North American populations, there are very few who address the fact that much of the scholarly work regarding issues particular to the United States are in fact issues of postcolonialism. At the same time, the kinds of academic attention that U.S. scholars give to postcolonial theory is being given to the writers and the cultures of, for instance, India, Sri Lanka, Pakistan, and so on, not to issues of the United States. What significance, if any, do you see in the academy refusing to validate the postcolonial nature of both the writers and the writing that has been and continues to be produced in the United State by peoples of color?

A: This is a problem of avoidance. This is a problem of linguistic and rhetorical and ideological avoidance of not acknowledging the degree to which this society's racist policies and practices are part of a deeper project of colonial and imperial expansion that happened on the backs of black peoples, on red peoples, and other native, indigenous peoples. But now, even as those scholars of color begin to interrogate its practices, the absorption of this discourse is put into a narrowly racialized frame that pays attention to black/white differences and so on without linking it to an international context of colonialism. When it does, it's only in regard to the presence of minorities in this country as opposed to its own practice. So partly what we're dealing with here is the self-identity of America as a colonial practitioner and an imperial power. What that signifies is the ability of America to absorb and redistribute dissent and the nomenclature that would name that dissent in ways that are less harmful. So that for America to conceive of itself as a colonial power, not simply *vis-à-vis* racial minorities, but as the expansion of its imperialist tentacles throughout the world, is so contradictory to its self-identity that people are discouraged from even talking about it in those terms.

What's also interesting is that during the '60s and '70s, people like Bob Blouner at Berkeley and other people who were talking about internal colonial theories, who were talking about the metaphoric relationship between America and colonial powers, were discouraged from doing so because it was said to be a narrow essentialist conception of the relationship between black and white or that it really wasn't exactly expressive of the caste dimensions between black and white in this country that happened in other spaces and places. In other words, as close as we got to any sense of America as a colonial power was this internal colonialism talking about the ghetto as this internal colonized space that drew upon Fanon, that drew upon other third-world theories to explain indigenous practices within America but never as largely America's colonial power.

To talk about America as colonial empire and as a beast is to really direct attention from domestic projects of civil rights that were dependent upon the *largesse* and *noblesse oblige* of white liberals to make a go of our own state. This is why even Martin Luther King, Jr., when he began to talk about America as a colonial power, empirical power, *vis-à-vis* Vietnam, was criticized not simply by white conservatives but by black so-called progressives and liberals who were upset that he was pilfering off the resources and entities of the domestic situation for the civil rights movement. His world view was of a piece and of a whole. What's interesting is that we've been discouraged from seeing America as a colonial and imperial power because of deference to a domestic conception of civil rights that was narrowly insular, that was concerned about the project of African-American freedom within the circumscribed limits and the discourse of American rights as opposed to seeing American imperialism, directed against black bodies, as part of an international project of colonial containment that American was the supreme arbiter of. Partly, that expresses attention to domestic situations that people were worried about pilfering the moral energies of the black movement in deference to this larger international perspective that would then reroute our energies into expressions that would lose our specific interrogation of the terrain that we found ourselves on, which is an America dealing with civil rights. But the genius of Martin Luther King, Jr. and Malcolm X was that they saw the international perspective. America has coded debates about race in terms of domestic territory and terrain alone so that we've obscured the international connection of America as an imperialist terrorist. The colonizing impulses of America were somehow safely contained within racial discourses when America would acknowledge its own containment of black people within its own culture as a buy off, as a way of purchasing scholars of color's silence about her materialist expansion internationally. In other words, the degree to which we're able domestically to reassign privileges within the territorial domestic space obscures the degree to which we are these international colonizers.

Now, those who have—besides bell hooks and those you mention—are those other scholars on the periphery of so-called intellectual life within black culture. These are people who are also going to talk about conspiracy theories. These are folk who are black nationalists, who are going talk about the expansion of the colonial project of American culture. So the high-falutin black public intellectuals don't really want to be associated with those black scholars on the margin who are willing to indict America for its imperialist expansion and its colonial project because those people are not seen to be at the heart of the project of rights and debates within African-American culture. So the irony of that is that America buys silence from black scholars and other scholars of minority standing by rearranging domestic space. The kind of topography of colonial space within American society obscures the kind of recognition of colonial expansion outside the United States. Our silence and recognition of the international expansion of American capital and power are bought precisely because America is willing to throw us a few bones inside. So our internal colonization, which is expressed by our ignorance of this international situation, is a paradox and an irony. And I think that with the explosion of postcolonialist theory of Homi Bhabha and others and resurgence of interest in Fanon forces us to have this international connection that people like Malcolm and other marginal scholars within African-American communities have invited us to see for quite a while.

Q: You write in "Benediction: Letter to My Wife Marcia" in *Between God and Gangsta Rap* that "many black men and women believe that placing questions of gender at the heart of black culture is an act of racial betrayal, a destructive diversion of attention away from race as the defining issue of black life." You continue, "I don't think race is the complete story. There's too much evidence that being gay, or lesbian, or female, or working poor makes a big difference in shaping the role race plays in black people's lives." In *Reflecting Black* you also write that "sex, race, and class have also caused considerable conflicts and tensions between groups who compete for limited forms of cultural legitimacy, visibility, and support." And, you write that you want to "help us to begin the process of open, honest communication about the differences within our race." I wonder about the critique that when race, class, gender, culture get discussed in the same breath that focus is denied to individual issues. You argue that race can't be looked at as an entity displaced from class, gender, or culture—that it doesn't exist in a vacuum—is this the same for gender? How would you respond to feminist theorists or class theorists who don't want gender or class swallowed up in discussions of race?

A: There are two things that are going on here simultaneously that I think we have to pay attention to. First of all, if we say that gender and race and class have their own intellectual integrity, that they have their own intellectual space from which they should be theorized, then I say "Amen." There are irreducible categories not only for social theorizing but for personal identity and for collective communal mobilization, no question about that. But if we suggest that they can somehow be divisible from each other, that questions of gender don't have any relationship to class and relationship to sexuality and so on, that is not the way it happens, because people experience themselves simultaneously. We have to say that questions of gender are implicated in questions of class, are implicated in questions of race and vice versa and all around. We should have specificity of analysis. I think the particularity with which these problems or categories of analysis or modes of identity manifest themselves have to be recognized and acknowledged and therefore taken seriously. I would be the first to suggest that we can't subsume one of these under the other. That kind of subsumption of race under class is ridiculous. We saw this in the Communist Party in the '30s and the '40s in this country; we see this in certain orthodox vogue or Marxist traditions where people want to subsume issues of race under class. They have their own intellectual integrity, their own kind of intellectual vitality, and their own kind of ideological portfolio that allows the political consequences of them to be interrogated under specific kinds of intellectual interventions and interrogations.

On the other hand, I think that they are fused more, that they are more bloody than that, and they bleed into one another in ways that we don't always pay attention to. I don't think we can divorce and divide them in as neat a way as we can do intellectually, or theoretically. For instance, what do we do with a person who happens to be gay and poor and black or a woman who's lesbian and poor and black and a single mother? They don't have the luxury of a kind of pre-theoretical interrogation of their identity so that they can assign the most merit based upon what part of their identity has more consequence. There's a whole range of identities that are competing for expression, that are being constituted in this one body. What we have to say to feminist theorists who would say, "I don't want gender to be subsumed by race" is "fine, but I want gender to be thought of in relationship to race." Because then, what we might end up having is, say, white feminists who pay no attention to the effect of race. So that when they interrogate the O. J. Simpson case, they see Nicole's body as a white woman's body or a universal woman's body being somehow marginalized in regard to the discussions about race, that race trumps gender. But what about for black women who see race and gender operate simultaneously? They want to say to black men, "listen, you're not paying attention to the ways in which black women's bodies have occupied a segregated rhetorical space within African-American popular and intellectual culture." They want to say to white women "you don't understand the way in which race has privileged white women's bodies against black women's bodies and the discursive terrain that white feminism operates on has all but excluded the geography of black identity for African-American women." I think that there's a way of paying attention to intellectual ideological specificity and particularity while understanding that's an intellectual intervention while understanding existentially and phenomenologically the intervention of, the fusion of, and the bleeding of these multiple identities into each other has to be acknowledged as well.

Q: You make clear your conviction that conversations of race frequently silence the voices of black women. You write "I agree with critics who argue that the rhetoric of black male suffering is often cobbled together from a distortion of black female troubles. Thus, the very language of black male crisis erases black women's faces and bodies from the canvas of social suffering. It is simply not true that black men's hurts are more important than the social horrors black women face." You also write in *Between God and Gangsta Rap*, "I think black women have learned, more successfully than black men, to absorb the pain of predicament and keep stepping. . . . I think brothers need to think about this more, to learn from black women about their politics of survival." In your religious work, too, you have contended that black men must recognize their own oppressive action toward black women if they are to be able to honestly criticize other oppressive forces in their lives. Black feminist intellectuals—such as bell hooks—have also called on black men to be more conscious of the struggles of black women. Would you talk about the rift, if you believe one exists, that has evolved between black women and black men in contemporary discussions of race, and how we might productively proceed as academics concerned with both race and gender?

A: I think the rift has developed as a result of the long elaboration of a whole host of factors that have been in black culture and American society from the beginning of our pilgrimage on American soil. The rift between black men and women expresses the gendering of internal differences and dissension within black culture and the way in which the gendered manifestation of those tensions has a particularly lethal effect upon our own communities. The rift between black men and women expresses the differential treatment accorded black men and black women in the political economy of slavery and how the extension and expansion of that political economy of difference manifests itself now in the material effects and on the intellectual self-understandings of black masculine and black female culture. And even more particularly, the rift between black men and black women is a remaking of a divide-and-conquer strategy that was ingeniously employed to undermine any sense of consensus, a kind of unity of integrity or a solidarity of principle, that might have provided black people a way out of the divisiveness that was introduced as a means and mechanism to destroy a black people's ability to come together and say, "We won't put up with this." We understand this now in our postmodernist, black space where tropes of unity and solidarity are highly questioned for good reason. The function of unity has to be interrogated for its ability to close out other voices and other visions that need to challenge that dominant hegemonic position within black culture. That's all for the good. But one of the negative consequences of that, culturally speaking, is the inability of black men and black women to embrace each other across the chasm of gender. I think that's an outgrowth of these political machinations to destroy any sense of unity and consensus among and between black people, to see their lives in the same boat.

What happens is that black men and women are often in the same bed, but at each other's throats. The rift between black men and women occurs precisely because black men have uncritically incorporated this narrow masculinist psychology as a kind of foolproof, fundamental structure of our consciousness in terms of combating not only white racism but what we consider to be the unjust manifestations of that white racism in black culture. Usually what we see as the most powerful rhetorical device to deploy against that racism is to see black women as the carriers of some particular strain or virus of exemption from white racism. As the story goes, black women are exempt from white racism because they have it better than black men. You don't only hear this in terms of black men, you hear it in terms of black women. Black women are less threatening; black women don't threaten white men in the same way. There's no doubting, I think, that given that we live in a patriarchal culture, in a way in which these codes of masculinity operate to legitimate certain forms of masculine power, that there is a specific dimension that black men occupy that certainly is a particular and special threat to white patriarchal power that black women wouldn't be considered to be.

There's no question that there's a hell of a difference in terms of specific manifestations of challenge from black men and black women. The underside of that argument is that it tends to privilege black masculine suffering over black women's suffering, as if they somehow almost genetically, or inherently, don't have the same kind of problems with white racism that black men have. And so you've got an internal resentment against black women. These things are at the back of the kind of collective imaginary of black masculine and black female identities being construed and constructed in one space, and this space happens to be the space of black American culture at the end of the century where racial millennialism is being refracted through the prism of this narrow patriarchal lens. That's why I understand black women's objections to the Million Man March, because it looked like warming up the same old patriarchal leftovers and feeding them to them as the new meal of black masculine identity, and that was really clearly a problem.

The rift between black men and black women has to do with the perception that black women are somehow exempt from the processes of white racism, that they are better off than black men materially, and that black men deserve to be talked about in specific ways because we live in this white patriarchal culture. The problem with all that, of course, as bell hooks and other feminists have warned, is that when we look at the liberty of black people and liberation through gendered lenses, we talk about not castrating the black man, not cutting off our penises because that is an exemplification of how the whole race has been treated. Those kinds of gendered metaphors miss the specific forms of female embodiment and how black women have been differentially treated within a political economy of privilege that has undermined their capacity to come to grips with their own forms of particular suffering because they're not named with the same sort of legitimacy that black masculine suffering is. That means that we're living in a hell of a time of contestation and conflict between black men and black women.

The academy, then, can do several things. First of all, it can begin to interrogate how masculinity, like race, is this artificial and social construction. It can articulate that there's no such thing as a necessary black masculine experience that has to be felt or interpreted a certain way. What academics can do is to begin to interrogate masculine identity as a gender. White people didn't have a race, and men didn't have a gender. Now men have a gender, and black men have a gender. The obsession with masculinity in our culture is an index of that. So what academics can do is help us understand the social production of gender and how it's constructed. Secondly, what they can do is help explain the obsession with masculinity in black culture and then begin to help map out a kind of cartography of masculinity and patriarchy that helps us understand why we are obsessed with it, why there are some good things about the obsession with masculinity, and why there are a whole lot of bad things about it. What we have to do as academics is to try to filter out the good and the bad and figure out how we can produce enabling understandings of masculinity and of gender. And third, we have to begin to not just leave it to feminist critics to theorize the negative impact of gender in black communities. Male critics, especially, and male academics, have to begin to think much more self-critically about the function of gender in American society and the relationship of gender and race and class and how the differences that gender would make in what we understand about race could help us in the long run. Perhaps if we begin to deconstruct and demythologize some of these narrowly masculinist patriarchal conceptions of gender and masculine identity, we could then move toward understanding and embracing different elements of identities that could then be embraced in much more constructive ways.

Q: As a public intellectual, you invite criticism; you seem to favor the idea of keeping your work and the work of other public intellectuals meaningful and effective through criticisms. In *Race Rules* you write: "We all slip. And our critics should be there to catch us." Are there any recent criticisms of your work that you'd like to address?

A: There have been some insightful criticisms of my work. For instance, people were quite interested in *Reflecting Black*. This book of cultural criticism was one of the first that tried to join both theoretical acuity with pop cultural expression and to try to take those two forms not only of interrogation but of expression seriously in the same text. But at the same time, there was a sacrifice of a certain sort of intellectual acuity. I think that there is a risk involved in trying to join and fuse genres. But I wanted to take that risk because I don't want to have a limited audience. I want to speak to the academy in very powerful and interesting ways, but I don't want to be limited to the academy. I have colleagues and I know people who limit themselves to the academy, and the academy becomes exaggerated in its importance in their lives. As a Christian, who was taught to really be suspicious of any form of idolatry, I don't want to make a fetish of critical consciousness. I don't want to make an idol of the capacity to intervene intellectually in the world and make that my entire life and the academy the shrine wherein I worship. At the same time, I want to have a mold of criticism that allows me to be mobile, to move from the academy to the street to the world. I want to be able to speak to that world, and I want to have a language that is clear—with all the problematic implications of clarity. I want to have the ability to be eloquent and clear and powerful and persuasive, because I've got a point to make, and I have a point of view. That point of view is worth more to me than what rewards I can reap in the academy; it's about making a difference in the lives of people who I meet and whose lives I intend to represent in my work, even if they disagree with much of what I say. Black poor people, black working-class people, black kids who are being demonized as nihilistic animals, black kids who are seen as somehow extraneous, unnecessary to America. I want to speak for and with them. I want to speak for intellectuals who feel that because they're theoretically dense and sophisticated they have nothing to say. I want to talk about the need to read those books and to struggle with them; anything worth knowing is worth knowing in a very difficult way. I would say to that criticism, I may not do it as well as it needs to be done, but I don't think that the project of trying to fuse those two genres is itself indictable.

There are also the more harsh criticisms by people like Adolph Reed. That kind of vitriolic criticism is a kind of vicious gangster rap in the guise of the academy, not even having the integrity of gangster rappers who import all forms of signifying and tropes and metaphors that indicate that they are not literally true, that they are engaging in a kind of metaphysical realm and a metaphorical world that collides on occasion. They are really artificially invoking an arena of experience that even though real in the world, they themselves realize that they're removed from it, because they are thinking about, rapping about, speaking about, something that they know they are once removed from. So they use *bitch* and *whore*, they use *gangsta* and *nigger* in all kinds of interesting ways. But there's a kind of literalism about Adolph Reed that is quite disturbing and destructive, or scholars of that ilk or an Eric Lott. What is interesting to me about Eric Lott is that he feels free as a white scholar to use words like *troglodyte* and to use terms like *caveman* and to use terms like *middlebrow imbecilism* in regard to a work. I think he's a very smart, sophisticated guy knowing the historic contingency of racial rhetoric and knowing the traditional content of racial rhetoric assigned to tropes, and metaphors that analyze black people. I would have thought he would have been a bit more careful about associating that, not that he had to worry about some PC police that would rigidly restrict his rhetoric, but that he would be more cautious about the historical inferences of race in assigning certain tropes and metaphors to a person's work. That doesn't in any way take away from the legitimacy of his criticism of my work as not being leftist enough, that by being involved in the public sphere you have to sacrifice certain radical dimensions. This kind of more-leftist-than-thou criticism has a limit in a way: in itself, it becomes cannibalistic. Authors feed off one another to prove that they are more leftist than the next person, and yet the political consequences of that kind of work is only to enhance the scholar' s position. It has no consequences upon the material effects upon the lives of people that they claim that they speak for more powerfully than a person like myself: poor black people, poor working-class white people, working-class people, and so on, or even radicals and progressives.

I think I've learned much from people who have taken issue with my work, who have said that there are certain sacrifices that one makes when one moves from the academy into the public sphere, and I think that's absolutely right. But my answer would be, then, you've got to do work for the academy that is important and that is integral to the perpetuation and production of scholarly, academic work. But, you've also got to do work that is accountable to a public, that also stands in need of the rich traditions of intellectual reflection that we can bring to bear upon those subjects. And my own mediating position then between the academy and the public sphere may never diminish the tension that I feel in terms of traversing those terrains and going back and forth. And I hope I won't lose that tension, because I think that tension in some ways informs and gives my work a certain moral authority and hopefully intellectual integrity that is if not always right at least is always intending to reflect those tensions in ways that help both the academy and the so-called public sphere. The public sphere needs the intellectual acuity of the academic world. The academic world needs the doses of material consequences and political effects that the public sphere can bring about. That's what I intend to do in my work: to bridge the gulf, to fuse the genres, and to swerve between the genres, and to really do something powerful in asking questions about how we can move beyond narrow disciplinary boundaries and narrow divisions between the "real" and the represented and get to the heart of the matter, which is to use powerfully clear work and to serve as a political interest that can be morally defended.

In Over Their Heads

Richard A. Posner*

A story is told about George Wald, a Nobel Prize recipient and biologist at Harvard, who in the 1960s had become one of those professors who no longer spoke much about his own field but instead provided ruminations on American foreign policy. After listening to one of these talks, the great Columbia physicist I. I. Rabi raised his hand and, upon being recognized by Wald, asked why homo sapiens had originated in Africa rather than on some other continent. Wald, startled, said, "But that was not at all the subject of my talk." "I know," replied Rabi, "but I thought it might be somewhat closer to your area of expertise."

Nothing has changed. Prominent academics continue to give public addresses, sign full-page ads, write op-ed pieces, and otherwise sound off in public on subjects remote from their fields. President Clinton's impeachment, the 2000 presidential election deadlock, and the terrorist attacks of Sept. 11 and their aftermath have provoked avalanches of such commentary. Much of this holding forth is ill-informed, inaccurate, and in the case of the terrorist attacks, often insensitive and offensive. Examples include: "The United States had it coming" because "world bullies, even if their heart is in the right place, will in the end pay the price" (Mary Beard, University of Cambridge classics professor), or "I'm not sure which is more frightening: the horror that engulfed New York City or the apocalyptic rhetoric emanating daily from the White House" (Eric Foner, Dewitt Clinton Professor of History, Columbia University), or "On the scale of evil the

*This article first appeared in the *Boston Globe*, January 27, 2002, C1. Reprinted with permission.

New York bombings are sadly not so extraordinary, and our government has been responsible for many that are probably worse. . . . The terrorist acts of victors are magically transformed into the early stages of a struggle for freedom or a mad but heroic blow for righteousness" (Thomas Laqueur, history professor, University of California at Berkeley).

Not that academics have a monopoly on fatuity. But when novelist Alice Walker says of Osama bin Laden that "the only punishment that works is love," we are more inclined to discount her statement as a flight of fancy. Likewise, that is true when Gloria Steinem reports that Afghan women have told her that "bombing would be the surest way to unite most Afghanis around them [the Taliban]."

Nor is it a surprise that daily journalists mispredicted the course of the war in Afghanistan, leading Jacob Weisberg of Slate.com to observe that the war "has made a whole coterie of dour windbags look like analytical midgets." One journalist, William Pfaff, writing in the *New York Review of Books* on Oct. 31, recommended that we suspend the bombing and allow "the situation in Afghanistan . . . to evolve over the winter months." What a disastrous error that would have been, selling out our Afghan allies and leaving the Taliban in control on the eve of victory. R. W. Apple Jr., writing the same day in *The New York Times*, expressed fear that Afghanistan would be another Vietnam.

In November, the *New Republic* published a long editorial explaining that the bombing had failed and that the Northern Alliance was hopelessly outnumbered and outclassed by the fierce Taliban fighters. Well, the journalists had to say something, and did their best. Academics did not have to open their mouths. They were gratuitous kibitzers.

Even those academics who should have known better, because they are experts on foreign or military affairs, made bad assessments. Not all of them, of course, but enough to raise serious questions about the ability of professors to comment on current events. Academic time is not real time. The intellectual skills honed in academia are poorly adapted to perceptive commentary on the confusing onrush of contemporaneous events.

Writing on Oct. 3 in the *New York Review of Books*, Stanley Hoffmann, a distinguished Harvard professor of political science, advised against military action in Afghanistan. He thought it would be futile because "it seems likely that by the time our planes and combat forces arrive, training camps and former hiding places for terrorists will be empty." In an article published in the *Wall Street Journal* on Oct. 31, Mackubin Owens, a professor at the Naval War College, advised that a winter offensive of 40,000 U.S. troops would be necessary to dislodge the Taliban. Edward Luttwak, a military specialist at the Center for Strategic and International Studies, wrote on Sept. 30 in the *Sunday Telegraph* that bombing Afghanistan would be futile because of a dearth of targets.

When President Bush on Nov. 13 ordered the establishment of military tribunals to try aliens accused of terrorism, the legal professoriat chimed in. In an open letter to Senator Patrick Leahy, Democrat of Vermont and chairman of the Senate's Judiciary Committee, 700 "law professors and lawyers" expressed opposition. Among the points made in the letter were that: "the United States has a constitutional court system of which we are rightly proud"; the president's order undermined the separation of powers because it did not have Congress's approval, as did President Franklin Roosevelt's order establishing similar tribunals in World War II; the order violated due process of law; it violated U.S. treaties, which "cannot be superseded by a unilateral presidential order"; and, issues of legality set aside, the order was unwise because it might encourage foreign countries to subject U.S. citizens to military tribunals.

In fact, not all the signers of the open letter are either lawyers or law professors. And most who are law professors are not experts on criminal procedure or international law, let alone military and foreign affairs. They are as much fish out of water as the biologists who signed an open letter to President Clinton opining that a national missile defense would be technically infeasible.

The reference in the letter to lack of congressional approval for the tribunals is a makeweight, since the signers would oppose congressional authorization of military tribunals. It is also a legal error: Bush's order establishing military tribunals has the same statutory basis that Roosevelt's order had. Due process, moreover, is relative to circumstances. And when the open letter was sent, the Defense Department had not yet issued regulations prescribing the procedures to be used by the military tribunals, so the complaint about the lack of procedural safeguards was premature. It appears that the regulations when issued will alleviate many of the due-process concerns expressed by the letter.

Nor does the letter consider the arguments for bypassing the ordinary civilian justice system to deal with foreign terrorists. These include delay, risks to jurors and witnesses, compromise of intelligence, the danger of hostage-taking, and the media circus to which high-profile trials give rise. And although the issue has never been definitively resolved by the Supreme Court, it is widely assumed that the president has authority to abrogate U.S. treaty commitments. At least one and possibly both of the treaties cited in the open letter are not self-executing, moreover. The second (the Geneva Convention) protects conventional prisoners of war rather than terrorists, who are illegal combatants within the meaning of the convention. In all likelihood, neither treaty is a legal obstacle to the tribunals.

Academic open letters are the most dubious form of public-intellectual activity in a field with many contenders for that honor. Shortly after the

November 2000 election, an advertisement appeared in the *Times* urging that Palm Beach County conduct a revote for president. The ad was signed by prominent academics in law, philosophy, and, rather incongruously, actors and other celebrities. The ad's almost certainly unlawful and in any event infeasible proposal was said to have been endorsed by 3,488 people, but a visit to the Web site where the endorsers are listed reveals a number of phony names, such as "Bush Won," "Comrade Al Gore," and "DIE, pinko scum!"

Is there a pattern in the reckless commentaries of academics on public affairs? I think there is. In "Public Intellectuals: A Study of Decline," published last month by the Harvard University Press but written before Sept. 11, I argue that the rise of the modern university, and the intellectual specialization that the rise has fostered, makes it increasingly difficult for intellectuals to comment constructively on ongoing public events. Most intellectuals now have safe berths as tenured professors.

The price of the safe berths for most is lifelong immersion in the academic hothouse and a degree of specialization that disables them from effective engagement with novel events occurring in the public world. And like George Wald, they incur no price, except occasional teasing, for being mistaken or even absurd in their public commentaries. They lack accountability, and lack of accountability is a formula for irresponsibility.

Paul Ehrlich, a biologist at Stanford University, predicted at the time of the first Earth Day in 1970 that by 1974 there might well be rationing of food and water in the United States, and that by 1980 there would be mass starvation, leading to hundreds of millions of deaths worldwide because of world overpopulation. He also suggested that U.S. life expectancy would have diminished by ten years because of DDT, rates of hepatitis and dysentery would have skyrocketed, and fishing might have disappeared because all the stock had died. Ehrlich remains a member in good standing of the Stanford faculty.

The academy values academics for their academic work. It is oblivious to the follies and pratfalls of their forays into the popular media.

As a first step toward promoting accountability by public-intellectual academics, I suggest that all academics post annually on their own or their university's Web site copies of all their public-intellectual forays in the preceding year. That would facilitate public evaluation of whether professors, when talking to the general public, come even close to complying with the standards of accuracy, care, and impartiality that govern academic work.

Forum

Patrick Saveau[*]

Since beginning my career as an intellectual in the American academy, I have had a strange feeling of discomfort and helplessness. A question haunts me, and I cannot answer it no matter how hard I try: Can I justify what I am and do as an intellectual? When I discuss this question with my colleagues, they typically respond with reassuring comments about our endeavors, but once I leave the academic realm, my undertaking is derided, pitied, and scorned. The source of my uneasiness lies in this gap between the intellectual's position and public opinion.

What people outside academia question and criticize is the intellectual's ideal of detachment, objectivity, disinterestedness, and autonomy, which intellectuals such as the French philosopher Julien Benda have defended. This ideal treats intellectuals as unidimensional beings, which they cannot be. As Pierre Bourdieu writes in "Fourth Lecture. Universal Corporatism: The Role of Intellectuals in the Modern World" (*Poetics Today* 12 [1991]), "The intellectual is a *bidimensional* being. . . . [O]n the one hand, he must belong to an autonomous intellectual world (a field), that is, independent from religious, political, and economic powers (and so on), and must respect its specific laws; on the other hand, *he must invest the competence and authority he has acquired in the intellectual field in a political action, which is in any case carried out outside the intellectual field proper*" (656; second italics mine). Since the Enlightenment, the balance between these two dimensions has never been stable: autonomy weighs at times more than engagement and vice versa.

---

*Reprinted by permission of the Modern Language Association of America from *PMLA* 112, no. 5 (1997): 1127.

As the end of the twentieth century approaches, American intellectuals appear to have entered a period of nonengagement, cherishing their autonomy over engagement and retreating into the ivory tower. Indeed, the attitude of today's intellectuals is a far cry from the radical stance that intellectuals adopted in the 1960s. Does this mean there is no consensual issue worth standing up for? Or is the oft-talked-about crisis in the humanities blunting intellectuals' ability to discern what is of consequence, dulling their desire to be engaged? Evidently, there is a strong tendency among intellectuals to be overly concerned with their own prerogatives and interests. To use a Baudrillardian image, intellectuals these days seem like fish that are happy swimming around their aquariums and looking out at the chaos plaguing the world.

This period of nonengagement is reinforced by two additional factors. First, as William Pfaff points out in "The Lay Intellectual (Apologia pro Sua)" (*Salmagundi* 70–71 [1986]), American intellectuals flourish most in a university setting, and they thereby become isolated from society. When was the last time vast numbers of American intellectuals formed one body to oppose a state or federal bill, as has just happened in France with the Debré laws to increase controls on immigration? Instead, intellectuals in the 1990s are content to remain within their university cliques, disseminating their ideas in a void they fail to notice because it engulfs them. The second contributing factor is the increasing popularity of new technologies such as the Internet, which, while fostering the exchange of ideas, draw intellectuals further inside, intensifying their separation from the world beyond the campus servers.

Those who try to define the place of the intellectual in the twenty-first century would do well to look to the past, in particular to the Enlightenment, and follow Voltaire, who in his article "L'homme de lettres" (*Dictionnaire philosophique*) contrasted engagement with "the scholastic obscurantism of decadent universities and academies" (Bourdieu 656–57). The reference to obscurantism—the "deprecation of or positive opposition to enlightenment or the spread of knowledge" (*Webster's Third New International Dictionary*, 1986 ed.)—rings true today. Is it not obscurantist to convey ideas obscurely, to judge the public unfit for knowledge? Isn't overspecialization cutting academics off from the public? Can a mind be wasted on matters so futile that only a negligible minority cares about them? Shouldn't intellectuals use their minds to reach out to the public and to espouse matters that directly concern their communities and their states? In Washington State, for example, the Commission for the Humanities sends intellectuals on tour to build bridges between people and ideas. This type of initiative is unfortunately too uncommon. The future of intellectuals in the twenty-first century depends on their ability and willingness to be "bidimensional," equally devoted to engagement and autonomy, the academy and the public.

Chapter 4

ON THE DECLINE OF
PUBLIC INTELLECTUALS

The Intellectual:
Will He Wither Away?

Merle Kling*

In accepting the Republican nomination to campaign for the Presidency a second time, Mr. Eisenhower, at the risk of blurring his stereotyped public image of conventionality, indulged in a rare literary reference and quoted Henrik Ibsen's letter of January 3, 1882, to George Brandes: "I hold that the man is in the right who is most closely in league with the future." With this phrase, Mr. Eisenhower, deliberately or accidentally, assumed the historically-sanctioned ethical posture of intellectuals. For intellectuals traditionally have rationalized and justified their vagaries precisely on the grounds that they were "in league with the future." Vilified for their beliefs or ridiculed for their literary and artistic innovations, intellectuals, like the devoutly religious who are confident of their rewards in the Kingdom of Heaven, have maintained faith in the "proof" of history.

Now the irony of this is that while Mr. Eisenhower associates himself with those "in league with the future," the contemporary intellectual has lost his claim on the future. It is my thesis (and one contrary to that which has been advanced in these pages recently) that the intellectual is isolated from the main currents of social change, and that he is incapable of comprehending or interpreting present directions of change. His predications in the past were not always right, but they were plausible. Today, thanks to the wholly unprecedented transformations wrought by science and technology, he lacks the most elementary and indispensable prerequisites for being in "league with the future."

*This article first appeared in the *New Republic*, April 8, 1957, 14–15. Reprinted by permission of *The New Republic*, ©1957, The New Republic, LLC.

When I conclude that the hook of intellectuals into the future has slipped, I of course employ the term "intellectuals" in a limited sense. I do not include the heterogeneous group of trained personnel, such as engineers, military officers, physicists and chemists, who are lumped together under the rubic *intelligentsia* by Soviet Communists. I am trying to identify primarily the conventional men of words who set themselves up as poets, philosophers, historians, teachers of literature—writers of what H. L. Mencken used to call beautiful letters, novelists, verbal interpreters of the social scene.

Let us take warfare and armed forces, for example. Need one be a literary scholar of medieval combat or a student of Tolstoy in order to appreciate the sources of inspiration that intellectuals have discovered on the battlefield? As late as World War I, perceptive intellectuals did not find the techniques of battle beyond their capacities for analysis and interpretation, as Hemingway, Barbusse, Remarque, Dos Passos, and E. E. Cummings—to name only a few—convincingly demonstrated.

However, World War II already placed significant arenas of military combat beyond the range of the intellectual. The plain truth is that one of the best books about the American army published since World War II is about the peacetime, pre–Pearl Harbor army! I mean James Jones' *From Here to Eternity*. Such books as *The Naked and the Dead* and *The Young Lions* captured nothing of the technological novelty of World War II and might have been written with a World War I setting.

The gulf between contemporary warfare and the intellectual, I suggest, is unbridgeable. The intellectual cannot master the technical knowledge required to understand the conduct of warfare by means of atomic bombs, thermonuclear weapons, and intercontinental ballistic missiles. In fact, his familiar moral and psychological categories—courage and cowardice, bravery and fear—have been extinguished by the nature of modern warfare. How does one conform to, or deviate from, a literary image of model military behavior when he kills his enemy by pouring the contents of one test tube into another test tube at a distance of more than 3,000 miles? Would William James advocate a moral equivalent to the atomic reactor today?

Or take industry and technology. The factory system and large-scale industry that superseded feudalism produced no insurmountable technical obstacles to imaginative, descriptive, and analytical works by intellectuals. The nineteenth century was densely populated with novelists, essayists, utopians, social philosophers, assorted reformers, self-proclaimed scientists of society, and visionaries who observed the new industrial society, confidently generalized its consequences and identified themselves with projects and doctrines they believed would supplant it.

During the first four decades of the twentieth century, the technology that spawned businessman and worker and research scientist still was not out of reach for the tenacious intellectual. Dreiser may have been as syntactically deficient as the literary critics insist, but he could perceive the American businessman beyond the boundaries of an executive suite. And as unsubtle as he may have been, Sinclair Lewis did not find it necessary to ignore the technical, professional, specialized problems of Doctor Arrowsmith.

We now squirm or sneer at the lack of sophistication in the so-called proletarian literature of the 1930s. But the intellectual polemics of that decade, which from our current perspective appear as obtuse and remote as some of the medieval quarrels, nevertheless reflected an intensity of concern for identification with the future for which there is no counterpart in today's intellectual life. In committing themselves to the "cause" of the working class, the "proletarian writers" were certain that they were riding the wave of the future. The Trotskyites, and the Socialists and the Communists and the Conservatives and the Fascists fought without quarter, because they assumed that there was a future which correctly oriented intellectuals could inherit. If John Strachey, an ideological hero of the political Left, wrote a book called *The Coming Struggle for Power*, then Lawrence Dennis, the intellectual spokesman of the extreme Right, likewise couched his appeal in the language of the future: he called his book *The Coming American Fascism*.

But how can the intellectual cope with today's new industrial developments in their functional realities? He cannot even peer appreciatively over the shoulders of the growing army of scientists and engineers that the new technology has recruited and absorbed. His technical incompetence paralyzes his capacity for insight. As novelist, therefore, he ignores the dynamic economy which he cannot fathom and writes reminiscences of archaic politicians (*The Last Hurrah*), or toys with simplistic formulas of political behavior (*The Ninth Wave*), or reverts to the fringe world of vice and perversion (*A Walk on the Wild Side*), or ponders the ancient behavior of Chinese riverboat people (*A Single Pebble*).

Or glance at the state of academic life—if you can stand the sight of carnage. Professors of literature and philosophy virtually have abandoned the struggle to maintain a grip on the future. They can only gape in admiration and envy as the financial support rolls in for their colleagues in the natural sciences (who so conspicuously and unceremoniously shape the future). With their faith shaken in the durable significance of their subject matter, teachers of literature now grasp at the straw of administration to save them from sinking further into the sea of irrelevancy. They serve on committees; they occupy themselves with the sterile details of curriculum revision; they daydream of deanships. On the basis of firsthand experience, painfully acquired at the expense of a colossal waste of time, I can testify with assurance that professors of literature and philosophy are the most diligent committee workers on a university campus; and professors of physics are the least reliable committee members. A professor of Latin or English or French rarely misses a committee meeting; a professor of physics usually refuses membership on committees or, if drafted, fails to attend meetings.

Some of my colleagues expressed surprise at the appointment of Dr. Robert F. Goheen, an Assistant Professor of Classics, to the Presidency of Princeton University. To me, however, it seemed symbolically appropriate that an energetic and capable young classicist should turn to administration. For what outlet is there today for an ambitious classicist who wishes to escape premature retirement from the relevant world? Administrative busywork has been—if I may be forgiven the pun—the classic response of frustrated creativity.

And what of social scientists? In a mood of hysteria and panic they cling to their semantic hold on science and thus hope to avoid the fate of colleagues in literature and philosophy. Confusing form for content, they assume that resort to the forms of the calculating machine, the questionnaire, the interview, and the quantified formula indeed will enable them to travel toward the future with the natural scientists and engineers rather than toward oblivion with their non-scientific colleagues. As a consequence, in intervals between plotting raids on philanthropic foundations, social scientists watch the IBM machines process their punch cards with the anxious fascination of superstitious customers awaiting the interpretation of a deck of playing cards by a wandering gypsy. Both social scientists and the gypsy's customers harbor the desperate hope against hope that the cards will spare them the fate of dreary irrelevance prescribed by the imperatives of their time.

Yet it should be acknowledged that economically, the intellectual is better fed, better housed, and more elegantly pampered than ever before. Despite the post–World War II vogue for things Italian, no cult of exile (or exile's return), such as followed World War I, has developed. With his visions blocked by a massive wall of technology, science, mathematics, and expertness that he is unable to penetrate, however, he stares blindly into the future and, with less complacency than Milton, can only stand and wait. Under the circumstances, it is fair to speculate that the role of the intellectual will come to resemble even more closely that of the archaeologist in our society. The archaeologist is not persecuted. He is subsidized, permitted to release his aggressions by spading ancient dirt, accorded token honors and courtesies, and—disregarded. Perhaps what Engels said of the state may be said of the intellectual: he will not be abolished; he will wither away. The intellectual is no longer a man without a country. But he may be man without a future. And if he is not in league with the future, can he be right?

The Graying
of the Intellectuals

Russell Jacoby*

In 1957 Norman Podhoretz participated in a symposium on "The Young Generation of U.S. Intellectuals." He was twenty-seven years old, already an editor of *Commentary*. He observed that his generation, which came of age in the Cold War, "never had any personal involvement with radicalism." His peers breathed an atmosphere of "intellectual revisionism," characterized by "an intensive campaign against the pieties of American liberalism, which for reasons we all know, had become the last refuge of the illusions of the '30s." Intellectual revisionism taught that liberalism lacked recognition of human and social limitations; nor did liberalism offer a "sufficiently complicated view of reality." Podhoretz concluded that for the young intellectual "the real adventure of existence was to be found not in radical politics or in Bohemia" but in accepting conformity and adult responsibilities. "The trick, then was to stop carping at life like a petulant adolescent."

Now, a quarter-century later, Podhoretz and many other intellectuals from the early and mid-'50s still loom large on the cultural terrain. Numerous commentators have sought to explain, and most often to approve, the conservative consensus that has settled over the country. Analyses abound of a skewed economy, the rise of a new Right, the appearance of the neoconservatives, and so on. Yet a disturbing truth is ignored or slighted: the face of today's cultural scene closely tallies with the landscape of the early '50s. Except for the age of the participants, little has changed in thirty years. To this a corollary can be appended: there is a

*This article first appeared in *Dissent* 30, no. 2 (1983): 234–237. Reprinted with permission.

marked absence of younger intellectuals. Where are they? Is America's cultural life graying?

References to a "return" to the 1950s risk instant clichés and nostalgia. Nevertheless, even when undeniable differences between the '50s and '80s are registered—gains in civil and sexual rights or the absence of McCarthyism—the convergences are striking. Public radicalism has disappeared, replaced by alarm over crime and delinquency. Anticommunism grabs the cultural limelight. Demoralized leftists slink off; puzzled liberals hang on the news. A sobering routine of jobs and careers chills dreams of refashioning America. Conservatism and conformism waft through the culture. C. Wright Mills, in an essay entitled "The Conservative Mood," judged in 1954 that the "tiredness of the liberal" and the "disappointment of the radical" reinvigorate conservatism. "There is no doubt that the conservative moods are now fashionable."

Yet to speak of a return to the '50s is misleading. The '80s signal a continuation, not a restoration. A wide-angled view of post-World War II America suggests that the movements of the '60s only temporarily rattled a liberal-conservative consensus that comfortably housed the intelligentsia.

The reconstitution of a '50s consensus is less startling than the virtually identical cultural program; not only the plot but after thirty years the actors themselves have not changed. This is most obvious in regard to the conservatives. The continuity is less evident for radicals, primarily because deaths, too, have diminished their small ranks. And in the case of the radicals, continuity may be valid for their work, which remains pertinent and frequently unsurpassed. Yet in the cases of both conservatives and dissenters the extended reign rests on a vacancy; a younger generation—the intellectuals of the '60s—is missing.

Peter Steinfels, in his acute study of the neoconservatives, misdates their appearance. If new recruits, reeling from the '60s, recently joined up, many key figures enlisted in the '50s. Not simply William Buckley and *The National Review*, but Irving Kristol, Norman Podhoretz, and Seymour Martin Lipset made their mark almost thirty years ago. Describing the cultural scene of the early '50s in *Making It*, Podhoretz might be reporting the current mood. "Revisionist liberalism" permeated the air. "The effort was to purge the liberal mentality of its endemically besetting illusions regarding the perfectibility of society." For Podhoretz and his friends, revisionist liberalism put to rest any lingering illusions about the Soviet Union and communism. Antiutopian in its core, it stressed "human imperfection as the major obstacle to the realization of huge political dreams." Even Daniel Bell, with a past steeped in radical politics, concluded in 1957 that the revolutionary illusions are finished. "What is left is the unheroic, day-to-day routines of living."

The '50s conservatives responded to events that would be roughly duplicated thirty years later. A revolutionary decade floated dimly in the past (the '30s and '60s), but its lessons—danger of utopia, communism, and political dreams—were very much alive; fresh events discredited Soviet communism (from the Berlin Blockade to Poland); American democracy was shining; a new anticommunist literature sprang up; radicals retreated and brooded.

The cast of '50s dissenters also has seen a few changes. From Irving Howe to Gore Vidal and Norman Mailer, they remain our cultural radicals. While there have been few additions, there have been many subtractions. The radicals of the '50s did not fare as well as the conservatives. Many died young, perhaps the cost of their isolation. If he had lived a full life, C. Wright Mills now would be 66. He died at 46, Paul Baran at 54, Robert Lindner at 41—all from heart disease. Precisely because they bucked a tide that has now returned, their contributions retain vitality and relevance.

Mills's *White Collar* (1951) reads almost as if it had just been completed. One might imagine that, after 30 years, a book drenched in empirical material would be impossibly dated. Not so. Much more than a dry study of middle-strata employees, it ranges over the mass media, new professional groups, academic entrepreneurs, and so on. *The Power Elite* (1956) contains more spunk and insight than much recent research. It also includes a chapter on the conservative atmosphere that speaks directly to the present. Many intellectuals "feel that they have somehow been tricked by liberalism, progressivism, radicalism. What many of them want, it would seem, is a society of classic conservatism."

That so many critical works of the '50s remain on target underlines the continuity of the '50s and '80s; it also throws into relief the uniqueness of the '60s. Its literature, such as Theodore Rozak's *The Making of the Counter Culture* or Philip Slater's *The Pursuit of Loneliness* seem hopelessly dated. To jump back a quarter-century, however to Paul Goodman's *Growing Up Absurd* or William H. Whyte's *The Organization Man* is to find works that seem current. For Whyte, a virulent conformism and careerism raced through the land. "In comparison with the agitation of the thirties," he wrote, college students do not "care too much one way or the other" about political and philosophical issues.

At least in tone, the '50s dissenters often differed from their successors. More isolated and beleaguered than their future compatriots, they were thrown back on their own resources. A note of hysteria frequently entered their voices. As Christopher Lasch has written, in a world partitioned by a discredited communism and an unpalatable liberalism, American radicals risked becoming "increasingly shrill, increasingly desperate." "A stench of fear has come out of every pore of American life," lamented Norman Mailer in 1957. "The only courage, with rare exceptions that we have been witness to, has been the isolated courage of isolated people." The isolation particularly afflicted academics and professionals. Unlike a loose community of poets and novelists, the professionals lacked a network of support and often complained of their isolation.

In both his strengths and weaknesses, Robert Lindner, today forgotten, exemplifies the '50s dissenter and perhaps illuminates the "missing" '60s intellectuals. In such books as *Prescription for Rebellion* (1952) and *Must You Conform?* (1956) he showed himself a trenchant, if sometimes strident, social critic. For Lindner a vast array of teachers, counselors, psychologists, priests, and officials systematically undermined an "instinct" to rebel that dwelled within the individual. A soporific existence oozed throughout America. Decades before R. D. Laing and "antipsychiatry" Lindner, himself a nonmedical psychoanalyst, blasted psychology for its blind ethos of adjustment. For the discontent of the original neurosis, psychology substitutes "the neurosis of conformity, surrender, passivity, social apathy, and compliance."

Lindner is important both for what he was and what he was not; the sharp limits of his work illuminate the course of American radicalism. A theoretical loner, his intellectual resources never equaled his moral and critical passion. It is almost as if he had to invent his radicalism from the ground up. Perhaps he did. For this reason, he sometimes succumbed to the clichés of the time. For instance, a thoroughly conventional kind of anticommunism and vision of the rise of the "mass man" marred his work.

In his theoretical boundaries and isolation, Lindner personified the deracinated American radicalism that later bewitched the '60s activists. Without an oppositional labor movement or an institutional base, American radicalism is always precarious and regularly disappears. Continuity between generations is frequently severed, compelling radicals to reinvent their radicalism. For this reason—to jump to the '60s—their radicalism, while novel and even vibrant, lacked the resilience of accumulated experience; it easily succumbed to creaking Stalinism and hip terrorism or literally vaporized into spiritualism. The absent '60s intellectuals may be a casualty of the discontinuous American radicalism.

I would suggest a more cynical response to the fate of the '60s intellectuals: there were none. Indeed, it is true that many intellectual luminaries of the '60s were hardly young. Earlier phases of radicalism informed the life and work of Isaac Deutscher, I. F. Stone, Herbert Marcuse, Paul Goodman, and Wilhelm Reich. That "under thirty" new leftists banked heavily on aging leftists is not surprising; it is surprising that they have not (yet) significantly supplemented the older works.

When the list of '60s intellectual luminaries is expanded—Paul Baran, Erich Fromm—another feature jumps out; not only were the '60s intellectuals aging, they were largely European-born and -educated. This indirectly confesses to the weakness of American radicalism. By the end of the 1950s only those personally rooted in a European experience could mount a compelling social critique. Often emigré scholars served as conduits, introducing American radicals to European texts—for instance, Hans Gerth for C. Wright Mills or Joseph Schumpeter for Paul Sweezy. That Americans radicalism often owes its existence or vitality to external infusion of theory and people confirms its vulnerability.

Nevertheless, the congenital fragility of American radicalism does not pinpoint the specific factors that have paralyzed '60s intellectuals as a historical force; this is the novel situation of the '80s, the dependency of its political culture on older intellectuals. Their continuity draws not only on the reestablishment of a political mood, which renders their contributions once again germane, but on the absence of new and younger voices.

Insight into this situation can perhaps be glimpsed from the following: when Paul Baran died in 1964, Paul Sweezy and Leo Huberman edited a memorial volume, "a collective portrait." It included some thirty-eight "statements" about Baran by friends and associates. Consistent with the orientation of American radicalism, perhaps 80 percent were by older foreigners or foreign-born and -educated Americans. The list of contributions ran from Bruno Betelheim to Isaac Deutscher, Ernesto (Che) Guevara, Eric Hobsbawn, Otto Kirchheimer, Herbert Marcuse, Ralph Milibrand, Joan Robinson, and many others. It also included statements by four younger intellectuals: Peter Clecak, John O'Neill, Maurice Zeitlin, and Freddy Perlman.

The first three, at the time all assistant professors, went on to make important contributions to radical scholarship. They now all teach at major universities and are familiar figures in their disciplines. The last, Freddy Perlman, founded an anarchist press in Detroit, Black and Red, which has published some fine pamphlets and books. Today his name is probably recognized by a few cognoscenti of left literature.

While this is hardly a scientific sample, it does suggest the trajectory of younger radical intellectuals. While journalism, publishing, editing, freelancing, and the legal and medical professions attracted many, the lion's share entered the universities. Today in several disciplines—sociology, history, political science, economics, anthropology—an identification with radicalism or Marxism by younger faculty is not unusual.

The foothold in the universities of radical intellectuals marks a fundamental change from the '50s. American radicals had been rarely or marginally academics. Or, from Veblen to Mills, the most significant were ostracized or sent packing by the universities. In the early 1950s only a handful of professors were publicly associated with Marxism or socialism. No longer. Not only do radicals teach at major universities, a series of dissenting journals (such as *Review of Radical Political Economics*, *Radical History Review*, *Insurgent Sociologist*, *Telos*, *New Political Science*, *Dialectical Anthropology*) serve as their forum.

The academization of the intelligentsia may mark a fundamental turn in American cultural life. It goes far in explaining the continuity of '50s intellectuals and the "disappearance" of those who succeeded them in the '60s. The two phenomena are inextricably linked. The intellectuals of the '50s and their works continue to speak to us not only because of the similarity of political culture. From C. Wright Mills to Paul Goodman, Gore Vidal, Paul Sweezy, and Dwight Macdonald they were independent intellectuals or marginal academics. They were and are committed primarily to a public universe and discourse and only secondarily, and often not at all, to a professional discipline. For this reason they lucidly addressed public issues to a cultural lay audience.

The successor generation of '60s intellectuals flowed into the universities. Consequently, in their writings, they have essentially reversed the loyalties of the independent intellectuals; they are devoted first to professional colleagues, and second to a wider public. This is not a judgment on the honesty and quality of left scholarship over the last twenty years, or on its quantity; neither can be denied. It is a judgment on the nature of the cultural discourse, now primarily directed to and read by colleagues.

A recent collection, *The Left Academy* (edited by Bertell Ollman and Edward Vernoff), surveys Marxist and radical thought in the universities. Surely, thirty years ago its content, taking up almost three hundred pages, would probably have been covered in ten; the change is startling. However, with the exception of some works in the field of history (significantly, the least technical of the disciplines)—works by Christopher Lasch, Eugene Genovese, William A. Williams, Herbert Gutman—and occasionally one by a sociology or political scientist, very few will be recognized outside a university community. Even the most important contributions, for instance, Immanuel Wallerstein's *The Modern World System*, do not tempt a wider public.

The monopolization of intellectual life by the universities is not simply a cultural but also an economic fact. The independent producer, inventor, or intellectual belongs to the past. The material existence of the nonacademic intellectual—always precarious—has become impossible; even painters, novelists, and dancers affiliate with institutions or find another trade. This structural tendency is compounded by the job squeeze. The migration into the universities ended some years ago and is slowly being reversed. Untroubled by a vigilant student movement and blessed by a conservative consensus, universities and colleges easily, and regularly terminate the employment of radicals.

This reality profoundly affects younger intellectuals. The situation is not entirely new, but the ante has been upped. The academic parks, already suffering purges by conservative managers, enclose the only patches of unregulated thought. And if they too are regulated, camping outside the park is risky, if not prohibitive. Obviously, this exacts a toll from those who like to think. The effort of maintaining the goodwill of colleagues supplants that of addressing larger issues, or, perhaps more crucially, a larger public. Anything can be written as long as it is unreadable. And so the missing '60s intellectuals are lost in the universities.

Some of these observations can be turned upside down; it could also be argued that the academization of the intelligentsia will break the curse of American radicalism, its lack of continuity. With a secure base in the universities—teachers, journals, students—the traditions that regularly dissipate will remain alive. Perhaps. An alternative, however, is equally plausible; the translation into disciplines and subdisciplines encapsulates radical thought in dead and arcane languages. This is the danger: when a public is ready to hear another message, the radical intelligentsia will have lost command of the vernacular.

The long view of post–World War II cultural life refutes belief in the perpetual rejuvenation of America. The political culture has not fundamentally changed in thirty years; nor have there been many new faces. While the aging industrial plan of America sparks much discussion, few mention the aging intellectual plan. The universities have occupied and preoccupied the most recent generation of intellectuals, depriving the wider culture of youthful talent. A future without independent intellectuals, now an endangered species, promises endless reruns.

Intellectuals After the Revolution

Paul Berman*

The year of the stock market crash, 1987, was also the year of the intellectual crisis. Afterward the stock market seemed to right itself, but that can't be said about the world of thought. Intellectual crises tend to be that way. Disorientation is never momentary.

The intellectual crisis has been amazingly widespread. The debates over curriculum at Stanford and Duke universities, Allan Bloom's *The Closing of the American Mind*, E. D. Hirsch, Jr.'s *Cultural Literacy* with its famous list of five thousand items every educated person is supposed to know—these show the crisis merely in its American pedagogical form. The debate in France over Martin Heidegger and his Nazi enthusiasms (conducted in an endless number of books and articles), along with the debate in this country over Paul de Man, reveals a deeper philosophical version of the same crisis, since the sudden worry about Nazi backgrounds bespeaks, I think, a loss of confidence in several of the main ideas that pass as most "advanced."

Russell Jacoby's *The Last Intellectuals*,[1] Alain Finkielkraut's *La défaite de la pensée*, Bernard-Henri Lévi's *L'Eloge des intellectuels*—these express the crisis as experienced by a younger generation of writers who can't help fearing that intellectual life is grinding to a halt. There was a book that came out in England in 1986, J. G. Merquior's *From Prague to Paris: A Critique of Structuralist and Post-Structuralist Thought*, which laid out aspects of the debate unobtrusively in advance. And still another book, Alain

*This article first appeared in *Dissent* 36, no. 1 (1989): 86–93. Reprinted with permission.

Renaut and Luc Ferry's *La pensée 68*, caused a stir earlier that same year and foretold much of what has now happened.

Intellectual crises are never easy to describe. Unlike stock crashes, they have no material manifestation. Book-buying doesn't diminish during an intellectual crisis; on the contrary. The whole event tends to be subjective, which is to say, it varies according to authorial predilection. Among the writers cited above, Russell Jacoby's predilection is Marxism, whereas Bloom's, if you read him closely, is pre-Periclean monarchy. Jacoby understands the crisis as a triumph of the academy, Bloom as its defeat. On the other hand, if many subjectivities yield an objectivity, one element of the crisis can reasonably be declared a fact. All of the American authors, left, right, and liberal, plus all of the French authors I have named, agree that the crisis had its origin in radical trends of the 1960s. Ferry and Renaut even specify a month: May 1968. What began then has either run out of steam, or never had any steam, or has gone off track. At least that is what everyone who succeeded in publishing a book seems to think.

Intellectual crises take place in the land of hyperbole, e.g., "God is dead," "The End of Ideology," "The Closing of the American Mind," "*La défaite de la pensée*." By definition, no bombast, no crisis. This makes for still another difficulty in identifying what is happening today. Hyperbole is easily laughed off. Anyone who wants to dismiss arguments about an intellectual crisis need only demonstrate hyperbole's difference from simple reportage and the arguments appear to sink. That may have happened a little too quickly in the reception given to Jacoby's *The Last Intellectuals*. Jacoby's way of describing the crisis is to announce a break in the chain of intellectual inheritance in America. "Where is the younger intellectual generation?" he wants to know. "Leading younger critics? sociologists? historians? philosophers? psychologists? Who are they? Where are they?"

They are nowhere, says Jacoby. The heirs to Edmund Wilson or to Lewis Mumford or to a figure like C. Wright Mills, whom Jacoby regards as a great sociologist, don't exist, and things have come to a very sorry pass indeed, with no sign of getting better.

Now, as reportage, that is a vulnerable claim, not to mention an irritating one. Jacoby says he has asked his friends to identify the younger writers and they can't think of any, and the possibility will arise in the minds of many readers that Jacoby's friends must live in California. For humble though they be, younger sociologists, historians, political writers, doctrinal polemicists, and columnists do exist. These younger intellectuals publish prominently. They read each other's work. They nod hello twice a year. Something exists and Jacoby ought to have taken the trouble to identify it correctly, if only to sharpen his denunciation.

He can't do it. It's a shame. His eye stops at all the wrong places. A reader of *The Last Intellectuals* might conclude that a publication called

Telos stands at the center of contemporary life. Journals that are not obscure—conservative, but especially liberal—almost disappear from his survey. Even the *New Republic*, Edmund Wilson's old home—the *Neuro* he used to call it—a very influential magazine, barely rates mention. Inconveniently for Jacoby's thesis, the *Neuro* is written and edited largely by members of the supposedly missing generation, who turn out not to be missing at all but, oddly enough, visibly prolific. And if Jacoby doesn't see this, how can we take his denunciations seriously?

Peculiar judgments fly every which way from his pages. He holds up political radicalism as a central obligation for intellectuals and then offers an idiosyncratic theory about Jewish intellectuals having been less firmly attached to their radicalism than bony WASP intellectuals. Who are these resolute WASPs? Among Jacoby's heroes from the older generation is Gore Vidal, the gentleman-crank. Possibly Jacoby feels drawn for some reason to the gentleman-crank style, which is, perhaps, more of a WASP than a Jewish style. Wilson had a bit of gentleman-crank in him—though he was a serious man of ideas, which can't be said of Vidal.

Anyway, what is this radicalism that resolute WASPs so stoutly champion? Jacoby never quite says. He admires the Fidelista writers; he actually praises the apology by C. Wright Mills for the Castro dictatorship; but then, some of his radical heroes are genuine libertarians, too, not that he discusses anything so relevant as dictatorship versus liberty. And if you add up these omissions and commissions, as Jacoby's critics have done, and factor in the admiration for Vidal and the empty spot where the *New Republic* should be, the details begin to weigh, and *The Last Intellectuals* begins to take on water, and then—but this is the danger—his argument sinks with a fearsome "glub" before your eyes.

Hyperbole's difference from simple reportage consists, however, in being bigger. The little specifics of past and present may get away from Jacoby, but around these specifics glows hyperbole's larger truth. I'll have to describe his truth in my own way. The business of the intellectuals, let us say, is to get up a discussion of how to live, what to feel, what to think. Discussions like that are hard to arrange. The participants have to share values, assumptions, purposes, at least sufficiently to allow for conversation. The participants have to form a group, even a squabbling group. If they don't, everyone will go baying each in his own corner and no one will make sense. Or else the participants will drift into groups that already existed when they came on the scene, discussion will be routine; and their own contribution will come off as slightly artificial.

Every generation produces critics and writers in the different fields of intellectual life—as even Jacoby acknowledges in a couple of sensible passages. But the intellectuals of every generation don't organize a group. Events have to organize it for them—big events, the size of the First World

War, preferably. Because with an event like that, the young writers come home from driving ambulances to discover that they no longer think and feel the way people thought and felt before, and the young writers can understand one another because of this, and have something new to say. It was the same during the Great Depression, and doubtless it was that way, too, for the writers who came of age during the Second World War.

Jacoby's generation, the people now in their thirties and forties, went through an earthquake like that. It was the revolution of the 1960s. But—here the larger truth comes up from the waves—for some reason their experience didn't translate into a serious discussion. The bright and accomplished intellectuals from the younger generation—the people whose bylines Jacoby doesn't know or doesn't respect—never quite organized a group. We have younger conservatives today, and younger liberals, and we have critics who sway back and forth according to what magazine assignment they receive. But the odor of experience is not on these younger writers, except in a few cases. The new tone that might have been expected from the younger generation, half-utopian, half-crushed, light and heavy at the same time, the radical shift that might have emerged, the maturation of student revolution into an intelligent intellectual life, the elaboration of what seemed twenty years ago to be great new inspirations—none of that, or not much, has come to pass.

Where are the intellectuals whose work does still reflect what was unique about the younger generation? That is the pertinent question, and Jacoby has given the answer. There are thousands of these people. But they are not old-fashioned intellectuals. They are, most of them, in the academy. They embrace narrow disciplines. They specialize. They write in jargon. Naturally some of them succeed in escaping the academic vices. The younger social historians, jewels of their generation, have produced brilliant volumes of social history—even if Jacoby, hobbled by his own discipline of hyperbology, won't acknowledge their achievement. Doubtless a tiny honor roll of exceptions to the rule could be assembled from other disciplines, too. But taking the academic radicals as a whole, Jacoby's assertion of mass disappearance is true enough. It is an astonishing thing. It is, in fact, a tragedy. The academic radicals have performed tremendous labors, yet the product of these efforts, the work of several varieties of university Marxists, of elegant deconstructionists, Foucaultians, Lacanians, structuralists, interpreters of the Frankfurt School, the criticism written by earnest people who regard someone named F. Jameson as a major literary figure, the harvest, all in all, of a left-wing academic generation—this product, vast, flat, infertile, dry, has the look of a Soviet wheat disaster.

It is a land of stubble. And whatever the flaws in Jacoby's survey, he was right, he was very brave, to stand up and say louder and more forcefully than any radical before him what conservatives have been saying with hypocritical glee for many years but radicals haven't wanted to concede. It may even be that *The Last Intellectuals* will prove historic. For if the subject of the sixties and its intellectual upshot has at least been broached from an honest standpoint that isn't seeking ideological advantage, maybe a serious discussion can finally begin, in English, without disciplinary guidelines.

What caused the remarkable march into the academy? Jacoby invokes "the economic winds that propel cultural life, and at times chill it." These winds have whittled away the traditional bases of independent intellectual life. Freelance writers make less money than before. Newspapers have shut down. Above all, the demise of modern cities has squeezed out the old bohemian districts that in the past created environments congenial to writers. As a result, intellectually minded people who grew up in the sixties had no alternative but to seek careers as professors, where they inevitably succumbed to academic values and ideas, especially the idea of ruthlessly rising through the departmental hierarchies.

I'm in no position to evaluate what Jacoby says about the corrupting aspects of academic life, though I'm ready to believe anything, especially remarks as modest as his. But his points about bohemia and the prospects for freelance intellectual work I can judge. The points are not foolish. In the twentieth century the center of intellectual activity has always been New York, and New York has become ever less hospitable to the kind of penury in which intellectuals must normally live. The process has been going on for sixty or seventy years. Edmund Wilson noticed the first stage in his Greenwich Village novel of 1929, *I Thought of Daisy*: "I did not know that I was soon to see the whole quarter fall a victim to the landlords and the real estate speculators, who would raise the rents and wreck the old houses." Then the speculators ruined the next quarter and the quarter after that.

Lately the situation has been aggravated by a second stage that Jacoby, as a Marxist, will surely acknowledge. That is the decline of the urban working class. New York bohemia existed in the past as a kind of adjunct to the proletariat. The bohemian neighborhoods were merely the eccentric parts of the old tenement and pretenement districts. Today the "economic winds" have blown the working class largely out of the city. The old neighborhoods have either risen into bourgeois splendor or sunk into lumpen squalor, and either way are no longer suitable for bohemian life. Aside from housing, the New York working class used to maintain a considerable intellectual culture, mostly in the left-wing parties. Many of the older intellectuals whose radicalism Jacoby thinks proved unreliable, plus some of the people whose radicalism never faltered, grew up in that environment. And this, too, has disappeared along with the class itself and the old streets and the affordable rents and the institutions that affordable rents allowed to flourish. A distressing situation.

But can this distressing situation explain what Jacoby wishes it to explain? The same urban conditions afflict people in the performing arts even more severely. Actors and musicians lose their careers entirely if they move far away, which is not the case with writers. There is no modem for the saxophone. And sure enough, the performing arts do suffer. Cultural historians of the future will not look kindly on the way America has let real estate speculators trample over what is best about New York. Even so, the performing arts haven't collapsed altogether. Is that because performing artists are more likely than intellectuals to come from wealthy backgrounds and can afford high rents? The opposite is more likely: performing artists feel less horrified than intellectuals at accepting the proletarian occupations that still survive. You see this in the strangely Thespian demeanor of Manhattan shop clerks, waiters, and taxi drivers.

The same distressing conditions afflict writers who did not flee into the corrupting embrace of the academy—the people who became old-fashioned intellectuals despite the rumors of their demise—the journalists, the contributors to the conservative magazines. The latter group sometimes benefits from the golden vaults of the right-wing think tanks. But the others have a hard time of it. I think their troubles may surpass those of predecessor generations, leaving aside writers from extremely oppressed circumstances. I know talented young writers who publish frequently and yet still bounce around from sublet to sublet without ever finding an affordable apartment of their own. A miserable way to live. Yet the distressing conditions haven't driven these people into paying equally expensive graduate school tuitions. Nor is it impossible to get into print. Jacoby complains that the *New York Review of Books* has failed to bring along a younger generation of writers, which may be true, though less and less. Even if it were true completely, surely there are other journals, more today than anybody could possibly read. Cities around the country still have radical weeklies with mass circulations and these weeklies are happy to publish young writers, the younger and more radical, the better. Conditions at these places are exploitative. But to find opportunities to learn how to write, to publish your views—that can be done. As for learned or scholarly journals, these have become a threat to the ecology. It is said that two thousand four hundred articles on sociology are published every year. (Of course, that may be part of the problem.)

The "economic winds" exist. But do they really "propel cultural life"? I don't think they propel the intellectuals—short of "in the last instance." If large numbers of people who came up in the New Left never took an interest in becoming old-fashioned intellectuals, if they became professors instead and undertook to write in jargon on topics an inch wide, if they abandoned playing a public role, I think the social factors merely smoothed the way. Ultimately these people made their own choice. No one herded the academic radicals into the universities. On the contrary: terrific efforts were expended at herding them out, and continue to be expended. The academic radicals entered because they wouldn't be stopped from entering. They wrote in jargon because they insisted on it. They became unintelligible because they believed that unintelligibility is profundity. They liked narrow topics. They thought they were making the revolution.

It's a pity Jacoby doesn't address himself to these beliefs. He might have been expected to.

In a very intelligent earlier book, *Dialectic of Defeat: Contours of Western Marxism*, he expounded on differences between "scientific Hegelianism" and "historical Hegelianism." Scientific Hegelianism results in a crude logic of determinism. Jacoby criticized this logic mercilessly. Crude determinism is bad. Historical Hegelianism leads to a sophisticated Marxist subjectivism. Sophisticated subjectivism is good. "Men do not make history just as they please, but they make their own history," Rosa Luxemburg said. But in *The Last Intellectuals*, though Jacoby echoes her maxim, writers don't make their own history. Landlords, tenure committees, and editors make the history.

Maybe that's what it was like in the Marxist thinking that came out of the sixties. In *La pensée 68*, Ferry and Renaut criticize Pierre Bourdieu, the sociologist, for following the same procedure in his own study of the intellectuals, *Homo Academicus*. Ferry and Renaut complain that Bourdieu foreswore vulgar Marxism in his introduction, then set about showing how French intellectuals express the larger social forces nonetheless. Jacoby goes further, actually, since the poor American professors that he belabors in *The Last Intellectuals* don't even get to express social forces. They merely get kicked around by them, like pebbles.

How to explain the radical professors, then? I think we have to put the economic winds to the side and look instead at the history of ideas in the sixties. That means recalling why the radicals became radical to begin with, and what their radicalism became.

Here is a rough sketch of a historical explanation. It begins by reversing Jacoby's question. He asks: Why hasn't the younger generation produced a lively intellectual life the way that older generations did? The question in reverse comes out: Why didn't the older generation produce heirs? What happened in the sixties that prevented the work of older writers (including writers who were fairly young at the time) from inspiring imitators, followers, critics, and detractors who would have formed an equivalent to the generations that came out of the thirties and the Second World War?

The answer should be obvious. The Second World War generation emerged from their youth ebullient in victory, perhaps a little exhausted, fearful of totalitarian dangers, confident in the values of liberal humanism for which the war had been fought. But by the middle sixties, each of these feelings had taken on a false quality. The victory had aroused hopes that were greater than the postwar achievements, which in the eyes of a younger generation that didn't experience the war, made the ebullience look hypocritical. The fear of totalitarian dangers became less and less realistic, more and more paranoid, producing ultimately the delusionary perceptions that led Americans into Vietnam. The confidence in liberal humanism seemed grotesque given the greatest of the postwar events, which wasn't the battle against totalitarianism but the global movement for decolonization. Ideas like democracy, human rights, and the freedom of the individual were mobilized precisely in order to maintain the continuity of imperial power. And the result was, by the middle sixties, that liberal humanism had in large measure lost the ability to make sensible judgments about its own performance.

Or possibly there was more to the generation gap than that. Possibly a gigantic underground shift had occurred from a culture of hardship to a culture of consumption. Possibly the successes of liberal humanism had proved so great that the old doctrines could no longer contain them. In any event, if there is an intellectual crisis today, there was also one in the middle sixties, a feeling that things had fallen apart, which on the part of the student generation took the form of revulsion against liberal humanism and its style. Jacoby may have forgotten this atmosphere when he regrets today the failure of that same generation to produce equivalents of Wilson or Dwight Macdonald. Yet these elderly figures were *New Yorker* writers. They were liberal humanists themselves, even if with some radical points of view. *New Yorker* writers had about as much chance as Frank Sinatra to articulate emotions of the middle and late sixties. The whole purpose of rebellion on the part of the student generation was to oppose people like that.

The young radicals followed other examples, European ones mainly, usually at the distance of five or ten years. New Left heroes of the late sixties were, as Jacoby recalls, writers of the fifties and early sixties—Sartre, Camus, Fanon, Marcuse, Deutscher, Reich. Then the radicals started flooding the graduate schools. Camus and the existentialism of Sartre disappeared, and what dominated instead was Althusserian Marxism, E. P. Thompson Marxism, Lacanian psychoanalysis, structuralism, the Frankfurt School, deconstruction later on, and so forth. The Thompson Marxists among graduate students were in the humanist tradition and therefore different from the others (and some of the younger historians, as I say, have continued to follow their own course, as has Thompson). But leaving the humanists aside and allowing for inconsistencies and exceptions on all sides, the various doctrines can be boiled down to a single grand metaphysic, which came to influence almost everyone in the left-wing graduate school environment. The metaphysic contained two fundamental points, plus a posture.

The fundamental points were: (1) What you see in front of you—for instance, a democracy, or the plot in a novel, or whatever—is an illusion. Reality is undecipherable, or else decipherable only with the aid of science. (2) Those who say otherwise do so because of who they are, not because of what they see. Who they are is probably a self-interested exploiter. Naturally, these points are expressed in different ways by each of the doctrines. Point One—the illusory quality of what lies before you—might, for instance, be stated in a semiotic or deconstructionist way (the distinction between signifier and signified, the impossibility of affixing a meaning), in a Freudian way (the governing role of the unconscious), in a Marxist way (the dominance of bourgeois culture), or in a structuralist way (the governing role of anthropological structures). In any case, the posture that followed from Points One and Two was the Great Refusal, the posture of absolute rejection, of final rupture with everything soft and humanist and subjective that had been thought before.

Were the two points absurd? No, they were an obvious place to begin criticizing smugness and blather. But the posture of the Great Refusal required turning these points into systems. And then, well: On the matter of writing style, for instance, it's obvious that any system of thought affirming the illusory quality of the visible world is going to exact consequences. The ordinary literary virtues of lucidity and straightforwardness do not seem like virtues to someone who regards the obvious world as an illusion. The philosophers of the sixties accordingly developed writing styles that were opaque, enigmatic, paradoxical, scientific-sounding, and complex. They refused to use simple narrative techniques, they abhorred old-fashioned lucidity. Ferry and Renaut mock these writers as "philosophists" and are dry about the results: "The philosophists of the sixties achieved their greatest success in managing to accustom their readers and listeners to the belief that incomprehensibility is the sign of grandeur." And five or ten years later, when incomprehensibility reached American shores, the consequences were, of course, even woollier. For bad writing in French is sometimes good. But in English, bad is worse. Not to mention inspirations from the German!

Point Two in the grand metaphysic—the idea that anyone who claims to see reality is doing so in order to dominate someone else—was at bottom a criticism of reason and the Enlightenment. Here again, the point could be expressed according to different systems. Foucault's version derived from Nietzsche. Foucault saw a link between rationality and repression. He argued that the development of reason in the seventeenth century led to persecution of the insane. The very idea of sanity began to look dubious from a Foucaultian perspective, as if words like sane and insane were mere conveniences of definition, brought into currency by the social need to dominate and exclude.

Alternatively, the criticism might derive from Marx, as in the work of Horkheimer and Adorno. There was Marcuse's famous argument that democracy's most obvious virtues, for instance, freedom of speech, are actually the hidden workings of bourgeois control. Or the criticism of the Enlightenment might derive from linguistics via Lévi-Strauss and structuralist anthropology. Lévi-Strauss argued that, since the same structures of belief underlie all cultures, no "better" or "worse" can be identified in comparing one culture with another. There is no "enlightened" versus "unenlightened"—except in the eyes of imperialists. The only barbarism, from this point of view, is the belief that there is barbarism.

Altogether stupid, these contentions? They offered sharp criticisms of abusive uses to which Enlightenment ideas had been put. Did we rain bombs on the peasants of Indochina? It was, after all, love of democracy that supposedly made us do it. Criticizing such a claim was an appropriate first reaction to the politics of the post–Second World War period. The anticolonialist ideas that derived from Lévi-Strauss were particularly powerful. On the other hand, if criticism of the Enlightenment was extended to mean that democracy and human rights are merely Western anthropological curiosities, what would prevent structuralist anticolonialism from turning into a defense of the most reactionary Third World dictatorships? If the only barbarism is the idea of barbarism, how can we identify any barbarism other than our own? If we are not the partisans of Enlightenment, what is to prevent us from becoming the partisans of every kind of obscurantism, especially when the obscurantists raise the flag of anticolonial resistance? On what basis, as Alain Finkielkraut asks, can even the most savage of customs be condemned?

The criticisms of reason and the Enlightenment spread into a criticism of all kinds of evaluation. If sanity isn't necessarily superior to insanity, if one culture cannot be said to be more advanced in important respects to another, can literature be said to have superior and inferior expressions? Can high culture be regarded as more serious or important than low or popular culture? These questions were likewise worth raising. The postwar era was a period of genius in certain popular arts, for instance, in black America popular music and its imitators; but it was a period also of snobbism among critics, who managed not to see these obvious achievements. The critical ideas that derived from structuralism and other doctrines of the sixties made a great battering ram for clearing away all kinds of snobbism and prejudice that obstructed genuine critical appreciation.

But when criticism of the Enlightenment had at last gone beyond countering the foolish and snobbish to become a thorough system in itself, what was to prevent tin-eared music critics from claiming, say, that a Duke Ellington on one side and a heavy-metal rock band on the other are really all on a plane? What would prevent professors from supposing that value in literature is merely an illusion fomented by the dominant class and end up teaching their students to feel content with reading Louis L'Amour, narrator for the masses? What was to prevent naive students from demanding, instead of an education, courses that would merely congratulate them on their ethnic background?

In short, what was to prevent the valuable and progressive criticisms of imperialism, snobbism, and prejudice from becoming reactionary defenses of tyranny abroad and ignorance at home? The criticism of liberal humanism, having turned into a systematic extreme, produced everything necessary for a thorough intellectual collapse—the collapse of lucidity and sense, the loss of the ability to distinguish the important from the ephemeral, the collapse also of leftism, in whose good name some of the fatuous claims were made. Even television came to be extolled. The defense of the masses thus evolved into a defense of the popular-culture exploiters of the masses. Finally, the whole enterprise caved in, and above the rubble hovered the dust of pretension that always hovers when earnest Americans try to imitate the French or the Germans.

What is to be done? Having said all this, I hate to invoke still other French writers as an alternative. But on a principle of fighting fire with fire, I note that in France, a counter-movement has begun among younger intellectuals who are calling, in effect, for a rehabilitation of liberal humanism, suitably updated. I've cited Ferry and Renaut, the authors of *La pensée 68*, and Alain Finkielkraut, who wrote *La défaite de la pensée*. Another writer from the same group is Pascal Bruckner, whose criticism of Third Worldism in France, *The Tears of the White Man*, has come out in English with a valuable introduction by the translator, William Beer, applying Bruckner's strictures to American attitudes.[2] The writers haven't received much press in the United States, and even less that is favorable. There's a tendency to compare them to the great masters of the sixties and be disappointed. They are not, in truth, great masters (though Finkielkraut in particular is very talented). But as one critic has observed, they're doing a fine job of dismantling the great masters. Anyone who reads their books will see how many of their ideas I've borrowed, not necessarily in ways they would applaud. Do the various American books and articles constitute a parallel effort on this side of the Atlantic? Bloom's *The Closing of the American Mind* raises questions about the influence of Heidegger that were raised a year earlier by Ferry and Renaut. Points of similarity to the French writers do exist. Bloom, though, is in the grip of cranky Straussian philosophical doctrines. He adopts the posture of a nattering curmudgeon and ends up grounding his arguments on a reactionary dislike for the reforms of the sixties. There's no future in Bloom, only a past. Jacoby, as the anti-Bloom, adopts an ultraradical sixties posture of the Great Refusal. This too is exasperating. But Jacoby has succeeded in focusing our attention on the method of criticism. As someone has said, the method of tailors is to sew a jacket, a shirt, a collar. The method of criticism is to stand up when occasion requires and say about a given body of work: Well, it's not wearing a jacket. It's not wearing a shirt. If you look carefully there's not even a collar. . . .

In that way and no other way the task of clarification goes on.

NOTES

1. Russell Jacoby, *The Last Intellectuals: American Culture in the Age of Academe* (New York: Basic Books, 1987).

2. Pascal Bruckner, *The Tears of the White Man: Compassion as Contempt* (New York: The Free Press, 1986).

Intellectuals—
Public and Otherwise

Joseph Epstein*

I cannot recall when I first heard or read the ornate term "public intellectual," but I do recall disliking it straightaway. I felt like a man who has been used to buying the same solid shirt for years—white oxford cloth, button-down collar—and one day enters his favorite store only to discover that someone has gone and added epaulets to it. When I noted the people who were being identified as public intellectuals, I knew that to superfluity had been added gross imprecision. Here was a phrase, in short, that absorbed no truth whatsoever.

Yet "public intellectual" seems to have taken stronger and stronger hold, popping up in print with little or no explanation of what it means. The late Lionel Trilling, one reads, "was the public intellectual and mainstay of *Partisan Review*." Edward Said, one learns, "is an American by default and a public intellectual by virtue of the mean accidents of political history." Richard A. Posner and Ronald Dworkin are "two of the nation's most admired public intellectuals," while the late Noel Annan was "as pure an example of the public intellectual as [one] could summon up." Best of all, I recently came across the news that at Florida Atlantic University in Boca Raton there is a full course of study designed to prepare you to become a public intellectual, providing a Ph.D. in whatever it is public intellectuals are supposed to do.

In Russell Jacoby's *The Last Intellectuals* (1987), the term gets a fairly good workout, and it may be that Jacoby first put it into circulation. In his own usage, a public intellectual "contributes to public discussion" and is also "an incorrigibly independent soul answering to no one," committed "not simply to a professional or private domain but to a public world—and a public language, the vernacular." This definition supplies a pair of pants baggy enough for both Walter Cronkite and Jackie Mason. In the usage of others, a public intellectual emerges as an academic specialist who can write the op-ed piece or do the political talk show. For still others, the public intellectual is someone vaguely intelligent who happens to appear before the public: Ted Koppel, say, or Frank Rich.

As for intellectual, plain and simple, that is, or was, something else altogether. I cannot recall when I first heard this term, either, but I do vividly recall my first experience of the phenomenon itself. In my third year as an undergraduate at the University of Chicago, I discovered the periodical room at Harper Library and what were then called little magazines. ("Our intellectual marines," wrote W H. Auden, "landing in little magazines.") The year was 1957, and these magazines were still at high tide. I read as many as I could find, but particularly *Partisan Review* (now often described as, in those days, the house organ of American intellectuals), *Commentary*, and *Encounter*. The last of these, which came out in England, was co-edited by the poet Stephen Spender and Irving Kristol (who had formerly been on the editorial staff of *Commentary*), and had only recently begun publication.

I find it difficult to do justice to the deep pleasure I took in these magazines. Education, as everyone knows, is a disorderly business. It is chiefly available through four different means: schools, new and used bookstores, conversation with intelligent friends, and good magazines. For me, coming to them pretty much *tabula rasa*, these intellectual magazines were easily the key element. Although the University of Chicago had taught me who were the essential writers and which were the perennially important questions—no small thing, granted—I had had no great teachers or important educational experiences in its classrooms and lecture halls. Serious learning commenced in the periodical room at Harper Library, and continued for a great many years afterward as I searched out back issues of the intellectual magazines and fell upon them with the combined ardor of a collector and a glutton. They made me want to be an intellectual, a term I then took as an unqualified honorific.

I was not wholly unprepared for the call. Max Weber's *The Protestant Ethic and the Spirit of Capitalism*, which I had recently read, had utterly dazzled me by the brilliance of Weber's historical connections and the power of his formulations. But what the intellectual magazines showed me was that not all brilliance was in the past—that some very interesting minds were still at work.

Some of the names I came across in the pages of these magazines were European and already known to me from my general reading: André Malraux, Ignazio Silone, F. R. Leavis, Bertrand Russell. (These were the days when Americans still existed in a condition of cultural inferiority vis-à-vis Europe.) Others I discovered there for the first time: Lionel Trilling, Isaiah Berlin, Philip Rahv, Sidney Hook, Hugh Trevor-Roper, Richard Crossman, George Lichtheim, Harold Rosenberg, Hannah Arendt, Saul Bellow, Mary McCarthy, Goronwy Rees, Gertrude Himmelfarb, Leslie Fiedler, Clement Greenberg, Delmore Schwartz, James Baldwin, Irving Howe, William Barrett, Hilton Kramer, Robert Lowell, Randall Jarrell, John Berryman. These writers introduced me to still others—Alexander Herzen, François Mauriac, Paul Valery, Max Beerbohm—and to scores of subjects of which I was still ignorant; and so the net of my intellectual acquaintance grew wider and wider.

Although *Commentary, Partisan Review*, and *Encounter* published fiction and poetry, some of it quite distinguished, at their heart was the discursive essay: ambitious in choice of subject, sometimes aggressively polemical in spirit, unhesitant in authority, often brilliant in execution. Looking back at representative American exemplars of the form, I would single out Robert Warshow and Dwight Macdonald. Warshow, an editor at *Commentary*, died in 1955 at the age of thirty-seven, and I read him only later, when I began rummaging through back issues. Macdonald had been an editor of *Partisan Review* and then, after breaking with his colleagues over World War II, to which he claimed moral objections, veered off to edit his own magazine, *politics*.

In his brief career, Warshow wrote more about the movies than about any other subject, but neither he nor Macdonald—who also wrote about the movies—can be said to have had an intellectual specialty. Nor was either of them a scholar, though Macdonald's best book, an anthology titled *Parodies*, contains much genuine scholarship. Neither man was remotely academic in either style or spirit; both were genuine freelances, writing about subjects they found interesting and attempting to draw out their widest implications.

Warshow's "The Gangster As Tragic Hero" (1948) provides a perfect illustration of what I have in mind. In this essay, Warshow sets out to discover both the real meaning of American gangster movies and the source of their attraction. The distillation is highly concentrated; it takes him fewer than three thousand words to make his case.

Inherent to our pleasure in gangster movies, Warshow asserts in "The Gangster as Tragic Hero," is the element of sadism: in watching them, "we gain the double satisfaction of participating vicariously in the gangster's sadism and then seeing it turned against the gangster himself." But the deeper significance of these movies lies in the way they encapsulate "the intolerable dilemma" we all feel about success. The gangster, in brief, is "what we want to be and what we are afraid we may become." And so the effect of the gangster movie "is to embody this dilemma in the person of the gangster and resolve it by his death. The dilemma is resolved because death, not ours. We are safe; for the moment, we can acquiesce in failure, we can choose to fail."

Warshow's essay is the act of an intellectual at its most characteristic. Here is an author who possesses no specialized knowledge, or even any extraordinary fund of personal experience. He does what he does with no other aid but the power of his mind. He has seen the same movies we have all seen. But he happens to have seen more in them than the rest of us recognized was there. "This interior need to penetrate beyond the screen of immediate concrete experience," wrote the sociologist Edward Shils, "marks the existence of the intellectuals in every society." A precise description, that, of Robert Warshow at work.

Very different from Warshow, Dwight Macdonald was dashing and slashing in his prose, more amusing than penetrating in his thought. In both culture and politics he assumed the stance of the immitigable highbrow. Whenever capitalism played a large part in any work of art or cultural production, he tended to attack it. He was death on middlebrow culture, writing rollicking blasts at Encyclopedia Britannica's *Great Books of the Western World* ("The Book of the Millennium Club") and the New English Bible. He could ambush a bestseller, and in the case of James Gould Cozzens ("By Cozzens Possessed") dealt so devastating a blow to the novelist that, even now, nearly forty-five years later, his literary reputation has yet to recover.

Macdonald's opinions were, however, less than original; they were those of the herd of independent minds, in Harold Rosenberg's withering phrase. Although Macdonald attempted a systematic formulation of his theory of culture in a lengthy essay, "Masscult & Midcult" (1960), it was riddled with contradictions and, theoretically, a mess. Late in life, at a symposium at Skidmore College, he acknowledged that he was at his best as a counter-puncher, writing against some work or idea. "Every time I say 'Yes,'" he remarked, "I get in trouble." His last big Yes was on behalf of the student rebellion at Columbia in 1968, where Yes was once again the wrong answer.

It was from Dwight Macdonald—whom I can hardly read today but who once gave me so much pleasure—as well as from Robert Warshow and a few other marines in little magazines (including Irving Howe and Paul Goodman) that I took much of my own notion of what constituted an intellectual. This exotic creature, they taught me, was a species of grand amateur—an amateur of the mind. He was distinguished from other mind workers, or intelligentsia, by his want of specialization. He knew not one but many things.

Unlike the scholar, for example, the intellectual did not work with primary sources, did not feel himself responsible for presenting the most accurate and detailed knowledge of his subjects, did not feel the need to back up his assertions with footnotes, did not seek out new factual material that might change the shape of a subject. True, there were scholars, scientists, occasionally artists, jurists, or even politicians who had the widest intellectual interests, but when they were functioning in their specialties they were not, strictly speaking, intellectuals.

The natural penchant of the intellectual was not to go deeper but wider—to turn the criticism of literature or art or the movies or politics into broader statements about culture. His lucubrations might have all sorts of consequences, but insofar as he was operating purely as an intellectual, he was less concerned with influencing policy, effecting change, or doing anything other than seeing where his ideas—and the boldness of his formulations—took him.

The intellectual, in the standard if unwritten job description, functioned best as a critic—be it stressed, an *alienated* critic—of his society. Guardian and gatekeeper, the intellectual had to be wary above all of the amorphous yet pervasive influence of Wall Street, Madison Avenue, the middle class, the middlebrow, the mainstream, the bourgeoisie, the big interests. In Dwight Macdonald's worldview, writers and intellectuals were always in danger of selling out to the devil, with the devil usually envisioned as Henry Luce and hell as Time, Inc.—where Macdonald once worked.

Where politics was concerned—and politics was always concerned—anti-Communism was permitted as an ideological component in the intellectual's makeup, or at least it was at the time my own intellectual aspirations took hold. (With the war in Vietnam, this, too, would become a contentious position.) But what was also assumed was a high reverence, theoretical and sentimental, for socialism. In those days—the late 1950s, the early 1960s—it did not seem possible to be an intellectual and not to be of the Left. This reverence for socialism was never entirely absent even in so otherwise independent-minded a figure as George Orwell.

If Warshow and Macdonald were representative intellectuals, Orwell was in many ways the perfect type, both in his strengths and in his limitations. He wrote well about politics, literature, and popular culture. He was devoted to truth-telling, even when that meant, as in the case of the truths he told about Communist totalitarianism, being cut off from the *bien-pensant* crowd of his day and from the journals that provided much of his income. He was also large-minded enough to be hospitable to ideas that went against his own, writing favorably, for example, about Friedrich Hayek's *The Road to Serfdom*. Although neither right about everything nor entirely able to evade self-deception, Orwell probably had a higher truth quotient—especially when it came to difficult truths—than any other intellectual of the past century.

But if Orwell represented the type of the intellectual at his best, he also manifested a number of its limitations. He was clever, he was penetrating, he was even prophetic—and that is a lot—but no one could claim that he was deep. Like most modern intellectuals, he was insufficiently impressed with the mysteries of life, which is why his fiction so often seems stillborn. T. S. Eliot famously remarked of Henry James, "he had a mind so fine no idea could violate it." Eliot meant by this not that James was ignorant of ideas but that he was after a different, a more elevated, form of knowledge than was available through mere ideas. Except at odd moments, Orwell never quite progressed beyond ideas: their stranglehold suffocates not only *1984* and *Animal Farm* but even his less directly political fiction.

Still, better to be in the grip of ideas that happen to be true—as Orwell, for the most part, was—than of ideas that are false and trivial, or odious and brutal. If the social and political speculations of intellectuals can lend charm to life—risky generalizations, especially those that sound cogent, are among the best stimulants to thought—the claim of the intellectual to be more than a high-order kibitzer often remains fairly thin. Like the kibitzer, the intellectual stands at the rim of the game, risking nothing by his assertions. An American intellectual once announced to my friend Edward Shils that, when it came to the politics of the state of Israel, he was of the war party. "Yes," Shils said in reporting this conversation to me, "Israel will go to war, and he'll go to the party."

But, then, intellectuals have never been known for their deep loyalty. This is a point underscored by the late Noel Annan in his recent book *The Dons*, in which he notes that intellectuals "vacillate and move gingerly to judgments about people, slide away at first hint of trouble, . . . and then decamp when their friend is in trouble, or worse, when he is in disgrace." Herman Wouk made essentially this point, a long while ago, in *The Caine Mutiny*, whose one really shameless character is the intellectual—played perfectly by Fred MacMurray in the movie—who goads the executive officer into wrongful action and then backs away when the going gets tough. The larger point is that you probably do not want an intellectual in your foxhole.

The historian Richard Hofstadter, noting the "passion for justice" of intellectuals, wrote that "one thinks here of Voltaire defending the Calas family, of Zola speaking out for Dreyfus, of the American intellectuals outraged at the trial of Sacco and Vanzetti." Yet such can be the fecklessness of many intellectuals that this same passion for justice has also surfaced as a penchant for mischief-making, and on a monumental scale. Next to alienation, one of the most enticing ideas to intellectuals has been revolution. This is no doubt partly because a number of actual intellectuals—Leon Trotsky, Zhou Enlai, Che Guevara—have played prominent (and in no way salubrious) roles in actual revolutions. As a young intellectual-in-training, I knew more about the Russian than about the American Revolution; after all, intellectuals had been much more conspicuous in the runup to the former. Most intellectuals have felt that when the revolution arrives, not the least of its important results will be a general recognition of the importance of you'll never guess who.

Even when they have not lent their energies to promoting schemes for human betterment that depend on the mass coercion of real human beings, the intellectuals' overdependence on ideas, and their consequent detachment from reality, have often turned them into little demons of ignorant subtlety. During World War II, a number of left-wing British intellectuals were convinced that what really lay behind America's entry into the war was the hope of stopping the spread of socialism in England—prompting George Orwell's acid remark that "Only an intellectual could be so stupid." When Barry Goldwater ran for president of the United States in 1964, Hannah Arendt, certain that America was on the edge of being taken over by fascists, sought an apartment in Switzerland. Susan Sontag, in 1982, announced to a New York audience her belated conclusion that Communism should no longer be the name of any thinking person's desire but was rather to be regarded as "fascism with a human face." To those who had troubled over the years to follow Sontag's own public imprecations against Western democracy or against the "white race" as the "cancer of human history," or her earnest championing of Communist North Vietnam as "a place which, in many respects, *deserves* to be idealized," her public change of mind, however carefully qualified, must have offered a moment of grim amusement. But her audience—in 1982!—was nevertheless shocked by even so calibrated a defection, and she herself never again ventured to say anything remotely so out of line.

Wrong or not, alienated or not, until the 1960s American intellectuals seemed to live easily if not prosperously enough, enjoying some of the comforts of a coterie existence. Not least among those comforts was the feeling of being vastly superior to their countrymen, of being among Stendhal's happy few. Unlike today's so-called public intellectuals, they were not invited to offer their opinions on radio and television, and their names were not much known outside the readership of the intellectual magazines.

Yet even in the 1940s and '50s, their influence was not negligible—though it might take a while to be felt. Edmund Wilson, perhaps the literary intellectual par excellence, had been a crucial figure in importing and explaining modernism in literature to an American audience, especially in his book *Axel's Castle* (1931), and in introducing readers to a vast international array of writers, living and dead. In the 1940s and '50s, Clement Greenberg had done something similar for Abstract Expressionism and the New York school in painting. Meanwhile, a number of men who wrote for the intellectual magazines—including James Agee, Irving Howe, and Louis Kronenberger—were also putting in time working for the devil himself at *Time* and *Fortune*; and so, in the sociological phrase, there was transmission of knowledge on this front, too. If one read both the intellectual magazines and that portion of the popular press that had intellectual pretensions, one saw how the ideas from the former began to percolate down to the latter.

By the early 1960s, "percolate" would no longer accurately describe the quickness of this transaction. In those years Harold Rosenberg became the art critic of the *New Yorker*, and Hannah Arendt, James Baldwin, and Mary McCarthy also published there. Dwight Macdonald not only became a *New Yorker* writer but signed on to write about movies for *Esquire*. In 1963 and '64 respectively, Mary McCarthy's *The Group* and Saul Bellow's *Herzog* were best-sellers. In 1964, Susan Sontag wrote an essay in *Partisan Review*, "Notes on Camp," that resulted within what seemed a matter of weeks in the spread of the word "camp" to just about everywhere, including *Vogue*. Intellectuals had suddenly gone public; they, or at any rate some of them, were on the Big Board.

At least as significant for the new integration of intellectuals into American life was another development, an early sign of which was the appointment of Philip Rahv, one of the founding editors of *Partisan Review*, and Irving Howe, then the editor of *Dissent*, to professorships at the newly founded Brandeis University. Neither Rahv nor Howe had a doctorate or anything resembling an academic specialty; what they had was intellectual authority, and that, apparently, was now deemed enough. The postwar expansion of the universities would soon siphon away a larger number of such people—until, in the end, American intellectual life was itself all but siphoned away by the universities.

Sometimes this was literally so, as when first Rutgers and then Boston University took over *Partisan Review*, with Rutgers installing a full-time academic, Richard Poirier, as one of the magazine's editors. More generally, the acceptance of intellectuals into the American university dealt a serious blow to the freelance spirit. The successors to the older generation of American intellectuals—among them Richard Sennett, Marshall Berman, Morris Dickstein, and Louis Menand—now tended to operate with a net under them, the net known as academic tenure; and, though their pretensions might be intellectual, their style tended to be highly academic.

Still, apart from the absorption of intellectuals by the universities, it was really the decade of the 1960s that finished off the old intellectual life. Before the '60s, the issue that had most divided intellectuals was Stalinism. That rancorous and deadly quarrel was much on the minds of some participants in the political disputes that arose during the 1960s over the war in Vietnam, the Black Power movement, the meaning of urban riots, and the nature of America itself. The effect was momentous. As Midge Decter has recently written in *Commentary*, "The 'partisan' community would become unstuck in the '60s, with several defections from among its ranks to the camp of the radical students, and would blow up even further in the '70s with the onset of neoconservatism."

In two of his memoirs, *Breaking Ranks* (1979) and *Ex-Friends* (1999), Norman Podhoretz has chronicled this sundering of the community of intellectuals he once dubbed the Family, as well as his own emergence as a neoconservative. Behind much of the anger that greeted at least the first of these books was the implicit charge that Podhoretz had betrayed the very essence of the intellectual vocation as it had come to be defined: that is, he had refused to consider it his first duty to be unrelentingly critical of his own country, to maintain his alienation, and to assert his disdain for middle-class life.

But Podhoretz was not entirely alone. Owing to the '60s, others of us were coming to regard the so-called intellectual vocation, at least as now construed, as outmoded if not downright dangerous, both to the life of the mind and to the life of society. The word intellectual no longer seemed such a clear honorific, and the baggage that went with the job—the pose of alienation, the contempt for the social class of one's origin, the pretense of distaste for the culture of one's country—seemed false to our experience of life. When it came to the breakdown of the universities, the racial bullying of the Black Power movement, and the general destruction of standards in society, the intellectuals had by and large run with the pack. Later, having long deserted such convictions as they might once have had, most intellectuals chose to stand aside when culture itself came under attack by the philistine forces of political correctness and radical feminism.

There were, admittedly, other factors at work in this decline. For one thing, recent decades have not exactly provided a hardy diet of ideas of the kind once on the intellectual's table. Consider Marxism in politics and modernism in the arts, the staples of the old *Partisan Review*. The former, with its prediction of ultimate revolution, is now a dead letter; party politics, once considered beneath the interest of an American intellectual, is now all that is left to him. Modernism, now more than a century old with many great discrete works to its credit, was always connected to an interest in the avant-garde; but the contemporary avant-garde, for the most part a mélange of political yahooism, in-your-face nastiness, and sexual liberationism, can hardly hold the interest of anyone seriously devoted to art. As for other big-system ideas once the meat and drink of intellectuals—including Freudianism—they have taken a ferocious drubbing over the past quarter-century, while structuralism, deconstruction, and the rest of the theory stew have proved digestible only by academics.

Then, too, the very notion of the sell-out, once so dear to intellectual thought, has become murky in the extreme. Nowadays, if one is sufficiently antinomian, one is likely to find one's art sponsored by Mobil Oil, one's novel receiving a six-figure advance from a major publisher, or oneself put on the faculty at Princeton. The problem for the talented is no longer selling out, but deciding where—and when—to buy in.

Another factor working against the idea of the traditional intellectual is the greater degree of specialization that infects the social sciences, literary studies, and philosophy. As recently as the 1960s, Lewis Mumford and Edmund Wilson, nonacademics both, could mount full-scale attacks on the heavily pedantic Modern Language Association editions of Emerson, Twain, and other American writers, inspiring sufficient discomfort among the officials in charge to make them feel the charges had to be answered. I am not sure there is an intellectual alive today who commands the authority to do anything similar.

And so the traditional intellectual has been replaced by a new type, the public intellectual, a figure who as likely as not retains all or most of the political attitudes of the '60s, suitably updated for the moment, and who has become adept at packaging them in fancy academic dressing. These are the Edward Saids and Ronald Dworkins of our time, the Richard Rortys and Cornel Wests, the Martha Nussbaums and Stanley Fishes, the Catharine MacKinnons and Peter Singers. Unlike the unattached intellectuals of earlier days, such people usually have university careers and arrangements at influential publications. Columnists, professors writing on subjects of putative contemporary relevance, soon, if Florida Atlantic University has its way, full-fledged Ph.D.s in public intellectuality itself—they are the inheritors of a mantle for which one now qualifies not by any particular mental power but by going public with one's intelligibility and one's mere opinions.

Words change for a reason, generally to fit changes in the world. We thus now have the empty term public intellectual, because the real thing, the traditional intellectual, is on his way out. As for me, harshly though I have written about the traditional intellectual, I now find myself—like Norman Podhoretz at the close of *Ex-Friends*—rather sorrowful at his departure from the scene. What once distinguished him was a certain cast of mind, a style of thought, wide-ranging, curious, playful, genuinely excited by ideas for ideas' sake. Unlike so many of today's public intellectuals, he was not primarily a celebrity hound, a false philosopher-king with tenure, or a single-issue publicist. An elegantly plumed, often irritating bird, the traditional intellectual was always a minuscule minority, and now he is on the list of endangered species. Anyone who was around in his heyday to see him soar is unlikely to forget the spectacle.

Forum

J. Hillis Miller*

Intellectual is not a word that readily springs to my mind or lips these days. The word has become a bit moldy. This degradation has no doubt been overdetermined. One important factor is surely the globalization of intellectual life (as well as other forms of human life), brought about by rapid travel all over the world, the internationalization of economies, the decline of the nation-state, and new communications technologies.

The old idea of the intellectual accompanied the culture of the book, newspaper, and journal that began in its modern form in Europe in the early eighteenth century and reached its heyday in the Romantic period and thereafter. This traditional concept of the intellectual, closely tied to nationalisms and to linguistic essentialisms, is exemplified by Coleridge in England and by the circles around Kleist and the Schlegel brothers in what was not yet a nationally unified Germany. These figures used periodicals and books to promulgate social and literary ideas. The followers of Kleist and the Schlegels gathered in salons to exchange ideas, as in Friedrich Schlegel's imaginary salon conversation "Gespräch über die Poesie" (["Dialogue on Poetry"], 1799–1800, *Kritische Schriften* [Munich: Hanser, 1964] 473–529).

That tradition remained a living ideal in Europe and America until after World War II. An intellectual was a distinguished specialist in some field—poetry, literary criticism, art or music criticism, history, political science, or even physics or biology—who also wrote for a broad educated

*Reprinted by permission of the Modern Language Association of America from *PMLA* 112, no. 5 (1997): 1137–1138.

public that shared a common culture. A certain mode of the essay was the intellectual's prime expressive medium. When Georg Lukács was only twenty-five, in 1910, he wrote an essay that identifies the role of this genre ("On the Nature and Form of the Essay," *Soul and Form*, trans. Anna Bostock [Cambridge: MIT P, 1974] 1–18). Walter Benjamin and Theodor Adorno would be examples of such intellectuals in pre–World War II Germany, as would G. B. Shaw and W. H. Auden in England, Paul Valéry and Jean-Paul Sartre in France, and Lionel Trilling, Edmund Wilson, and Hannah Arendt in the United States.

This tradition is severely etiolated or even dead now. All the factors that sustained it are vanishing, at least in the United States. There is no longer a common culture in the United States, or it is recognized that there never was one. Nor are there central cities that can play the role Berlin, Dresden, and Jena did for the German Romantics, London and Paris did for nineteenth- and early-twentieth-century England and France, or New York did for the early-twentieth-century United States. Capitals today, like Oslo, sufficiently unified and small that representative artists, writers, professors, journalists, and politicians might meet at the same party or reception do not have international cultural influence.

It is not that journals in the United States have all become politicized. They have always been political. No one, however, confidently expects to find in the *New York Review of Books* or the *New Yorker* essays of the caliber of Benjamin's or Arendt's, nor do such periodicals represent the views of more than a small segment of the educated class. From an outsider's perspective they often seem as much anti-intellectual as intellectual. No large, highly educated public with common interests and goals exists in the United States. If Bill Clinton had quoted a great American poet during the last presidential campaign—Walt Whitman, say—he might not have been elected. To a considerable degree universities have lost their social role as advisers and shapers of opinion for the government and the public. Scholars now commonly have more solidarity with international groups interested in their specialties than they do with any national constituencies or even with their own local university communities. Talk show experts, even on public radio, are as likely to be drawn from conservative think tanks as from universities.

The most drastic force putting an end to the old tradition of the intellectual is the popular visual and aural culture of radio, television, cinema, videos, CDs, CD-ROMs, and the World Wide Web, which has replaced print culture as the crucible of public opinion, of the ethos and values of citizens in the West. This popular culture is creating what Jon Katz, in a recent provocative essay, calls the "netizens" of the new "digital nation" ("The Netizen: Birth of a Digital Nation," *Wired* Apr. 1997: 49+, online, World Wide Web, available at http://www.wired.com/5.04/netizen/).

As he explains, netizens disdain those who lecture them about the shallowness of mass-marketed music, cinema, and so on. "The digital young . . . ," says Katz, "share a passion for popular culture—perhaps their most common shared value, and the one most misperceived and mishandled by politicians and journalists. On Monday mornings when they saunter into work, they are much more likely to be talking about the movies they saw over the weekend than about Washington's issue of the week [or, I might add, about what a wonderful poem *Paradise Lost* is]. Music, movies, magazines, some television shows, and some books are elementally important to them—not merely forms of entertainment but means of identity" (184). Poems and novels used to be means of identity; now it is the latest rap group. Media culture, disseminated globally, has the power to drown out the quiet voice of the fading book culture and also to blur the specificities of local and national societies, just as people everywhere wear blue jeans and carry Walkmen. The old ideal of the intellectual will be replaced by a netizen figure whose profile is as yet but dimly discernible.

Chapter 5

A CONTINUING PRESENCE: PUBLIC INTELLECTUALS AND CHANGE

Intellectuals in Politics

Theodore Draper*

"Intellectuals in politics" immediately raises two questions: What intellectuals? What politics?

Instead of trying to define these terms, which are so broad and loose that they defy exact definition, I prefer to start by name-dropping. To begin with, the names are Woodrow Wilson, Raymond Moley, Patrick Daniel Moynihan, Henry A. Kissinger, and Zbigniew Brzezinski. These names indicate the type of American intellectual with which I will be largely concerned. Three things can be said about them immediately. They went into politics, full-time or part-time, after they had established themselves professionally as intellectuals. The intellectual in politics is most often the professor in politics. And politics here does not refer merely to the realm of ideas or intellectual influence; it requires actual service in government. There are other types, such as intellectuals in revolutionary politics, but they are so different that they need a quite different approach.

The late Richard Hofstadter wrote an admirable book called *Anti-Intellectualism in American Life* (1963), much of which dealt with anti-intellectualism in American politics. He may have chosen anti-intellectualism rather than intellectualism because he thought that the former had deeper historical roots. Intellectuals in American politics are, in fact, a relatively recent phenomenon, limited almost wholly to the present century. Their history remains to be written.

*This article first appeared in *Encounter* 49 (1977): 47–60. Reprinted with permission.

In the eighteenth and early nineteenth centuries, from Thomas Jefferson to John Quincy Adams, the United States had intellectual politicians rather than intellectuals in politics. The distinction is important. The intellectual politician is a type of politician; the intellectual in politics is a type of intellectual. One makes his career in politics; the other comes to politics after making an intellectual career. The most happy reconciliation between intellectualism and politics was achieved by the intellectual politicians in the first half century of American life. It was not to be approached for another century.

Beginning with the Jacksonian Era in the 1830s intellectualism and politics drifted apart. Despite a few notable exceptions, intellectuals considered politics alien, politicians considered intellectuals politically useless. The historian George Bancroft, served as secretary of the navy and minister to Great Britain and Germany. Edward Everett, a professor of Greek at Harvard University, was later governor of Massachusetts, minister to Great Britain, and U.S. senator. Henry Cabot Lodge was an assistant professor of history at Harvard before becoming a senator. One nineteenth-century President, James A. Garfield, not one of the most distinguished, was for a short time, a teacher of classics and president of Hiram College, a small institution in Ohio. With one exception, these careers signified no trend. The exception was a tradition even in the nineteenth century of appointing intellectuals to diplomatic posts. But presidents varied even in this respect, and it was at most a marginal affair.

The intellectuals' distaste for politics was, for most of the nineteenth century, matched by the politicians' disdain for intellectuals. An intellectual-political movement, known as "the genteel reformers," arose in the post–Civil War period but had little success. A Tammany Hall boss in the last quarter of the nineteenth century put the case against intellectuals in politics in this way:

> Some young men think they can learn how to be successful in politics from books, and they cram their heads with all sorts of college rot. They couldn't make a bigger mistake. Now, understand me, I ain't sayin' nothin' against colleges. I guess they have to exist as long as there's bookworms, and I suppose they do some good in certain ways, but they don't count in politics."[1]

It is said that the first—or one of the first—American uses of the term "intellectual" appeared in a letter by the philosopher, William James, in 1899.[2] James used the term in a context that had a direct bearing on the American attitude toward intellectuals in politics. Commenting on the Dreyfus case in France, James sympathized with the French intellectuals' "aggressively militant" role and hoped that they would grow "stronger and stronger." But then he turned around and thanked God for an America in which "intellectuals"—he still thought it necessary to put the word in quotation marks—could stay out of all corrupting "big institutions," which he blamed for Captain Dreyfus's ordeal. Except for the American "party spirit," James believed, American sources of corruption were trivial compared with the European. He did not say so in so many words but he seemed to imply that American intellectuals should stay out of politics and instead "work to keep our precious birthright of individualism" and seek fulfillment in "free personal relation." His emphasis on "freedom from all corrupting institutions" must have included the political in view of his conviction that "the only serious permanent force of corruption in America is party spirit."[3]

Nevertheless, it was at the turn of the century that the institutionalization of intellectuals in American politics began. Its birthplace was the state of Wisconsin where, under the leadership of Governor Robert M. La Follette, the outstanding political figure of the Progressive movement, the first successful experiment in achieving a symbiosis between a university and a government was attempted. A comprehensive program was worked out to put academic "experts" of the University of Wisconsin at the service of the state government. Scientists, engineers, agronomists, economists, historians, political scientists, and the like were systematically called on for advice and information. The Wisconsin system was nominally nonpartisan; in fact, it was the servant of Progressive politics which was the only kind of politics willing and able to engage in such an experiment. Thus the Wisconsin experience produced a familiar type of intellectual in politics—the reformer working for a reform movement.

The next great step forward by an American intellectual in politics was taken by Woodrow Wilson. In fact, he took the greatest step forward that any American intellectual has ever taken—right into the White House. Wilson was an authentic intellectual if ever there was one—Professor of Jurisprudence and Political Economy, President of Princeton University, author of basic works on the American political system. The story of how Wilson became a politician suggests the function sometimes reserved for intellectuals. When he was approached in 1910 to accept the Democratic nomination for governor of the State of New Jersey, his stepping-stone to the presidency two years later, he examined his overworked conscience to find a good reason why he should give in to the temptation. He came up with the idea that "a new day had come in American politics." He interpreted the proposition, in effect, as the opening of a new era in American politics—the era of the intellectual in politics. Wilson later realized that he had naively deceived himself. His biographer notes that the New Jersey politician who masterminded Wilson's nomination "hoped to use Wilson as a respectable front behind which he could operate." It was not a role that Wilson could or would play, but he might never have started on his political career if some politician had not chosen him to play it.

I do not imagine that Wilson was the last intellectual whom politicians have intended to use as a "respectable front." But Wilson learned fast. One of the first things he had to do to win the governorship was to repudiate virtually everything he had stood for on the issue of trade unionism, which he had previously opposed.[4] In short, he had to learn how to act like a politician, not an intellectual, to gain power. For better or worse, however, Wilson unlearned this lesson in the course of his presidency. He was always more the schoolmaster than the politician. The more power Wilson had, the less he was willing to compromise—a trait attributed to his intellectualism but perhaps more attributable to his character.

Far more than Wilson personally, the First World War opened the political door to intellectuals.

> The war itself, ironically, raised many of them to heights of influence as no domestic issue could [Hofstadter observed]. Historians and writers were mobilised for propaganda, and experts of all kinds were recruited as advisers.[5]

They became so prominent that one Republican senator protested, "This is a government by professors and intellectuals." He warned, not for the last time, that "intellectuals are good enough in their places, but a country run by professors is ultimately destined to Bolshevism and an explosion."[6] The high point of this academic invasion came in 1919 when a group known as "The Inquiry" was organized to prepare the ground for American policy in the peace negotiations. It brought together 150 scholarly experts from many different fields, ranging from history to ethnology, aided by a staff of several hundred more of similar background.

The First World War, then, might have been the decisive breakthrough of American intellectuals into political or at least governmental service. They were welcomed in unprecedented numbers and variety. Some lessons can be drawn from this experience. One is that the first large-scale incursion of American intellectuals into political life needed a national crisis that united the nation, including the intellectuals. The second is that intellectuals were drawn into government in large numbers when the functions or responsibilities of government were enormously enlarged. By vastly expanding the reach of government in the economic and social as well as the military sphere, the First World War temporarily created a need to tap a new and sizable reservoir of special training. Such a reservoir for a quick, massive infusion existed only in the universities and other schools. That a professor was president did not hurt, but another war showed that it was not necessary to have a professor as president to produce the same result.

The First World War did not constitute the decisive breakthrough because it was immediately followed by national disillusionment and Wilson's repudiation. The next administrations of Presidents Harding,

Coolidge, and Hoover went back to the older system of using intellectuals selectively and even exceptionally. This war-time and post-war experience introduced an aspect of intellectuals in politics that has forcefully struck students of the subject. It is the cyclical nature of the phenomenon. This was the first time that American intellectuals went in and out of the revolving door of politics. For the first one hundred and fifty years of the Republic, then, it may be said that intellectuals in politics were not a common commodity and had not established a firm tradition. We can see gradual changes, but they were more of degree than of kind. The real breakthrough was still to come.

It came with Franklin D. Roosevelt in the 1930s. The story is familiar to students of Rooseveltiana, but it is worth repeating for what we can learn or relearn from it.

The intellectual breakthrough was a byproduct of Roosevelt's presidential campaign before he was elected president. According to the most circumstantial version, candidate Roosevelt and his faithful factotum, Samuel I. Rosenman, were sitting around in March 1932 talking about how to organize the campaign. Roosevelt was a quick learner, but he had much to learn about national problems and policies. As Rosenman later recalled, he told Roosevelt that they ought to get some people together "and see whether we can come up with some answers or at least some good new intelligent thinking, pro and con, and some new ideas. . . ." Whom did Rosenman have in mind? Rosenman's answer suggests something important about the whole phenomenon:

> Usually in a situation like this, a candidate gathers around him a group composed of some successful industrialists, some big financiers, and some national political leaders. I think we ought to steer clear of all those. They all seem to have failed to produce anything constructive to solve the mess we're in today. Now my idea is this: why not go to the universities of the country? You have been having some good experiences with college professors. I think they wouldn't be afraid to strike out on new paths just because the paths are new. They would get away from the old fuzzy thinking on many subjects, and that seems to be the most important thing.[7]

Rosenman's version lends itself to a broad generalization about the necessary social condition for such an intellectual breakthrough. "The mess we're in today" was, of course, the greatest economic crisis in American history.

A different kind of crisis had brought the Wilsonian intellectuals into politics. The Rooseveltian crisis was far deeper, implying the bankruptcy of the whole social system, and the successful industrialists, big financiers, and national political leaders who dominated it. Roosevelt as governor of New York had already used professorial experts for specific problems and projects. Rosenman wanted to use professors to fill a general political vacuum—that was what was new about it. The way was opened for the early Rooseveltian intellectuals into politics not so much because Roosevelt was so different at that stage from previous American politicians but because the period in which he wanted to become president was so different. The economic crisis was the midwife of the Rooseveltian breakthrough for the intellectuals.

The first intellectual to be recruited into the Brain Trust, Professor Raymond Moley of Columbia University, did not like Rosenman's version because it gave Rosenman too much credit for the historic innovation. Moley's account also lends itself to a larger consideration. The real reason for the Brain Trust, according to Moley, was Roosevelt's and Rosenman's extreme limitations in national affairs. They brought in the professors because they had found them so useful during Roosevelt's governorship and had merely expanded the practice to broaden their political education.[8] No doubt the original Brain Trust—which soon included Professor Rexford Guy Tugwell and Professor Adolf A. Berle (both of Columbia), with Professor Felix Frankfurter (of the Harvard Law School) lurking in the wings—started as a curious sort of private seminar for Franklin D. Roosevelt. Tugwell called it a "course in socio-economics."[9] It thus served an educational purpose for which professorial intellectuals were particularly well fitted. Another presidential candidate might not have been so responsive. Nevertheless, it may be doubted whether Roosevelt would have had the incentive and patience to meet with the professors in long night sessions if economic conditions had been less ominous.[10]

The learning process, however, was not a one-way affair. One of Moley's admitted reasons for accepting the invitation to teach the future president was that the teacher was also going to learn—learn about politics from the inside or, as Moley put it, "satisfy my desire for wider experience in politics." He was not the last professor who has dealt with politics in the classroom and has sought to increase his knowledge of politics in the back rooms. Max Weber said that "either one lives 'for' politics or one lives 'off' politics."[11] Many an intellectual has lived for politics before living off politics, and then managed to live both for and off politics.

The Brain Trust did not long remain an informal educational institution. Politically, its key members served three main functions—as idea men, as talent scouts, and as speech writers. These functions have continued to be typical of those intellectuals whom we might call "generalists." Roosevelt himself once defined the Brain Trust's role in these words:

> "You study the problems, work out the best answers you can, and bring them to me. Don't mix in politics—it is unpleasant, sometimes a dirty business. Leave that to me."[12]

The tasks of intellectuals may also seem more glamorous from the outside than from the inside. Moley later complained that he was called to work on a speech "just as I'd be called in if I were a plumber and a pipe needed fixing."[13] Tugwell referred to himself as an "errand boy."[14]

The early Brain Trusters had grave misgivings about switching from Professor to Politician. Moley fervently protested that he had no intention of giving up his intellectual freedom, his aspiration to be accepted "on the basis of what I had to say, rather than because I was part of a governmental machine," and his conviction that "honest teaching and writing about public affairs precluded not only White House cup-bearing and administrative paper-shuffling, but party goose-stepping"—before being prevailed on by Roosevelt to give them up. Tugwell had a similar struggle with himself. When he first considered the prospect of an official post in Washington, he told himself that "from professor to the government is a great transformation." He also reflected: "If I am in the administration, I'll have to make endless compromises—a far different position from that of critical observer." But he soon capitulated and went to Washington. Berle held out the longest. He told a colleague that "all of us can be a good deal more useful hoeing our own row than monkeying with obscure under-secretaryships or commissionerships." Incidentally, Berle used to write letters to the president addressed to "Dear Caesar." Roosevelt once replied that he did not mind being called *Caesar* but hated being thought of as *Napoleon*.

The Rooseveltian Brain Trust as such was relatively short-lived. Raymond Moley, the key figure, defected from the New Deal in 1935. He disagreed on a matter of high policy, and I suppose his case might be taken to mean that intellectuals cannot be trusted to be unconditionally loyal to politicians, at least not as much as other politicians. Rex Tugwell, next in line, became the chief whipping boy of the anti-Roosevelt opposition; the attacks on him were easily as disgraceful as any later unleashed by Senator Joseph McCarthy. Not the least reason for Tugwell's vulnerability was his status as a professor and intellectual. By 1936, Tugwell had become such a political liability that Roosevelt did not try to save him. His case may illustrate another function of intellectuals in politics—as scapegoats and sacrificial lambs. A. A. Berle stayed out of Washington until he accepted an appointment as Assistant Secretary of State in 1938 but lasted only about half-a-year in that office. (His real political career came somewhat later, a circumstance that enabled him to last longer and go further than the other two.)

So the political careers of the most famous early Brain Trusters were not too promising. Nevertheless, much more was happening during the first Roosevelt years to intellectuals lower down on the scale. Professor Arthur Schlesinger, Jr., described the New Dealers in terms of the following occupations—"they were mostly lawyers, college professors, economists, or social workers." Lawyers had long had a virtual monopoly of the American government, but college professors in second place—that was something new. Presumably some of the economists as well as the social workers were intellectuals, too. The Brain Trust received most publicity but it was only the tip of the New Deal's intellectual iceberg. The Moleys and Tugwells played for big stakes and eventually lost; many others, less well-known or less exposed, came and stayed. The larger influx had a more stable structural foundation; the New Deal brought into existence a whole series of government agencies and bureaucracies devoted to public works, social security, energy and reclamation, and reforms in many other fields. New agencies and new policies demanded new people and new capabilities. If professors did not get most of the new jobs, their students did.

The New Deal, however, was only the first stage of the Rooseveltian breakthrough for the intellectuals. As the New Deal waned, the influence of its intellectuals declined. But for the Second World War, the United States might have gone through another cyclical movement of intellectuals in and out of government favor. The war completed the process that the New Deal began. With or without the New Deal, the war would have brought in intellectuals *en masse*. The First World War had already shown the way, but it had not gone so far because it had not lasted long enough (for the United States) and had not ended with the assumption of American responsibility for the fate of the world or at least the Western world. American intellectuals supported the Second World War with greater unity and enthusiasm. The new war agencies swallowed up thousands of older and younger intellectuals. Well over a hundred new agencies of the executive branch were formed during the course of the war. Many of the post-war intellectuals were infected with the political virus in these agencies, never to recover. The distinguished politicized intellectuals who came out of the Office of Strategic Services (or O.S.S., predecessor of the C.I.A.) could easily staff one or more good-sized universities.

The war and its aftermath produced a new type of American intellectual in politics. The earlier variety had almost always been brought in to advise on domestic policies, such as financial reform or criminal justice. "The Inquiry" of Wilson's day had been devoted to foreign affairs, but it had not been given an opportunity to do much beyond preparing documents and memoranda for the peace negotiations; and it had not been able to perpetuate itself.

Now a new breed of politicized intellectuals appeared—the foreign-affairs intellectuals. What had been a fairly small field became a minor industry with branches in international politics, international economics, international arms proliferation and control, foreign aid, area specialization, and the like. Exotic fields could attract hundreds of specialists virtually overnight and flourish as long as the government or foundations were willing to subsidize them. If anything more were needed to reinvigorate the war-time and post-war boom in the procreation, care, and feeding of politicized intellectuals, the Truman Doctrine of 1947 and the Marshall Plan of 1948 came just in time. They enabled large numbers of American intellectuals to fan out all over the world at government expense, scattering their largesse and advice far and wide. It was also a time for some to learn the difference between Meursault and Montrachet. All this has nothing to do with whether the war, the doctrine, or the plan were good or necessary; most American intellectuals thought they were. What is more to the point for our purpose is that they provided the political, structural, and material foundation for the new breed of intellectuals. A different kind of United States was needed to produce a different kind of intellectual in politics. The rise of the United States as a pre-eminent world power was a necessary condition for the rise of the intellectual as an eminent political force in the United States.

Nevertheless, the pendulum continued to swing. The upsurge of McCarthyism in 1950 and the defeat of Adlai Stevenson by General Eisenhower for the presidency in 1952 gave intellectuals in general and politicized intellectuals in particular a feeling of rejection if not persecution. Writing in the midst of the Eisenhower period, C. Wright Mills did not consider intellectuals to be part of "the power elite," barely bothered to discuss them at all, and then only to dismiss them contemptuously as "hired men."[15]

Toward the end of Eisenhower's administration, a survey of opinion of social science professors showed that most of them were convinced that the professoriat was not "much appreciated" by businessmen and congressmen.[16] In 1959, Professor Seymour Martin Lipset was impressed by the self-pity and the self-image of low status among intellectuals, neither of which he believed was justified by the evidence. Other indications supported a more optimistic view. By 1958, of the fourteen U.S. senators who had taught in some college or university, nine might be classified as professors, a higher percentage than ever before. One writer claimed that the Eisenhower administration employed more professors than the New Deal had ever done. In 1959, one of the most astute observers, Professor David Riesman, held that the status of intellectuals was "good and getting better." And soon after the end of the Eisenhower years, the one authority on the American Establishment revealed that "the presidents and senior professors of the great Eastern universities frequently constitute themselves as *ad hoc* Establishment committees." Since he also confessed that the only thing we can apparently know about the Establishment is that it exists, it was not altogether clear just what importance should be attributed to these self-constituted committees. Still, even to be mentioned in such high and mighty company suggested that the status of some university presidents and senior professors had risen spectacularly despite all the pessimism and discontent of the Eisenhower period.[17]

An article of particular interest, owing to the future career of its author, appeared in 1959. It was called "The Policymaker and the Intellectual" and was written by Henry A. Kissinger, at the time of publication a Lecturer in Government at Harvard and already knowledgeable from personal experience about the vicissitudes of intellectuals in politics.[18]

Kissinger thought that a case could be made even then that "in some respects the intellectual has never been more in demand" by policymakers. As much autobiographical as anything else, most of the article was a cry of pain at the way policymakers mishandled and misunderstood intellectuals. Kissinger's catalogue of woes was revelatory—

> [T]he intellectual is rarely found at the level where decisions are made. . . . It is the executive who determines in the first place whether he needs advice . . . : he [the intellectual] is asked to solve problems, not to contribute to the definition of goals . . . in short, all too often what the policymaker wants from the intellectual is not ideas but endorsement.

The great problem for the intellectual, according to Kissinger, was to decide whether to participate in the political process as an intellectual or as an administrator. If he chose the role of intellectual, it was essential for him

> to retain the freedom to deal with the policymaker from a position of independence, and to reserve the right to assess the policymaker's demands in terms of his own standards."

Kissinger in 1959 had already had a good deal of experience dealing with policymakers from a position of independence which, in practice, meant staying out of the administration and dispensing advice to those in both parties who asked for it. The Kissinger of 1959 still thought like an intellectual in politics; it took ten more years and the temptation of office to make him more like an intellectual politician. As one reads the 1959 article, one is not sure that the earlier Kissinger would have approved of the later Kissinger.

In any case, the cyclical theory as interpreted by Professor Arthur Schlesinger put the 1950s on the downward swing. It may well be, however, that the cyclical theory operated, but on a higher and higher plane. Thus the Eisenhower period was a letdown from the heady Roosevelt and Truman years but still represented an advance over pre-Roosevelt times. Another possibility is that intellectuals in politics do not count other intellectuals who have the wrong kind of politics.

Professor David Riesman proved to be right. It did not take long for the political status of intellectuals to get better, indeed, better than ever. When John F. Kennedy was elected president in 1960, he was not the intellectuals' first choice. Most of them preferred Adlai Stevenson and distrusted Kennedy. By winning over two of Stevenson's most important intellectual backers (Arthur Schlesinger and John Kenneth Galbraith), Kennedy turned the intellectual tide in his favor. They preferred to pick a winner, an urge not conspicuously characteristic of previous generations of liberal intellectuals. In fact, the Republican presidential candidate, Richard M. Nixon, tried to stigmatize the Democrats as "the party of Galbraith and Schlesinger and Bowles"—not a bad score for the intellectuals, if only it had been more accurate. This line of attack showed that intellectuals were still functioning as political whipping boys. In Schlesinger's view, Kennedy himself was a latter-day intellectual politician "as politicians go"—possibly fainter praise than was intended. Schlesinger also explained why the intellectuals had changed their attitude toward Kennedy from cold to hot—"their gradual recognition of his desire to bring the world of power and the world of ideas together in alliance."[19] A better diagnosis of the passion for politics by Kennedy's intellectuals would be hard to find; it suggests that the older faith in the power *of* ideas had given way to the newer preference for power *and* ideas. Kennedy's closest aide, Theodore C. Sorensen, claimed that Kennedy had appointed to important posts a higher proportion of academicians (including sixteen Rhodes scholars) than any other president in history and even more than any European government had ever done. Sorensen also boasted that Kennedy's appointees had written more books than the president—a fast reader at twelve hundred words a minute—could read in a four-year term.[20] One dreads to think how long it would have taken a president like Eisenhower to read the same number of books.

The White House was not the only source of political advancement for intellectuals in the transition from the 1950s to the 1960s. A former Rhodes Scholar, Representative John Brademas of Indiana, has related how he was told to play down his Harvard-Oxford background when he first ran for office in 1954. Four years later, his local backers were urging citizens to "vote for Brademas because he has a fine education."[21] By the mid-1960s, almost a seventh of the members of the U.S. Senate were former professors.[22] It may be said without exaggeration that professors, ex-professors, and would-be professors were all over Washington—in the White House, in the bureaucracy, in Congress and congressional staffs, in almost all levels of government.

Then the cyclical theory began to work again. President Lyndon B. Johnson had inherited many of Kennedy's intellectuals, but they could never be as happy with Johnson as they had been with Kennedy, if only for stylistic reasons. It is hard to imagine Johnson concluding an informal talk with representatives of national organizations by reading to them Blanche of Castile's speech from *King John*, beginning with the words: *"The sun's o'ercast with blood; fair day, adieu! . . ."*[23]

Johnson's intellectuals were enormously productive during his first two years of domestic reforms; the Viet Nam war destroyed him politically and isolated them morally. One historian of the period asserts that the defection of "liberals and intellectuals"—it is sometimes hard to tell them apart in the literature—finished off Johnson as a party leader and forced him to abdicate.[24] For once, a president needed intellectuals more than they needed him.

Lyndon Johnson lost the intellectuals; Richard Nixon never had them. Nixon would have had trouble with intellectuals even if he had not been Nixon. He was a Republican, and intellectuals have been allergic to Republicans at least since the New Deal. Nixon even had trouble giving away jobs to well-known intellectuals. Those few who took them felt as isolated and embattled as if they had decided to sacrifice themselves in a lost but somehow necessary cause. Indeed, the best of Nixon's intellectuals accepted his call to duty because he was the president and had a right to summon them to serve the country, not because they were particularly fond of him. Professor Kissinger was notoriously dubious about Nixon's qualifications before proximity in the White House made him change his mind. After Nixon's disgrace, the intellectuals who had enjoyed his favor in better times felt that be had betrayed them—not that they had betrayed themselves. What disturbed them was Watergate, not Viet Nam. In a sense, intellectuals never had so little and yet so much power as under Nixon—so little because most of them did not want it from him and so much because they could now take it or leave it.

It is too soon to say much about President Carter's intellectuals, except that they are all over Washington again. By this time, intellectuals seem to have pre-empted some key governmental positions—assistant for national security affairs, science advisor, and chairman of the Council of Economic Advisors, among others. Academic economists have done especially well in the Carter administration. If we may trust that high authority, Professor Galbraith, a hard man to please, President Carter has appointed no fewer than four "professional economists of full academic qualifications" as secretary of the treasury, secretary of commerce, secretary of labor, and chairman of the Council of Economic Advisers.[25] It may be surmised, however, that presidents have been turning to professional economists not merely for their academic qualifications but because they enable them to avoid appointing a businessman who might annoy labor or a labor official who might annoy business. The new science adviser, Professor Frank Press, recently declared, "Jimmy Carter doesn't have the fear of academics and intellectuals" that several previous presidents are said to have had.[26] Presumably we will now find out whether intellectuals are better off when they are not feared.

By now, the sub-species which Dr. Ralf Dahrendorf, director of the London School of Economics, recently called "the important group of those who 'straddle' academia and decision making" has been recognized internationally. The latest and most conspicuous straddler is Professor Zbigniew Brzezinski, Dr. Kissinger's successor in the White House. The typical straddler is most frequently found in research institutes such as the Brookings Institution of Washington, D.C., whose members must sometimes be confused about whether they are coming from or going into the government. Straddlers have become so indispensable in the modern state that we may soon have, according to Dr. Dahrendorf, a Social Science Research Council institute for policy research and a more modest "LSE Brookings" in Britain as well as a "European Brookings" and a "Third World Brookings."[27] Professor Brzezinski prepared for his present position by straddling in not one but two such organizations— his own Research Institute on International Change (originally Communist Affairs) at Columbia University and his brainchild, the "Trilateral Commission," in which he first attracted the attention of Governor Jimmy Carter and vice versa. Straddling has now been institutionalized to such an extent that it must be considered the highest form of life among intellectuals in politics.

Some deep structural changes must have taken place in American society to account for the change from the nineteenth century, when intellectuals were alienated from American politics and politicians from intellectuals, to the latter half of the twentieth century, when a kind of symbiosis has taken place between intellectuals and politics. These changes are not uniquely American but they have probably gone further in the United States than anywhere else.

One of the deepest aspects of the change is the shift in perspective from the past to the present. The native habitat of scholars used to be the past; real scholars did not go beyond 1789 or, in extreme cases, the Renaissance or even the Middle Ages. A few such purists remain but they are a vanishing breed. The cult of the present has almost replaced the cult of the past. When intellectuals go into politics they go into the world of the present, the pragmatic, the manageable. As a result, fields such as economics, political science, and sociology, which are themselves concerned almost wholly with the present or recent past, make the most fertile breeding grounds for intellectuals in politics. Such intellectuals do not have to jump from the past to the present; they jump from the study of the present to the practice of the present—and then jump back to the study of their own practice. The university has become a preparatory school for government, and government has become the ultimate in post-professorial education. Professor Moynihan is an extreme case in point. He spent thirteen of the twenty years between 1950 and 1970 in government. Reflecting on this background, he has confided that "as a teacher I find these experiences are the largest store of knowledge on which I have to draw. . . ."[28] Teachers have long taught politics; some now teach their own experiences in politics. It becomes virtually impossible to draw a line between intellectual work and political work.

The fields I have mentioned are not the only ones that have made this temporal leap. They at least were always located mainly in the present. But what shall we say of the transformation that has taken place in anthropology? When I went to school it was still thought to be the study of primitive societies. Not long ago, however, I sat next to a young woman studying at a large American university. I politely inquired what she was doing. "Anthropology," she said. "And what kind of anthropology?" I asked. She replied she was doing a dissertation on one of the "new towns" that have sprung up in the United States—so new that it is still not quite finished. The anthropologists, having exhausted or having been expelled from the society of primitives, have invaded the society of the present, thus creating an awkward situation for the sociologists, who presumably should have taken revenge by moving from the present to the past. We are obviously in the presence of an intellectual transmutation that goes far beyond politics but is particularly conducive to participation in politics.

Sociologists know when they have a good thing and have no intention of giving up their stranglehold on the present. An American sociological journal recently asked a group of sociologists what they expected from the Carter administration. Some replies were euphoric. Congress, one experienced practitioner jubilated, "is increasingly dependent on the products of social science research." Some Congressional committee reports are stuffed with it. The executive branch increasingly finds that it can hardly get along without sociological research.

> In learning to live with an all-volunteer army, for example, the army is calling on social scientists to study how to deal with race and sex. The Army Corps of Engineers is calling on social scientists to help it understand the impact of its projects on communities. The State Department needs sociological research not only for briefing foreign affairs officers, but also in administering Agency International Development programs. . . .

Another sociologist lamented that the government was driving out "the amateur in the social science business" by supporting large-scale research institutions that

> are geared to the major consumer—the government—. . . understand the cost guidelines . . . know how to do business in Washington.

He was, however, somewhat cynical about the outcome—"the bulk of academics will be used as window-dressing for the proposals that are written." Another professor thought that "the long latent lust for being close to power—or at least the trappings of power," which gripped academics and intellectuals during the Kennedy-Johnson years, and went underground with Nixon and Ford, was staging a comeback with Carter. He looked forward to the emergence of a new type of "born-again" social scientist, committed to political action with "open political values." A fourth foresaw the evanescence of "a good many of the former reservations about government funds and consultancies, expressed in academia with such fervor in the late 1960s and 1970s." Well-known scholars were worrying that the government would not lavish enough of its largesse on the academic community. "Gone, apparently, are all the qualms." Here, apparently, is a new generation of intellectuals awaiting its turn at the political trough.[29]

Thus far I have emphasized the intellectual shift from the past to the present. Intellectuals who go into politics, however, make an even greater leap in time. After all, intellectuals almost always work for politicians—and politicians live *in* the present *for* the future. I am always astonished at the kind of questions that government officials and politicians ask. What they want are prophets, not historians. Politicians are always worried about policy—what to do to meet this-or-that problem or eventuality. They want to know what is going to happen if they take this action or adopt that strategy. Policy is the politician's game, and policy is future-oriented. Intellectuals cross an invisible line into politics whenever they get into policy. Yet it is at that point that they really begin to interest politicians, who may listen patiently to the background of a problem but wish desperately to get to the foreground.

As a result, intellectual trends and fashions have been following political needs and conditions. We now have, for example, an academic field known as "public policy" or "policy studies." In one branch of this field, a school of thought interprets the making of foreign policy largely in terms of "bargaining" between bureaucrats in the government hierarchy. Whatever we may think of this "Bureaucratic-Politics model," as it is called, it is clearly an intellectual child of the times. It reflects the preoccupation of intellectuals with policy, in part because intellectuals are increasingly called on to pronounce on policy, in part as a result of their increased experience with it.

Or consider the ups-and-downs of the field known as "Area Studies." It shot up in the 1950s when the United States was drawn in—or drew itself in—to virtually every area in the world often without preparation, personnel, or policy. For about a decade, no self-respecting university could get along without "area specialists"—Southeast Asia, East Africa, West Africa, Middle East, Far East, Latin America, etc., or any portion thereof. By the end of the 1960s, area studies went into decline; many of its former practitioners have turned to more promising fields. One reason for the popularity of area studies had been the availability of funds from the government or wealthy foundations; as soon as these lost interest, the programs shriveled. Another reason for their decline was the growing reluctance of many areas, especially in Africa, to let Americans, particularly anthropologists, roam freely in villages, asking all sorts of suspicious or outlandish questions—from the point of view of the natives. The rise and decline of Area Studies was at least as much politically as intellectually motivated.

The same intellectual cycle of rise and decline has characterized Russian studies, Chinese studies, Latin American studies, and guerrilla-warfare studies—to name but a few. Government policy has not always been the main reason for such fluctuations. In the case of Russian studies, the New Left wave at the end of the 1960s was partially responsible for their decline by spreading the word that the Soviet Union had become conservative, unfashionable, boring. These academic trends behave like the stock market; their intellectual stocks go up and down depending on the public's interest and investment in them.

Other structural changes in society have also changed the role of intellectuals in government. In the past half century or so, three great proliferations have taken place, so familiar that I need only mention them—the proliferation of government, of the so-called knowledge industries, and of colleges and universities. Each of these proliferations produced a demand for more and more trained personnel, at least some of whom may be classified as intellectuals. By now the American government has become so pervasive that even the Carter administration, which came in committed to cutting it back, seems to be giving up in despair. The three proliferations add up to a new or at least a very different social order, for which no one has yet been able to come up with a good name. The most popular name—"the Post-Industrial society"—tells us what it followed, not what it is. A crisis in the social order brought American intellectuals into politics; a change in the social order has kept them there in larger and larger numbers.

How important are intellectuals in American politics?

The short answer is, I think, that they are generally as important as politicians want them to be. Intellectuals may have influence but they almost never have power. President Truman is supposed to have said: "I think intellectuals in government are great as long as there's an old pro to tell them what to do." Intellectuals may find this Trumanesque candor offensive or demeaning, but it comes out of long, hard experience and cannot be easily rejected. Politics demands 60–40 decisions, even 55–45, and in extreme cases 51–49. Politicians who cannot make such decisions do not get to or stay at the top. For intellectuals, such decisions may be agonizing, often impossible. If the odds are so close, it is intellectually better to reserve judgment, wait for more evidence, report results without prejudice. Thus it has become the accepted function of intellectuals in government to present the available options as fairly and fully as possible, but to let the "old pro" decide on which option to adopt. The way options are presented may influence the decision. Still, presenting is not the same thing as deciding, and responsibility goes to the political decision-maker, not the intellectual option-merchant.

On the other hand, intellectuals are not likely to do much good until they lose their awe for the "old pro."

The experience of Professor Schlesinger in the case of the ill-fated Bay of Pigs expedition in 1960 should be a warning to all intellectuals new to government. Arthur Schlesinger was officially designated a Special Assistant to President Kennedy without specific duties; he thought of himself as a "historian-participant," itself a new intellectual-political role. As a newcomer to the government, he was given the assignment of writing a White Paper to justify the attempt to overthrow Castro. It was a pretty good paper, but it had little relation to the political realities behind the enterprise: Schlesinger himself thought that the project was ill-conceived and privately expressed his opposition to President Kennedy. In the critical discussions at which the heads of the CIA, the Joint Chiefs of Staff, and Departments of State and Defense were present, Schlesinger said little. Later he explained why:

> It is one thing for a Special Assistant to talk frankly in private to a President at his request and another for a college professor, fresh to government, to interpose his unassisted judgment in open meeting against that of such august figures as the Secretaries of State and Defense and the Joint Chiefs of Staff, each speaking with the full weight of his institution behind him.

The fiasco changed all that. "The Bay of Pigs gave us license for the impolite inquiry and the rude comment," Schlesinger recalled, no doubt with grim satisfaction.[30] That was probably the last time he was overawed by anyone.

One of the things an "old pro" tells intellectuals to do is to write speeches for him. Professor Raymond Moley, the original Brain Truster, will probably be remembered most for inserting three words, "the Forgotten Man," in a campaign speech for Franklin D. Roosevelt in April 1932. The phrase was not original with him; it had first been used in a different context by the sociologist William Graham Sumner; presumably, however, it took an intellectual to remember the words in the first place. But would they have reverberated in the same way if Moley, the intellectual, not Roosevelt the politician, had spoken them in his own name?

Then there is the Professor Galbraith who wrote a draft for the inaugural address of President Kennedy in January 1961. Kennedy seems to have used little more than one sentence. Galbraith later commented ruefully on the fate of his draft:

> A ghost-writer is like an unloved dog in a poor family. He must be content with scraps.[31]

More than one intellectual has felt like an unloved dog in a politician's extended family. Still, intellectuals must get a great deal of satisfaction from ghost-writing—they do so much of it. It may well be the ultimate expression of the intellectual's role in politics—words, not actions; ideas without responsibility.

Intellectuals as idea men and as talent scouts—their two other favorite occupations—obey the same rules of the game.

Intellectuals propose; politicians dispose. To be successful, the intellectual must often propose just what the politician wants him to propose. "I've been an adviser of the President," Professor Paul A. Samuelson, the eminent economist, recently confessed:

> You sometimes have the impression that you call the shots, but as you think about it you realise that you are selected because your brand of moonshine, of snake oil, sits well on the scalp or in the stomach of the President.[32]

To say that intellectuals have become important is largely to say that they have become important to politicians. To gain real power, the intellectual must become a politician. The only independent source of power in the American system comes from having a constituency, and most intellectuals have a constituency of one—themselves. Thus Senator Moynihan, after having suffered repeated frustrations in appointive offices, sought and won an elective office. His case suggests how really powerless—if real power is understood to be the power of decision—an appointed intellectual can be and what he can do about it. One sociologist was so elated by Dr. Moynihan's election to the Senate that he celebrated it as the beginning of "a new era of seeking and winning office" by social scientists. In this latest of new eras for the intellectual in politics, "if social scientists want to, they may begin appointing the lawyers—a long overdue switch in roles."[33] One might almost imagine that the real struggle for power was between intellectuals and lawyers.

Professor-Ambassador-Senator Moynihan is one of our two most celebrated intellectuals in politics. His career merits a little closer examination because he illustrates a number of different types of the species. For years he went in and out of university and government; in this phase, he was what may be called an "in-and-outer," which is what most intellectuals in government are. In this capacity, he set something of a record by impartially serving presidents as different as Kennedy, Johnson, and Nixon in succession. Professional politicians must envy his survival rate; no politician has ever given a better exhibition of how to survive the downfall of at least two presidential patrons and come out on top on his own. As senator, Pat Moynihan is presumably in politics to stay, though one cannot be sure of anything in his case—he recently referred to himself, perhaps jokingly, as a "displaced professor." In effect, he illustrates two paths of the intellectual—from in-and-outer to stay-in, and from the appointive to the elective.

The question arises whether Senator Moynihan is still an intellectual in politics. This question was implicitly raised by Mr. James Reston, who holds the Chair of Political Commentary endowed by the *New York Times*. Mr. Reston recently remarked that Dr. Moynihan had markedly changed since he was elected to the United States Senate. Before putting on his senatorial toga (according to Reston) Moynihan "saw the world as a whole and was almost recklessly honest in defining America's widest possible interests." Now, as senator from New York, Moynihan has been advocating a limitation on foreign imports on behalf of the hard-pressed garment industry in New York. As a result, Reston concluded sorrowfully, Moynihan is fighting for the interests of his particular rag-trade constituents and "defending their local, personal and political concerns," as he apparently would not have done in the old days when he could still afford to see the world as a whole and be almost recklessly honest.[34] Now (if we believe Mr. Reston) Senator Moynihan has to see the world through the eyes of his constituents and be as honest as their interests will permit. Thus Moynihan illustrates the distinction between an intellectual in politics and an intellectual politician.

Senator Moynihan figured in another recent incident that tells much about the difference between a pure-and-simple intellectual, an appointed intellectual, and an elected intellectual. The story is worth relating in some detail because it concerns two intellectuals in politics in the same field but cast in different roles.

Dr. Moynihan went to work for President Nixon in 1969 as assistant for urban affairs. His job entailed responsibility for drawing up a plan for the reform of the welfare system. It took almost seven months for the Nixon administration to present Congress with a project, known as the "Family Assistance Plan," which provided for a guaranteed annual income. The plan was shot down in the United States Senate, and Dr. Moynihan published a book in 1973 (*The Politics of a Guaranteed Income*) about the politics that had killed it. In that same year, Professor Henry J. Aaron put out a staff paper entitled *Why Is Welfare So Hard to Reform?* for the Brookings Institution. Moynihan's book might have had the same title.

During the 1976 presidential campaign, Dr. Moynihan as a member of the Democratic platform committee was instrumental in writing into the platform a commitment for an "income maintenance system," another form of his old guaranteed-annual-income plan. The newly elected Senator Moynihan also succeeded in getting a seat on the important Senate Finance Committee and in heading its Subcommittee on Public Assistance to consider the promised Carter reform of the welfare system. Meanwhile, Professor Aaron was appointed assistant secretary of the Department of Health, Education, and Welfare (HEW) in charge of welfare. Thus the two authors of 1973 found themselves in different political positions in 1977.

On 25 April of this year, Senator Moynihan learned that the administration bill would not be ready by 1 May as he had expected and that only a statement of principles would be forthcoming by that date. The delay was sorely disappointing. It meant that his subcommittee would not be able to hold early hearings on the bill as he had planned. The urgency of such hearings was not apparent inasmuch as the Majority Leader, Senator Robert Byrd, had already put off welfare reform in favor of energy legislation for at least that session of Congress. In any case, Senator Moynihan blew up at the news of the administration's delay. In his wrath, he told reporters that "you can draft that bill in the morning"—the sort of bill which had taken him almost seven months to draft for President Nixon without getting Congress to approve it and which the Carter administration was expected to draft in only four months.

The chief culprit, according to Senator Moynihan, was Assistant Secretary of HEW Aaron. Referring to Professor Aaron's staff paper of 1973, Senator Moynihan exploded, "This is *HEW* at it again. They produce wonderful books telling you why you can't do things." Senator Moynihan seemed to have forgotten that Professor Moynihan had also produced a wonderful book in 1973 telling why he couldn't do the same things.

After Senator Moynihan's public denunciation, Assistant Secretary Aaron was clearly in trouble. So Assistant Secretary for Public Affairs Eileen Shanahan came to Assistant Secretary Aaron's assistance by announcing that the staff paper of 1973 no longer reflected the latter's views.

This cautionary tale shows how dangerous it is for intellectuals to write books before becoming government officials. But if they did not write books, how would they become intellectuals? There is no easy way out of this dilemma. We have here two former professors who, as intellectuals, were not so very far apart. As senator and assistant secretary, however, they moved into positions of antagonism. The senator forgot how embarrassing the written word had more than once been for him. The assistant secretary decided—or had it decided for him—that it was better to repudiate his book than endanger his job.

Three months later, the Carter administration finally produced its new welfare program. Senator Moynihan immediately called it "magnificent, superbly crafted," without waiting for any hearings on the proposed bill by his subcommittee.[35]

Senators, then, have political "muscle" and "clout." Assistant secretaries do not. Senator Moynihan had himself been an assistant secretary not so long ago. It is interesting to speculate what would have happened if the roles had been reversed—if Senator Aaron had denounced Assistant Secretary Moynihan. Probably they would have acted out their respective roles in much the same way; the rules of the game put an assistant secretary at a disadvantage in confrontation with a senator, especially the head of just the subcommittee that must pass on the assistant secretary's handiwork.

That less polymorphous but even more celebrated intellectual in politics, Henry A. Kissinger, suggests another side of the phenomenon. The species is apt to suffer from a rare form of psychological conflict. As Secretary of State, Dr. Kissinger lived with an acute case of this subtle affliction. In an interview with James Reston, Dr. Kissinger said that he thought of himself as a historian more than as a statesman. For our present purposes, we may interpret this to mean that he thought of himself as an intellectual more than as a politician. As a historian, Secretary Kissinger explained, one had to be a pessimist or, to use his exact words, "one has to live with a sense of the inevitability of tragedy. . . ." But as a statesman, he said, one had to be optimistic or, again in his own words, "one has to act on the assumption that problems must be solved. . . ."[36] Who was the real Kissinger, the pessimistic historian-intellectual or the optimistic statesman-politician? One suspects that the real Kissinger thought of himself as an intellectual pessimist but felt that he had to pretend to be a statesmanlike optimist. In any case, Kissinger could not lose. If he succeeded, the statesman-politician was right; if he failed, the historian-intellectual was right.

Nor was this the only evidence of an unresolved conflict in Kissinger's intellectual makeup. On the one hand, he was forever calling for "concepts" in the formation of foreign policy. On the other hand, he insistently maintained that "nuances" were what really counted. He never explained how concepts can be crucial if nuances are all-important.

It may be objected that Dr Kissinger was an exception to the rule that appointed officials lack real power of decision. If he was an exception, however, no great generalities can be drawn from him. It is not yet possible to be sure just how exceptional he was throughout the eight years that he served under Presidents Nixon and Ford. We are most likely going to find out that he did what Nixon wanted him to do, and he did not do what Nixon did not want him to do, until the Watergate crisis of 1973. He became more and more independent of the presidency as the president came closer and closer to self-destruction. Kissinger was the product and beneficiary of an afflicted system. Yet he somehow contrived to be in and out of it at the same time. The sicker the system became, the more indispensable he appeared to be. He was its symptom far more than its cure.

In any case, it will take some time to disentangle Kissinger's publicity from his power. Favored writers paid him back to the point of inanity. For example, one virulently anti-Israel book on the Arab-Israeli conflict (based in large part on some twenty-five interviews with Kissinger and two of his closest aides as well as on secret documents secretly leaked) told readers that "Kissinger was in real measure running the world" during the Yom Kippur war in October 1973.[37] The *whole* world? Brezhnev's Russia? Mao's China? Castro's Cuba? Even Indira's India? Still, one can only regard with awe an intellectual who was voted "the greatest person in the world today" by the Miss Universe contestants in 1974.[38]

I am inclined to think that Kissinger's power over the American media was greater than his power over anything else. I doubt whether future historians will agree with a court biography which was written with his help and which flattered him in these terms: "He is a professor who had been given the unique opportunity to put his theories into practice and to shape history."[39] The pre-Nixonian Kissinger had anti-*détente* theories but did not put them into practice; the Nixonian Kissinger improvised one theory of *détente* after another to suit his practice; the post-Nixonian Kissinger warned in effect that *détente* in theory was Soviet expansionism in practice, as demonstrated by the Soviet-Cuban intervention in Angola. How much history was actually shaped by Kissinger has become more and more dubious as less and less of his handiwork remains. It looks as if the further we get away from Kissinger's accomplishments, the more insubstantial and ephemeral they appear to be. The more illusions a statesman inspires about himself, the more disillusionment he invites from future historians. The latter may even have trouble figuring out what all the excitement was about or what Kissinger did to earn it. As a shaper of history, Kissinger was most successful in shaping his own histrionics, not history.

Yet Kissinger's self-aggrandizement paid off in a little noted way. In the transition from the Nixon to the Ford presidency, Kissinger emerged as the critical element of continuity and stability. That President Ford should have had to announce without delay that he was keeping Kissinger in office testified to the independent role that Kissinger had achieved. Unfortunately, this feat was predicated on the degeneration and disintegration of the political régime of which he had been an integral part and to which he had lent some respectability. How he managed to save his political skin was a tribute to the political, not the intellectual, side of his personality. Whatever the reason or the means, he was thereby able to help the country though a dangerous moment. It may well come to be regarded as the time when he did the least and gave the most.

What does the future hold for intellectuals in politics? The high point for the species was probably reached during the Kennedy years and for and individual by Henry Kissinger during the Nixon years. The intellectual component in the Carter administration is still large enough to indicate that there has been no great change for the worse. The ubiquity and complexity of the modern state assure a continuing need for intellectuals— fully licensed, semi-, quasi- and pseudo-.

But American intellectuals themselves have changed. When they first invaded the government in large numbers, they were filled with self-confidence. The economists forged into the lead, setting an example of worldly success and mathematical precision. Much that happened in the other social "sciences" was imitative of or at least inspired by them. By 1973, the economists again led the way—in retreat. That year the new president of the American Economic Association, Professor Walter Heller, former chairman of the Council of Economic Advisers, spoke for the profession when he said:

> Economists are distinctly in a period of re-examination. The energy crisis caught us with our parameters down. The food crisis caught us too. This was a year of infamy in inflation forecasting. There are many things we really don't know.

Such uncertainty still characterizes the intellectual mood, and not only of economists. One of our best sociological minds, Professor Daniel Bell, has recently put into words what is common knowledge—"the social-science knowledge to design a proper health system, or a housing environment, or a good educational curriculum, is inadequate."[40] If intellectuals cannot cope with these tasks, they are in much greater trouble than at any time since the great breakthrough almost half-a-century ago. The quantity of intellectuals in politics may not change much, but the quality of their work is being downgraded by the intellectuals themselves.

If the intellectuals do not watch out, they may bear out the low opinion of experts expressed exactly one hundred years ago by Lord Salisbury, who knew something of politics:

> No lesson seems to be so deeply inculcated by the experience of life as that you should never trust in experts. If you believe the doctors nothing is wholesome; if you believe the theologians nothing is innocent; if you believe the soldiers nothing is safe.

He might have gone on to say: if you believe the intellectuals, nothing is right.

The difficulty is that there is no good substitute for "experts" and "intellectuals." If they are not to be trusted, who should be? They may not be trusted as much as before, but society and government are likely to be just as dependent on them in the foreseeable future. The reason is that the intellectuals are but the most articulate, self-conscious repositories of the accumulated learning and experience of a society. If the intellectuals are in trouble, they are not the only ones; the society is in trouble.

NOTES

1. Richard Hofstadter, *Anti-Intellectualism in American Life* (New York: Knopf, 1963), 187.

2. Hofstadter, *Anti-Intellectualism . . .*, 39. Hofstadter says that the term *intellectual* first came into use in France and was "soon exported—at the time of the Dreyfus case" (38). This seems hardly likely in view of the fact that the *Oxford English Dictionary* has an English usage of the term as far back as 1652, and three perfectly recognizable uses in the nineteenth century, one by Byron in 1813.

3. *The Letters of William James*, Vol. II, ed. Henry James (Boston: Atlantic Monthly Press,1920), 100–101.

4. Arthur S. Link, *Wilson: The Road to the White House* (Princeton: Princeton University Press, 1947), 149–50, 158.

5. Hofstadter, *Anti-Intellectualism . . .*, 211.

6. Senator Lawrence Sherman, 65th Congress, 2nd sess., *Congressional Record*, (3 September, 1918) 9877.

7. Samuel I. Rosenman, *Working with Roosevelt* (New York: Harper, 1952), 57.

8. Raymond Moley, *After Seven Years* (New York: Harper & Brothers, 1939), 5–6.

9. Rexford G. Tugwell, *The Democratic Roosevelt* (Garden City, NY: Doubleday, 1957), 218.

10. These meetings are vividly described by Moley, 20–21, and Rosenman, 63–64.

11. "Politics as a Vocation" (1918) in *From Max Weber: Essays in Sociology*, trans., ed., and with an introduction, by H. H. Gerth and C. Wright Mills (New York: Oxford University Press, 1947), 84.

12. These words were said by Roosevelt to Berle but intended for the entire group. See Adolf A. Berle, *New Republic*, 7 March 1964, in *Navigating the Rapids*,

1918–1971: From the Papers of Adolf A. Berle, ed. Beatrice Bishop Berle and Travis Beal Jacobs (New York: Harcourt Brace Jovanovich, 1973), 114.

13. Arthur M. Schlesinger, Jr., *The Coming of the New Deal* (Boston: Houghton Mifflin, 1957), 549.

14. Bernard Sternsher, *Rexford Guy Tugwell and the New Deal* (New Brunswick, NJ: Rutgers University Press, 1964), 308.

15. C. Wright Mills, *The Power Elite* (New York: Oxford University Press, 1956), 351.

16. Paul F. Lazarsfeld and Wagner Thielens, Jr., *The Academic Mind* (Glencoe, IL: Free Press, 1958), 12.

17. *Daedalus* (Summer 1959): 469. *New York Times*, 9 November, 1958. John Fischer, *Harper's* (March 1958): 18. *Daedalus* (Summer 1959): 492. Richard H. Rovere, *The American Establishment and Other Reports, Opinions and Speculations* (New York: Harcourt, Brace & World, 1962), 8–9.

18. *The Reporter* (5 March 1959): 30–35.

19. Arthur M. Schlesinger, Jr., *A Thousand Days: John F. Kennedy in the White House* (Boston: Houghton Mifflin, 1965), 109.

20. Theodore C. Sorensen, *Kennedy* (New York: Harper & Row, 1965), 246.

21. *The Intellectual in Politics*, ed. H. Malcolm Macdonald (Austin: Humanities Research Center, University of Texas, 1966), 103–104.

22. Arthur M. Schlesinger, Jr., *The Crisis of Confidence: Ideas, Power, and Violence in America* (Boston: Houghton Mifflin, 1969), 79.

23. Schlesinger, *A Thousand Days*, 725.

24. William L. O'Neill, *Coming Apart: An Informal History of American in the 1960s* (Chicago: Quadrangle Books, 1970), 146.

25. *Esquire* (May 1977): 70.

26. *New York Times*, 2 May 1977.

27. *The Times* (letter), 4 August 1977.

28. Daniel P. Moynihan, *The Politics of a Guaranteed Income: The Nixon Administration and the Family Assistance Plan* (New York: Vintage Books, 1973), 13.

29. Professors Jessie Bernard, George Sternlieb, Brady Tyson, and William Glade, *Society*, May–June 1977, 8–21.

30. Arthur Schlesinger, *A Thousand Days*, 249–55, 297.

31. John Kenneth Galbraith, *Ambassador's Journal: A Personal Account of the Kennedy Years* (London: Hamilton, 1969), 16.

32. Interview in *Challenge* (March–April 1977): 31.

33. Irving Louis Horowitz, *Society* (May–June 1977): 22.

34. *New York Times*, 16 April 1977.

35. This story can be followed in the *Washington Post*, 26 and 27 April 1977, 8 August 1977, and the *New York Times*, 26 April 1977.

36. *New York Times*, 13 October 1974.

37. Edward R. F. Sheehan, *The Arabs, Israelis, and Kissinger: A Secret History of American Diplomacy in the Middle East* (New York: Readers Digest Press, 1976), 38.

38. Leslie H. Gelb, *New York Times Magazine* (31 October 1976): 79.

39. Marvin Kalb and Bernard Kalb, *Kissinger* (Boston: Little Brown, 1974), 544.

40. "The Future World Disorder: The Structural Context of Crisis" in *Foreign Policy* (Summer 1977): 120.

The Intellectual as Celebrity

Lewis Coser*

A new intellectual type has risen on the American scene, the *celebrity in-tellectual*. He addresses a semi-educated mass public that makes little claim to expert knowledge or refined taste, and that adheres to no commonly shared cultural standards. The celebrity intellectuals, figures like Erich Segal, Charles Reich, and Marshall McLuhan, come to the fore under identifiable conditions and exhibit a distinct set of relations with an admiring public.

Societies like our own are characterized by a pronounced segmentation of social and intellectual circles.[1] Florian Znaniecki has developed the notion that thinkers are likely to speak not to the total society but to a selected public. Specific social circles, he argued, bestow recognition, provide material or psychic income, and help shape the self-image of the thinker as he internalizes their normative expectations. Men of knowledge are supposed to respond to or anticipate certain demands of their circles and these in turn grant certain rights and immunities. Men of ideas, he argued further, define data and problems in terms of actual or anticipated audiences. Thus thinkers may be classified in terms of their public and of the performances expected of them within these contexts. Such circles, in short, provide the setting for informal social control.[2]

An academic intellectual seeks his audience among fellow academics, and his contributions are shaped through exchanges with academic colleagues.[3] He is relatively unconcerned with the evaluation of, say unattached and nonacademic intellectuals; he does not grant them the claim to

*This article first appeared in *Dissent* 20, no. 1 (1973): 46–56. Reprinted with permission.

make judgments about his intellectual work. At the most, such outside appraisals are given only peripheral attention. Even the message conveyed by the "unattached intellectuals" described by Karl Mannheim,[4] who are less tied to specific circles than the types described by Znaniecki and whose audience is not as rigorously defined or confined, is mediated by a closer group of peers and expert judges of status. It is these peers and judges whose opinions the "unattached intellectuals" esteem and to whom they grant near-exclusive claims for critical evaluation of their work.

By contrast, the celebrity intellectual does not address a delimited circle of peers, or an appreciative public of specifically trained connoisseurs, but an educated or semi-educated public at large. He short-circuits, so to speak, the arduous and complicated process through which other intellectuals attempt to gain recognition among qualified judges. Instead, he appeals to an amorphous general public from which he craves acclaim.

Since his audience has no specific expert knowledge and is not held together by common canons of taste, the celebrity intellectual is able to escape the social controls habitually exercised by intellectual or social circles. His public does not have enough in common to be capable of judging his intellectual work in the way, for example, an academic public judges the products of academic research, or in which cultured groups judge a novel.

The fact that this general audience makes no claim to expert knowledge or cultivated taste does not mean that it has no effect on the celebrity intellectual. Quite the contrary. Although it can hardly influence the quality of his work by applying substantive standards, it is likely to judge it in terms of what may be called "appeal qualities," such as "novelty" or "brilliance." This has important consequences. Since such qualities are not likely to afford long-term satisfaction, they foster a well-nigh insatiable appetite for "more" of the same. Novelty, brilliance, and abundance may, then, be taken provisionally as some of the hallmarks of the celebrity intellectual.

The emergence of the celebrity intellectual in the postwar years can be traced to three related occurrences. First, the coming of age of an unprecedentedly large college-educated middle class, providing a market for new and relatively sophisticated cultural commodities. This new public differs from the older college-educated stratum in significant ways. The relative homogeneity of cultural standards among the older college graduates has been replaced by an enormous heterogeneity whose only common denominator is the certification by which these men or women are said to be Bachelors or Masters of Arts or holders of professional degrees. These people regard the acquisition of status through the consumption of some "high" culture a basic requirement. But a genuine immersion in high culture requires considerable effort, and all these people desire is an effortless acquisition of its outward trappings,[5] an easy and quick way of being "in the know," or "with it." Whether in the realm of drug-induced stimuli or of cultural consumption, what they crave is instant gratification. This is precisely what the mass media attempt to provide. The development of the new media of communication corresponds to the emergence of a wide college-educated public. These new media, especially TV, are able to service an enormous mass market at relatively low cost, realizing appreciable economies of scale; and they can provide the required cultural commodities for both low-brow fare and for the more sophisticated repertoire desired by the college educated. Moreover, competition with the new media leads to the rapid transformation of older media to serve the needs of the new half-educated public. Robert Brustein summarizes these developments very well:

> Soon, Hollywood discovered there were big grosses to be had from movies based on serious literature, and not just "Anthony Adverse" or "Gone with the Wind". . . . the literary and academic celebrities thus created were being toasted on a host of television talk shows; *Playboy* and *Esquire* started folding short stories and short literary interviews between the pages of their cartoons and nude photographs, while *Vogue* and *Harper's Bazaar* slipped in poetry, stories and reviews among their clothing, cosmetic and jewelry ads; and prominent personalities began enjoying incomes of more than $100,000 from lecture tours alone. We were into an age where the appetite for fame joined the hunger for money as the decisive factor in the direction of many careers and everybody who could hold a pen was in a position to be as famous as a movie star.[6]

This being the demands of the new market, a host of intellectuals who had previously considered themselves to be serious rush in to supply cultural commodities in tune with the needs of the new audience. Some are still marked by ambivalence in regard to their new roles, and given to comparing their old reference anchorage in restricted circles with their new roles and audience. Others manage fully to internalize the demands of the new public and hence escape the torture of ambivalence.

The products of the celebrity intellectuals are not mediated through an intellectual give-and-take in identifiable circles. Their appeal is to an unidentifiable and heterogeneous audience that has no other way of responding than through popularity ratings. Without shared cultural standards, this audience relies overwhelmingly on cosmetic rather than substantive criteria. What counts is not content or truth, but "novelty" or "brilliance."

To be sure, in itself the introduction of such formal criteria in the evaluation of intellectual products is not new. It has developed gradually with the spread of intellectual products to an increasingly wider and more undifferentiated audience. Robert Nisbet has shown that the search for "brilliance" was already quite marked in the eighteenth century,[7] flourishing in the salons of Paris and the coffeehouses of London at a time when for the first time a broad audience emerged for men of ideas. This wider public—though it did not yet abandon other criteria of evaluation such as mastery of a subject, depth, and accuracy—was peculiarly fascinated by those aspects of style that could be seen as "brilliant" or "novel." Even in writers as great as Voltaire, Diderot, or Samuel Johnson, this new public criterion became one of the reasons for their enormous success.

The structural conditions pressing for the emphasis on novelty and brilliance, though already partly at work a century or two ago, have become perfected only in recent times, so that in our days, "Brilliance has become . . . the most cherished, sought-after, carefully calculated, and profitably traded adjective in the lexicon."[8] Although eighteenth- or nineteenth-century intellectuals tried to come to terms with the new public that appeared with the increase in literacy, they were still tied to their own circles of cultural producers and consumers, as I have attempted to show elsewhere.[9] Whether they be salons or academies, bohemias or particular publications catering to identifiable consumers or peers, these circles helped to structure intellectual life in distinctive ways and insured the differentiation of cultural offerings. As late as the first half of our own century, distinctions between high-brow, middle-brow, and low-brow culture were still clearly in evidence. Although such criteria as "novelty" and "brilliance" began to be introduced with the emergence of a wider public, they continued to be held in check through the elaboration of more substantive standards of excellence, institutionalized in particular circles in which men of knowledge continued to live and work.

In more recent times, however, the path has been opened up for a type of intellectual who can free himself from the control of standards embedded in distinct cultural circles and personified by distinctive status judges. He can bypass them, so to speak, and address himself directly to an undifferentiated public of superficially educated consumers. These large masses of men and women are not equipped to judge the accuracy, the mastery or depth of a contribution, but they are sufficiently well-educated to judge a work in terms of surface characteristics of style and presentation. They are likely to ask not whether what is asserted is true or significant, but whether it is startling. What counts among them is not whether a work contributes understanding or knowledge, but whether it provides the shock and *frisson* of brilliant novelty.

While older, highly institutionalized circles tended to be conservative in their judgments and were so disinclined to recognize innovation as to become a source of neophobia—the loose and general public of the mass media provides the conditions for *neophilia*, that is, a one-sided value emphasis on what is new. In otherwise heterogeneous audiences, only the new and the brilliant can provide suitable conversation pieces, allowing everyone to display his recently acquired knowledge as a badge of status. And since members of the new public sometimes suffer from boredom in the quotidian routines of their lives, they particularly value those cultural producers who engage in a search for new stimulants to revive jaded intellectual or aesthetic palates. Brilliant novelty becomes a tension-reducing anodyne.

It might be objected that celebrity intellectuals do not address their generalized public directly, but that their contributions are mediated through television commentators, talk-show hosts, media executives, and the like. This objection only strengthens my point. Such intermediaries, far from being independent evaluators, are in fact gatekeepers who will allow entrance to all whom they judge as agreeable to the audience they serve. Far from being cultured judges of the intellect, like some literary critics, they are of uncertain cultural background, live above their intellectual means, and are disposed, like the public they serve, to value the new above the significant. They are forever in pursuit of red-hot novelty.

Given this "tradition of the new," to reshape somewhat Harold Rosenberg's phrase, it stands to reason that the time span in which celebrity intellectuals can hold the limelight is extremely short. The new of yesterday rapidly becomes the old of today, so that the effective exposure time of the celebrity intellectual is likely to be very brief. To the extent that he is aware of this, he is inclined to make the most of the moment allotted to him and to pile into it as much as he possibly can. This, as well as the insatiable demands of the public, may account for the frantic pace characteristic of these men, who compress into a few years an output of writing, lecturing, interviews, and TV appearances that for others could be spaced over a lifetime. What is more, since intellectuals can produce significant work only when it is matured over fairly long periods of incubation, the celebrity intellectual has to repeat himself and produce variations of essentially the same idea. He is under structural pressure to go off half-cocked, that is, to offer opinions and ideas that have but little grounding in mature reflection. He must keep trying to raise the ante so that subsequent utterances often seem like self-parodies of earlier ones. No longer guided, if he ever was, by the disciplined criteria of inquiry and assertion emanating from a circle of colleagues and peers, he is pushed, and not just by happenstance, to make a fool of himself in the effort to grab the mike.

Forced at all times to compete for attention with celebrities who are not intellectuals, the celebrity intellectual runs in a very crowded field. The *Celebrity Register* lists its 2,200 biographies in alphabetical order so that Polly Adler comes after Mortimer Adler and Bertrand Russell is followed by Jane Russell.[10] Given such competition, the celebrity intellectual is driven to stunts and feats that will keep attention focused on him. Since he tends to become a performer among other performers, these, and not other intellectuals, become his reference group. Even if he has attained his position in the limelight by what serious intellectuals judged to be an intellectual accomplishment, he may soon be reduced to performances that are no longer intellectual at all. Here Gordon Allport's principle of functional autonomy comes into play: specific forms of behavior become, under certain conditions, ends or goals in themselves, although they were only means at an earlier stage.[11] Whereas the cultivation of brilliance may at first have been a device to draw attention to the qualities of the intellectual product, it tends later to be cultivated in itself.

TV, as well as "sophisticated" illustrated magazines such as *Esquire* or *Playboy*, is the medium par excellence for performers. They all offer rewards of exposure and applause, not an intensive exchange of ideas. Consequently, once the intellectual becomes a performer he no longer gains gratification from reciprocal exchanges with his audience, nor does he experience the delight that emerges through consensus between author and public. He derives most of his gratification from an ever-renewed exhibitionism, as insatiable in him as in his audience. This exhibitionistic behavior, it needs to be stressed, is not necessarily part of his psychological makeup; it is a response to his structural position.

To keep up with the competition, the celebrity intellectual must constantly refashion his personality in a way that appeals to the consumer. Hence he comes to resemble the salesgirl on the personality market of whom C. Wright Mills wrote that she "must not only sell her time and energy; she must also 'sell herself.' For in the personality market, the personality itself, along with advertising, becomes the instrument of an alien purpose."[12] In our case, since the celebrity is "known only for his well-knownness,"[13] this purpose is simply the need for keeping one's competitive standing within the ranks of celebrities. The celebrity intellectual must forever try to be "with it" because his status depends on his ability to contribute brilliantly to the set of ideas currently defined as "novel," "advanced," or "progressive." But precisely this leads to the ever-present danger of becoming rapidly obsolescent. As Dean Inge noted a while ago, he who would marry the spirit of the times is soon likely to become a widower. The more the celebrity intellectual proclaims his allegiance to whatever conceit is currently the latest, the more likely it is that he will soon be surpassed by a new celebrity, intellectual or not, who manages to attach himself to ideas that are even more recent and hence even more "advanced."

In the romantic age there arose the idea of the genius, the direct ancestor of the creative hero of avant-garde modernism. It was then assumed, as Hegel once put it, that in case of "conflict between genius and his public, it must be the public that is to blame . . . the only obligation the artist can have is to follow truth and his genius."[14] But with the celebrity intellectual this statement has to be reversed. In case of a conflict between him and his public, it is he who is felt to deserve the blame. Having failed to satisfy the public's taste, he deserves the penalty of oblivion.

The contributions of the celebrity intellectual, it turns out, tend to be judged in terms not of their use value but of their exchange value on the market of intellectual commodities. They assume a fetishistic character, being weighed not for their intrinsic worth but for their public rating. As literary critic Leonard Kriegel has put it, the cultural market is "gobbling up the contemporary before it can even establish its presence."[15] Or, as another literary critic, William Phillips, writes,

> Ideas are dissolved into styles, and everything is gobbled up by publicity and co-opted . . . into entertainment. . . . When I heard Germaine Greer was guest host for Dick Cavett, all I could think of was that she was a natural for TV. . . . But can you imagine Rosa Luxembourg [sic] on Johnny Carson's show?[16]

The promotion director of a large publishing house, Simon and Schuster, summed it all up in a recent interview in the *New York Times* (Dec. 31, 1971): "The more an author is known as a celebrity, the more personal promotion helps. The more serious, the more scholarly, the more literary a book is, the less author appearances matter." The first thing broadcast interviewers look for, he suggested, "is an author who is a celebrity, somebody whose name is known beyond the book."

Here follow the portraits of three celebrity intellectuals.

Erich Segal, a professor of classics at Yale, was fairly inconspicuous until recently. His scholarly work was mainly concerned with translations of Roman plays and commentaries on Latin authors. But in the last few years he suddenly started writing successful pop songs, collaborated on screenplays for such movies as *The Yellow Submarine*, and, more recently, achieved bestsellerdom (almost 500,000 copies sold) with the sentimental novel *Love Story*, which was soon made into an even more successful movie. In recent years, Segal, usually attired in the latest mod style, has been seen on innumerable talk shows, delivering a variety of "with it" comments. As Robert Brustein writes, "In Segal, the media interviewers had found the perfect patsy—a performer willing to play the fool on demand in return for continued exposure in front of the public."[17] His case is of interest not because Segal in his new persona pretended to major contributions in the world of ideas, but because it illustrates the tensions that arise in men suddenly caught between old and new standards.

To interviewers who asked him why and if he had given up his scholarly calling he replied that he had by no means done so, that he was still a scholar at heart. To others he would say that his trashy novel was in fact a contribution to literature. At times he is known to rant at "a lot of

pseudointellectuals in New York, who put me down at cocktail parties."
After students who at first admired him as a teacher who had managed to
work with the Beatles now put him down as having sold out to the mass
media, Segal availed himself of further recourse to TV shows and film festivals in order to "explain himself." It is all rather sad. In the words of
Robert Brustein, "he remains a victim of the culture he had fed on, schizoid
to the last, stranded between two worlds, able to sacrifice neither."[18]

While Segal is a transitional type, nearer in certain respects to an older
type of man, once found on the fringes of Hollywood, who succumbs to
the lure of the media and craves celebrity status while yet being unwilling to sever connections with the world of serious ideas, the other two intellectuals to be discussed are closer to the new type. Operating without
visible pangs of conscience as celebrity intellectuals, they seem to feel that
they offer the public not just entertainment but profound and novel intellectual fare.

When Charles A. Reich's *The Greening of America* burst upon the scene
in 1970, its author was practically unknown to the larger public. A professor of law at Yale, his contributions were restricted mainly to the law
journals. His publisher initially seems not to have expected major sales for
this book, and orders for the first as well as for the second printing were
only for 5,000 copies. Nor was there a concerted commercial promotion
campaign. But all of a sudden the *New Yorker*, for reasons unknown, decided to reprint large excerpts from the book and, within a week, it became a tremendous success, the talk of the town. The *New York Times* in
turn gave the book its accolade by reprinting excerpts and running a
number of comments pro and con, in addition to its regular review. The
austere *London Times* soon followed suit. For a few months it was all but
impossible to look at a mass culture magazine or a TV show without en-
countering the theme of *The Greening of America*. What then had Reich
wrought?

What he had provided was essentially a pop version of an interpretation of human destiny that has been part of the underground currents of
mythical ideas ever since the late twelfth century. At that time the semi-
heretical Calabrian abbot Joachim of Fiore had prophesized the imminent
coming of a new historical order, in which the Church of Christ would be
superseded by the reign of the Holy Ghost on earth, and most of
mankind's ills would be cured. The reign of the Son was born of the reign
of the Father, he taught, and it would soon be followed by a new order of
perfection, the reign of the Holy Ghost on earth. Love on earth, love from
the heart would replace the stern laws of both Testaments and usher in a
millenarian age of human bliss. Reich duplicated this vision by his peri-
odization of history into the old orders of Consciousness I and II, soon to
be followed by redemption in Consciousness III.

Marx once remarked that historical happenings tend to repeat themselves, that which was enacted once as historical tragedy being reenacted as farce. Exactly what happened here. The millenarian desires for a perfect universe of love reappear in Reich's pop version, but the earnest yearnings of the millenarians have become utterly trivialized. The term "consciousness" is never clearly defined; it is, among others, so we are told, "the whole man; his 'head;' his way of life. It is that by which he creates his own life and thus creates the society in which he lives." As to the rest, it is, above all, an embarrassingly crude celebration of the "new"—of protest, drugs, Woodstock festivals, and liberated life styles. It is a rhapsody to the antinomian, a pathetic celebration of spontaneity and pastoral bliss. The reasoning is shoddy to the extreme and the evidence painfully wanting. "We know," says Reich, "what causes crime and social disorder, and what can be done to eliminate those causes."

The very reception of the book utterly falsified some of its premises, such as the plaintive assertion that "the media systematically deny any fundamentally different or dissenting point of view a chance to be heard at all." The book feeds parasitically on other modish writers, from Marcuse to Keniston to Cleaver. Yet it was hailed as a major breakthrough in puffs by John Galbraith and Justice William Douglas. Senator McGovern found it "one of the most gripping, penetrating and revealing analyses of American society I have yet seen," and the *Washington Post* believed it to be a "brilliant synthesis of contemporary ideas."[19]

The point is not that all reviews were laudatory. *Time*, for example, called it, "A colloidal suspension of William Buckley, William Blake and Herbert Marcuse in pure applesauce." It is rather that the book was nowhere, among friends and foes alike, submitted to the kind of critical scrutiny that would have been normal had it emerged within a specific intellectual circle. Once it had been publicized in the *New Yorker*, the influential taste-makers of the media treated it as the work of a celebrity, as a book primarily known for its well-knownness. But such fame is short-lived. Some six months after the appearance of the book, a British writer, Henry Fairlie, met the editor of the *New Yorker* and made a passing allusion to the greening of New York during the St. Patrick's Day parade. William Shawn, the *New Yorker* editor, remarked in reply: "That all seems so long ago. I don't mean only in time, the months that have passed. The whole mood is so remote now. It was a last whimper."[20]

One doubts whether Reich himself would consider his work a major breakthrough in the world of ideas. But such is clearly the case with Marshall McLuhan, who seems the purest incarnation of the celebrity intellectual yet to appear on the American scene. Not only have others compared him to Darwin, Pavlov, Freud, Newton, and Einstein,[21] but he gives the impression of having made their judgment his own.

McLuhan was born in Edmonton, Alberta, in 1911. His father made his living as a real estate salesman. His Scottish-Irish parents were of Baptist and Methodist faith, but he became a Catholic convert in his twenties. After initial studies in English literature at the University of Manitoba, McLuhan went abroad to Trinity Hall, Cambridge University, to study under such figures as I. A. Richards and F. R. Leavis. He received his Ph.D. with a dissertation on the Elizabethan writer Thomas Nashe. In the next fifteen years, McLuhan followed a fairly conventional academic career. He began his teaching at the University of Wisconsin and joined the staff of a Catholic institution, St. Louis University, after his conversion in 1937. He returned to Canada in 1944 to teach at Assumption University in Windsor, Ontario. Two years later he joined the faculty of St. Michael's College, the Roman Catholic unit of the University of Toronto, with which he has been associated ever since, having been promoted to full professor in 1952.

Up to the 1950s McLuhan published almost exclusively in scholarly and literary reviews, contributing papers on Poe, Tennyson, Kipling, Pound, Joyce, Eliot, as well as on Elizabethan writers, to such magazines as *Sewanee Review* and *Kenyon Review*. His first book, *The Mechanical Bride: Folklore of Industrial Man*, appeared in 1951, just a year before he received his promotion. A vividly written assault on the mass media in general and on advertising in particular, it attacked the "pressures set up around us today by the mechanical agencies of the press, radio, movies, and advertising." Though a sharp departure from his previous writings, the book may still be considered a not untypical product of a Catholic intellectual steeped in the classics of English literature and the prophets of modernity, who reacted with horror to the decline in standards and taste during the age of mass consumption. At that time McLuhan clung fastidiously to the somewhat elitist cultural standards he had absorbed at Cambridge. *The Mechanical Bride* is a book that Ortega y Gasset would have appreciated. The book was sparsely reviewed, and only attained an underground reputation among critics of mass culture.

In the 1950s McLuhan directed a seminar on culture and communications at the University of Toronto sponsored by the Ford Foundation and, together with the anthropologist Edmund Carpenter, edited the periodical *Explorations*, largely devoted to unconventional and highly imaginative analyses of mass communications. Late in the '50s McLuhan's reputation as a specialist in communications had spread across the Canadian border, bringing him an appointment for 1959–60 as director of a media project for the U.S. Office of Education and the National Association of Educational Broadcasters. In the '50s, then, McLuhan had broadened his audience, moving from the world of English literature to circles interested in communications—a subject that attracted widespread attention at that time.

But only in the 1960s did McLuhan emerge in the limelight. *The Guten-berg Galaxy*, his first successful book, was published in 1962; here he first expounded his well-known thesis that when print replaced oral com-munication, the eye rather than the ear became the principal sensory or-gan. With the dawn of the electronic age, however, linear thinking based on print was pushed into the background. This brought about a height-ening of sensory awareness. Two years later, in *Understanding Media*, he extended his previous thesis and attempted to show why and how the new electronic media restructured modern civilization in a profoundly revolutionary sense. Another volume, *The Medium Is the Massage*, fol-lowed in 1967.[22]

With the publication of *The Gutenberg Galaxy* McLuhan became a celebrity. In addition to addressing innumerable gatherings ranging all the way from the PEN Congress to the Public Relations Society of Amer-ica and the Modern Language Association, he was a sought-after guest at talk shows and other TV events. CBS produced a recording of *The Medium Is the Massage*, NBC presented an hour-long documentary on his work, and CBS interviewed him on its top-rated Sunday night public-affairs show. To cap it all, he was appointed to the Albert Schweitzer Chair in Humanities at Fordham University, which pays $100,000 a year for salary and for staff expenses (to my knowledge no commentator at the time pointed to the irony that this chair was meant to honor one of the great in-trospective, "withdrawn" figures of our time).

In the 1960s there was hardly a magazine [not *Dissent*–Ed.] that failed to deal extensively with McLuhan's theses. Whether *Time* or *Life*, *The Na-tional Review* or *Commentary*, *Popular Photography* or the *Times Literary Sup-plement*, all made an attempt to interpret him. *Understanding Media* quickly went from a hard-cover edition priced at $8.50 to a paperback edi-tion priced at $1.95 to a drugstore paperback edition selling at 95 cents. More than 100,000 copies were sold. *The Medium Is the Massage* sold about 200,000 copies.

Corporation executives, in the advertising industry and elsewhere, soon clutched McLuhan to their collective bosoms. IBM, General Electric, Bell Telephone, The Container Corporation flew him from one city to the next to talk to their hierarchs about the electronic future. A San Francisco advertising executive, Howard Gossage, became his unofficial publicity agent, advertising him as "an Archimedes who has given the ad industry levers to move the world."[23] One corporation offered him $5,000 to pres-ent a closed-circuit television lecture on how the products of its industry would be used in the future. Two national magazines offered him perma-nent offices in their buildings, plus fees, to do occasional consulting work. He had an office at Time, Inc., and wrote articles for *Look* on such topics as "The Future of Sex" (co-authored by a *Look* editor).[24]

Tom Wolfe, the fashionable journalist, once witnessed a conversation between McLuhan and Gossage, the publicity agent. Gossage: "Listen, there are so many people willing to invest money in your work now, you'll never have to grade papers again." McLuhan: "You mean it's going to be fun from now on?" Gossage: "Everything's coming up roses."[25]

What accounts for this craze? To begin with, as a perceptive critic has remarked, "Fame and adulation of this proportion are only granted to someone who tells people something they already want to hear."[26] *The Mechanical Bride*, with its savage indictment of modern mass culture, it will be recalled, had only a very modest impact. The more recent books, in contrast, celebrate the electronic revolution and indicate, to quote Bernard Rosenberg,[27] that its author has now married the mechanical bride. The public at large took to McLuhan only after he had taken to the mass culture that public espoused. His celebration of the electronic media served to allay residual feelings of inadequacy the public may still have harbored over its immersion in the delights of nonlinear sensory stimulations. McLuhan legitimized pleasures that were heretofore indulged in only with greater or lesser uneasiness.

Yet legitimation of the media had been attempted earlier by others, with much less success. McLuhan had an advantage over them; he legitimized the existing state of affairs by having recourse to the language of novelty. "Newness as a norm or a criterion of value," the literary critic Geoffrey Wagner has written, "is the quickest and most convenient concession to the dominant technology."[28] By using a deliberately new vocabulary of sloganized and easily remembered catch phrases like "The Medium Is the Message," McLuhan gave his public the impression of learning something profoundly new while exerting minimal effort. He seemed to give instant knowledge, an immediate shock of recognition.

Many critics have pointed out the innumerable logical fallacies, the almost ludicrous distortions, to which McLuhan had recourse. Thus when he says, for example, that "with film you are the camera . . . but with TV you are the screen," this may seem very perceptive at first—until you realize that something like 80 percent of TV material consists of film. "The content of a movie," says McLuhan, "is a novel or a play or an opera." This sounds at first blush like a fine illustration of the thesis that the medium is indeed the message since, if the content of a medium is always derived from another medium, the only real innovation is the technology of each. Upon reflection, however, it turns out that many of the greatest achievements in film-making, like the works of Bergman, Fellini, or Antonioni, or the comedies of Keaton and Chaplin, are not based on novels, plays, or operas.[29]

When such outrageous examples are cited to defenders of McLuhan, the reply always turns out to be that his insights are not meant to be right or wrong; they are meant to be "stimulating." McLuhan himself refers to his writings as "probes." But what is a probe? More often than not, a statement for which there is no evidence or which flies in the face of obvious facts.

At this point a personal reminiscence might be in order. A few years ago I attended a small seminar in which McLuhan asserted, *inter alia*, that new technological inventions are reflected in the writing styles of great literary figures, so that "you cannot understand the style of Swift without realizing that he wrote in the age of the spinning jenny." When I pointed out to him that Swift had died several decades before the invention of the spinning jenny, there came the amazing reply, delivered with great self-assurance, "So, he anticipated it."

Closer textual analysis than can be attempted here would reveal that the ratio of sense to nonsense in the writings of McLuhan has steadily decreased from the days of *The Gutenberg Galaxy* to his more recent work. The questionable "The Medium Is the Message" gave way to the absurdity of *The Medium Is the Massage*. In an effort to keep raising the ante, McLuhan increasingly parodied himself. But there comes a point for celebrity intellectuals when such tactics are counterproductive. The half-life of most of them is short indeed. Some of my freshman students have recently asked me with puzzled expressions, "Who is Marshall McLuhan?" McLunacy, having lasted some eight years, is over. What next?

Though particular celebrity intellectuals pass from the scene, the type, I venture to think, is here to stay. Individuals are used up, but the institutionalized settings exerts pressures for their rapid replacement. "The particular," wrote Hegel, "is for the most part of too trifling a value as compared with the general: Individuals are sacrificed and abandoned."[30] Such is the cunning of reason, or, as the sociologist has it, the power of institutions.

NOTES

1. Cf. Kurt H. Wolff, ed. *The Sociology of Georg Simmel* (New York: Free Press, 1950), *passim*. For a modern extension of these views see Charles Kadushin, "The Friends and Supporters of Psychotherapy: On Social Circles in Urban Life," *American Sociological Review* (December 1966): 786–802.

2. Florian Znaniecki, *The Social Role of the Man of Knowledge* (New York: Harper Torchbooks, 1968, new ed.), and my introduction to Znaniecki's volume.

3. Cf. Lewis A. Coser, *Masters of Sociological Thought* (New York: Harcourt Brace, 1971).

4. Karl Mannheim, *Ideology and Utopia* (New York: Harcourt Brace, 1936), and "The Problem of the Intelligentsia" in *Essays on the Sociology of Culture* (London: Routledge and Kegan Paul, 1956).

5. On the notion of effortlessness, cf. David Riesman, *The Lonely Crowd* (New Haven: Yale University Press, 1970), and *Abundance for What?* (Garden City, NY: Doubleday, 1964).

6. Robert Brustein, "If an Artist Wants to Be Serious and Respected and Rich, Famous and Popular, He is Suffering from Cultural Schizophrenia," *New York Times Magazine*, September 26, 1971.

7. Robert Nisbet, "What Is an Intellectual?" *Commentary* (December 1965): 93–101.

8. *Ibid.*

9. Lewis A. Coser, *Men of Ideas* (New York: Free Press, 1965).

10. See Daniel J. Boorstein, *The Image* (New York: Atheneum, 1962), 58.

11. Cf. Robert K. Merton, *Social Theory and Social Structure* (New York: Free Press, 1968, enlarged ed.), 15.

12. C. Wright Mills, *Power, Politics and People* (New York: Oxford University Press, 1963; Ballantine Books, n.d.), 271.

13. Boorstin, *The Image*, 57.

14. Quoted in Irving Howe, *Decline of the New* (New York: Harcourt Brace, 1970), 8.

15. Leonard Kriegel, *Edmund Wilson* (Carbondale: Southern Illinois University Press, 1971), 88.

16. William Philips, in *Partisan Review* (Spring 1971): 142.

17. Brustein, "If an Artist Wants to Be Serious. . . ."

18. Brustein, "If an Artist Wants to Be Serious. . . ."

19. All these puffs can be found on the back cover of the paperback edition.

20. Henry Fairlie, "The Practice of Puffers," *Encounter* (August 1971): 3–13. I have relied heavily on this fine essay.

21. Gerald E. Stearn, ed., *McLuhan Hot and Cool* (New York: Dial, 1967), xv.

22. For biographical information, see, Raymond Rosenthal, ed., *McLuhan: Pro and Con* (New York: Funk & Wagnalls, 1968), 15–22.

23. Harry H. Crosby and George Bond, eds., *The McLuhan Explosion* (New York: American Book Co., 1968), 167.

24. Crosby and Bond, 166; see also Tom Wolfe, *The Pump House Gang* (New York: Bantam Books, 1968), 110, 130.

25. Wolfe, *The Pump House Gang*, p. 129.

26. Neil Compton, "The Paradox of Marshal McLuhan," in Rosenthal, ed., *McLuhan: Pro and Con*, 107.

27. Personal communication.

28. Geoffrey Wagner, "Misunderstanding Media: Obscurity as Authority," in Rosenthal, *McLuhan: Pro and Con*, p. 159.

29. Dwight McDonald, "Running It Up the Totem Pole," in Rosenthal, ed., *McLuhan: Pro and Con*, p. 33.

30. G. W. F. Hegel, *The Philosophy of History* (New York: Bohn Library, n.d.), p. 34.

Forum

Howard Young*

The precursors of today's intellectuals were the *philosophes* who propagated the Enlightenment, using lodges, salons, cafés, journals, theaters, and academies to express ideas on progress, the primacy of reason, and the rights of the individual. According to Enlightenment belief, energetic minds could organize, categorize, and ultimately assimilate knowledge in its totality, as the seventeen volumes of the *Encyclopédie* (1751–66) were designed to show. Although founded a century earlier, the Académie Française sought to prescribe correct French well into the Enlightenment. Of course, modern linguists have destroyed the ideal of fixed proper usage (ironically, the Académie's only significant progeny, the Real Academia de la Lengua Española [founded in 1713], faced an enormous lexicographical invasion from the Americas), and a knowledge explosion has made conventional encyclopedias acutely provisional. Television and cyberspace have provided new outlets for expression, and CD-ROMs contain previously unimaginable fonts of information.

The term *philosophe* designated writers, thinkers, and scientists; in 1818 Coleridge called learned persons the clerisy; and early-twentieth-century Russia created the word *intelligencija*. Is there an analytic definition of what these terms designate in common? For Edward Shils (*"The Intellectuals and the Powers" and Other Essays* [Chicago: U of Chicago P, 1972]) and Daniel Bell ("Intellectuals," *The Harper Dictionary of Modern Thought*, ed. Alan Bullock and Oliver Stallybrass [New York: Harper, 1977] 314–15), an

*Reprinted by permission of the Modern Language Association of America from *PMLA* 112, no. 5 (1997): 1126–1127.

intellectual is someone who is intensely attached to cognitive, moral, and aesthetic symbols outside immediate experience. Foucault provides a useful distinction between the "specific" intellectual, or scholar, and the "universal" intellectual, who derives from the jurist or notable and finds fullest manifestation in the writer ("Questions of Geography," *Power/ Knowledge*, ed. Colin Graham [New York: Pantheon, 1980] 128). It recognizes the great flowering of experts produced by universities. Foucault is more charitable than Ortega, who would have dubbed the respected and valued expert on Foucault or Virginia Woolf—as distinct from Foucault and Woolf themselves—a *sabio-ignorante* ("learned ignoramus").

At the close of the twentieth century, intellectuals do not appear to be a dying breed. On the contrary, their spectacular increase in numbers makes one long for an Ortega to analyze this new revolt of the masses. While public rendezvous in salons, Masonic lodges, and cafés are gone, journals have multiplied a hundredfold, although some have less-than-dutiful gatekeepers; academies have given way to universities; and guilds are now professional associations with a Byzantine range of interests. Today intellectuals are liable to begin as teachers in classrooms (there are no journalist or jurist intellectuals as in the time of Lippmann or Holmes) and to progress to publication of their writing, provided that—if the publisher is a university press—their discourse reflects the specialized interests of certain other intellectuals. At the same time, for a few academics, trade books, television talk shows, and cyberspace lurk in the wings to offer an audience even Bertrand Russell never imagined. One result is an intensification of the star system. T. S. Eliot, Ortega, and Croce were stars in their time (in his prime Eliot drew 13,700 spectators to a football stadium in Minneapolis to listen to a lecture on criticism, and Ortega talked to packed if often uncomprehending audiences in Madrid). But today's stars enjoy more fame and popularity than before and reach a wider audience.

Tension among intellectual groups and the dangers of dogma are nothing new. What is novel today is technology and the money it provides to intellectual stars as they flash across the horizon for three to five years before their celebrity wears off and they go from the pages of the *New York Times Magazine* back to the learned journal, to be sighted thereafter only when they write a letter to the editor.

I cannot imagine a society in which groups of people did not distinguish themselves by an intense attachment to cognitive, moral, and aesthetic symbols outside immediate experience. And I cannot imagine a society that did not recognize intellectual acuity or merit, however defined. It is ironic that the Enlightenment, which led to Ortega's *sabio-ignorante*, also generated the zeal to apply reason for the betterment of society and enhanced the value placed on learning and on intellectual curiosity. These are gifts difficult to despise.

Ortega wrote, "Sorprenderse, extrañarse, es comenzar a entender. Es el deporte y el lujo especifico del intelectual." "To be surprised, filled with wonder, is the beginning of understanding. It is a sport and a luxury specific to the intellectual" (*La rebelión de las masas*, 1929 [Madrid: Revista de Occidente, 1959] 5 I; my trans.). In this remark, sport conveys the playfulness and elasticity of mind valued in intellectual activity, while luxury suggests that such activity provides society with wealth that comes from no other source.

Chapter 6

SPEAKING TRUTH
TO POWER

On Knowledge and Power[1]

C. Wright Mills*

I.

During the last few years I have often thought that American intellectuals are now rather deeply involved in what Freud once called "the miscarriage of American civilization." I do not know exactly what he meant by the phrase, although I suppose he intended to contrast the eighteenth-century ideals with which this nation was so hopefully proclaimed with their sorry condition in twentieth-century America.

Among these values none has been held higher than the grand role of reason in civilization and in the lives of its civilized members. And none has been more sullied and distorted by men of power in the mindless years we have been enduring. Given the caliber of the American elite, and the immorality of accomplishment in terms of which they are selected, perhaps we should have been expecting this. But political intellectuals too have been giving up the old ideal of the public relevance of knowledge. Among them a conservative mood—a mood that is quite appropriate for men living in a political vacuum—has come to prevail.

Perhaps nothing is of more immediate importance, both as cause and as effect of this mood, than the rhetorical ascendancy and the intellectual collapse of liberalism: As a proclamation of *ideals*, classic liberalism, like classic socialism, remains part of the secular tradition of the West. As a *theory* of society, liberalism has become irrelevant, and, in its operative way, misleading, for no revision of liberalism as a theory of the mechanics of

---

* This article first appeared in *Dissent* 2, no. 3 (1955): 201–212. Reprinted with permission.

*This article first appeared in *Dissent* 2, no. 3 (1955): 201–212. Reprinted with permission.

modern social change has overcome the trade mark of the nineteenth century that is stamped upon its basic assumptions. As a political *rhetoric*, liberalism's key terms have become the common denominators of the political vocabulary, and hence have been stretched beyond any usefulness as a way of defining issues and stating positions.[2]

As the administrative liberalism of the 1930s has been swallowed up by economic boom and military fright, the noisier political initiative has been seized by a small group of petty conservatives, who, on the middle levels of power, has managed to set the tone of public life. Exploiting the American fright of the new international situation for their own purposes, these political primitives have attacked not only the ideas of the New and Fair Deals; they have attacked the history of those administrations, and the biographies of those who took part in them. And they have done so in a manner that reveals clearly the basis upon which their attractive power rests: they have attacked the symbols of status and the figures of established prestige. By their attack upon men and institutions of established status, the noisy right has appealed not at all to the economically discontented, but to the status-frustrated.[3] Their push has come from the *nouveau riche*, of small city as well as larger region, and, above all, from the fact of the rankling status-resentment felt by these newly prosperous classes who, having achieved considerable wealth during and after World War II, have not received the prestige nor gained the power that they have felt to be their due.

They have brought into dramatic focus the higher immorality as well as the mindlessness of the upper circles in America. On the one hand, we have seen a decayed and frightened liberalism, and on the other hand, the insecure and ruthless fury of political gangsters. A Secretary of the Army, also a man of older family wealth, is told off by upstarts, and in public brawl disgraced by unestablished nihilists. They have brought into focus a new conception of national loyalty, which we came to understand as loyalty to individual gangs who placed themselves above the established legitimations of the state, and invited officers of the U.S. Army to do likewise. They have made plain the central place now achieved in the governmental process by secret police and secret "investigations," to the point where we must now speak of a shadow cabinet based in considerable part upon new ways of power which include the wire tap, the private eye, the widespread use and threat of blackmail. And they have dramatized one political result of the hollowing out and the banalizing of sensibility among a population that for a generation now has been steadily and increasingly subjected to the shrill trivialization of the mass means of entertainment and distraction.

As liberalism sat in these "hearings," liberals became aware, from time to time, of how close they were to the edge of the mindless abyss. The status edifice of bourgeois society was under attack, but since in America there is nothing from the past above that established edifice, and since those of once liberal and left persuasion see nothing in the future below it, they have become terribly frightened by the viciousness of the attack, and their political lives have been narrowed to the sharp edge of defensive anxiety.

Post-war liberalism has been organizationally impoverished: the prewar years of liberalism-in-power devitalized independent liberal groups, drying up their grass roots, making older leaders dependent upon the federal center and not training new leaders round the country. The New Deal left no liberal organization to carry on any liberal program; rather than a new party, its instrument was a loose coalition inside an old one, which quickly fell apart so far as liberal ideas are concerned. Moreover, in using up, in one way or another, the heritage of liberal ideas, banalizing them as it put them into law, the New Deal turned liberalism into a set of administrative routines to defend rather than a program to fight for.

In their moral fright, post-war liberals have not defended any left-wing or even any militantly liberal position: their defensive posture has, first of all, concerned the civil liberties.

Many of the political intelligentsia have been so busy celebrating formal civil liberties in America, by contrast with their absence from Soviet Communism, that they have often failed to defend them. But more importantly, most have been so busy defending civil liberties that they have had neither the time nor the inclination to *use* them. "In the old days," as Archibald MacLeish has remarked, freedom "was something you used . . . [it] has now become something that you save—something you put away and protect like your other possessions—like a deed or a bond in a bank."[4]

It is much safer to celebrate civil liberties than to defend them, and it is much safer to defend them as a formal right than to use them in a politically effective way: even those who would most willingly subvert these liberties, usually do so in their very name. It is easier still to defend someone else's right to have used them years ago than to have something yourself to say *now* and to say it now forcibly. The defense of civil liberties—even of their practice a decade ago—has become the major concern of many liberal and once leftward scholars. All of which is a safe way of diverting intellectual effort from the sphere of political reflection and demand.

The defensive posture, secondly, has concerned American Values in general, which, quite rightly it has been feared, the petty right seeks to destroy. Quite unwittingly, I am sure, the U.S. intelligentsia has found itself in the middle of the very nervous center of elite and plebeian anxieties about the position of America in the world today. What is at the root of these anxieties is not simply international tension and the terrible, helpless feeling of many that another war is surely in the works. There is also involved in them a specific worry with which many serious-minded Americans are seriously concerned.

The United States is now engaged with other nations, particularly Russia, in a full-scale competition for cultural prestige based on nationality. In this competition, what is at issue is American music and American literature and American art, and, in the somewhat higher meaning than is usually given to that term, The American Way of Life. For what American has got abroad is power; what it has *not* got at home or abroad is cultural prestige. This simple fact has involved those of the new gentility in the curious American celebration, into which much scholarly and intellectual energy now goes. The celebration rests upon the felt need to defend themselves in nationalist terms against the petty right; and it rests upon the need, shared by many spokesmen and statesmen as urgent, to create and to uphold the cultural prestige of America abroad.[5]

The noisy conservatives, of course, have no more won political power than administrative liberals have retained it. While those two camps have been engaged in wordy battle, and while the intellectuals have been embraced by the new conservative gentility, the silent conservatives have assumed political power. Accordingly, in their imbroglio with the noisy right, liberal and once-left forces have, in effect, defended these established conservatives, if only because they have lost any initiative of attack, in fact, lost even any point of effective criticism. The silent conservatives of corporation, army, and state have benefited politically and economically and militarily by the antics of the petty right, who have become, often unwittingly, their political shock troops. And they have ridden into power on all those structural trends set into motion and accelerated by the organization of the nation for seemingly permanent war.

So, in this context of material prosperity, with the noisy little men of the petty right successfully determining the tone and level of public sensibility; with the silent conservatives achieving established power in a mindless victory; with the liberal rhetoric made official, then banalized by widespread and perhaps illicit use; with liberal hope carefully adjusted to mere rhetoric by thirty years of rhetorical victory; with radicalism deflated and radical hope stoned to death by thirty years of defeat—the political intellectuals have been embraced by the conservative mood. Among them there is no demand and no dissent, and no opposition to the monstrous decisions that are being made without deep or widespread debate, in fact with no debate at all. There is no opposition to public mindlessness in all its forms nor to all those forces and men that would further it. But above all—among the men of knowledge, there is little or no opposition to the divorce of knowledge from power, of sensibilities from men of power, no opposition to the divorce of mind from reality.

II.

Once upon a time, at the beginning of the United States, men of affairs were also men of culture: to a considerable extent the elite of power and the elite of culture coincided, and where they did not coincide as persons they often overlapped as circles. Within the compass of a knowledgeable and effective public, knowledge and power were in effective touch; and, more than that, this classic public also decided much that was decided.

"Nothing is more revealing," James Reston has written, "than to read the debate in the House of Representatives in the Eighteen Thirties on Greece's fight with Turkey for independence and the Greek-Turkish debate in the Congress in 1947. The first is dignified and eloquent, the argument marching from principle through illustration to conclusion; the second is a dreary garble of debating points, full of irrelevancies and bad history."[6] George Washington in 1783 read Voltaire's "Letters" and Locke's "On Human Understanding;" Eisenhower, two hundred years later, reads cowboy tales and detective stories.[7] For such men as now typically arrive in the higher political, economic, and military circles, the briefing and the memorandum seem to have pretty well replaced not only the serious book, but the newspaper as well. This is, perhaps, as it must be, given the immorality of accomplishment, but what is somewhat disconcerting about it is that these men are below the level on which they might feel a little bit ashamed of the uncultivated level of their relaxation and of their mental fare, and that no intellectual public, by its reactions, tries to educate them to such uneasiness.

By the middle of the twentieth century, the American elite have become an entirely different breed of men from those who could on any reasonable grounds be considered a cultural elite, or even for that matter, cultivated men of sensibility. Knowledge and power are not truly united inside the ruling circles; and when men of knowledge do come to a point of contact with the circles of powerful men, they come not as peers but as hired men. The elite of power, wealth, and celebrity are not of the elite of culture, knowledge and sensibility. Moreover, they are not in contact with it, although the banalized and ostentatious fringes of the two worlds do overlap in the world of the celebrity.

Most men are encouraged to assume that, in general, the most powerful and the wealthiest are also the most knowledgeable or, as they might say, the smartest. Such ideas are propped up by many little slogans about those who "teach because they can't *do*," and about "if you're so smart, why aren't you rich?" But all that such wisecracks mean is that those who use them assume that power and wealth are sovereign values for all men and especially for men "who are smart." They assume also that knowledge always pays off in such ways, or surely ought to, and that the test of genuine knowledge is just such pay-offs. The powerful and the wealthy *must* be the men of most knowledge; otherwise how could they be where they are? But to say that those who succeed to power must be "smart," is to say that power *is* knowledgeable. To say that those who succeed to wealth must be smart, is to say that wealth *is* knowledge.

These assumptions do reveal something that is true: that ordinary men, even today, are prone to explain and to justify power and wealth in terms of knowledge or ability. Such assumptions also reveal something of what has happened to the kind of experience that knowledge has come to be. Knowledge is no longer widely felt as an ideal; it is seen as an instrument. And in a society of power and wealth, knowledge is valued as an instrument of power and wealth, and also, of course, as an ornament in conversation, a tid-bit in a quiz program.

What knowledge does to a man (in clarifying what he is, and setting it free)—that is the personal ideal of knowledge. What knowledge does to a civilization (in revealing its human meaning, and setting it free)—that is the social ideal of knowledge. But today, the personal *and* the social ideals of knowledge have coincided in what knowledge does *for* the smart guy: it gets him ahead; and for the wise nation: it lends cultural prestige, haloing power with authority.

Knowledge seldom lends power to the man of knowledge. But the supposed, and secret, knowledge of some men-on-the-powerful-make, and their very free use thereof, has consequence for other men who have not the power of defense. Knowledge, of course, is neither good nor bad, nor is its use good or bad. "Bad men increase in knowledge as fast as good men," John Adams wrote, "and science, arts, taste, sense and letters, are employed for the purpose of injustice as well as for virtue." That was in 1790; today we have good reason to know that it is so.

The problem of knowledge and power is, and always has been, the problem of the relations of men of knowledge with men of power. Suppose we were to select the one hundred most powerful men, from all fields of power, in America today and line them up. And then, suppose we selected the one hundred most knowledgeable men, from all fields of social knowledge, and lined them up. How many men would be in *both* our line-ups? Of course our selection would depend upon what we mean by power and what we mean by knowledge—especially what we mean by knowledge. But, if we mean what the words seem to mean, surely we would find few if any men in America today who were in both groups, and surely we could find many more at the time this nation was founded than we could find today. For, in the eighteenth century, even in this colonial outpost, men of power pursued learning, and men of learning were often in positions of power. In these respects we have, I believe, suffered grievous decline.[8]

There is little union in the same persons of knowledge and power; but persons of power do surround themselves with men of some knowledge, or at least with men who are experienced in shrewd dealings. The man of knowledge has not become a philosopher king; but he has often become a consultant, and moreover a consultant to a man who is neither king-like nor philosophical. It is not natural in the course of their careers for men of knowledge to meet with those of power. The links between university and government are weak, and when they do occur, the man of knowledge appears as an "expert," which usually means as a hired technician. Like most others in this society, the man of knowledge is himself dependent for his livelihood upon the job, which nowadays is a prime sanction of thought control. Where getting ahead requires the good opinions of more powerful others, their judgments become prime objects of concern. Accordingly, in so far as intellectuals serve power directly—in a job hierarchy—they often do so unfreely.

The characteristic member of the higher circles today is an intellectual mediocrity, sometimes a conscientious one, but still a mediocrity. His intelligence is revealed only by his occasional realization that he is not up to the decisions he sometimes feels called upon to confront. But usually he keeps such feelings private, his public utterances being pious and sentimental, grim and brave, cheerful and empty in their universal generality. He is open only to abbreviated and vulgarized, pre-digested and slanted ideas. He is a commander of the age of the memo and the briefing. He is briefed, but not for longer than one page; he talks on the phone, rather than writes letters or holds conversations.

By the mindlessness and mediocrity of men of affairs, I do not, of course, mean that these men are not sometimes intelligent men, although that is by no means automatically the case. It is not, however, primarily a matter of the distribution of "intelligence"—as if intelligence were a homogeneous something of which there may be more or less. It is rather a matter of the quality of mind, a quality that requires the evaluation of substantive rationality as the key value in a man's life and character and conduct. That evaluation is what is lacking from the American power elite. In its place there is "weight" and "judgment" which count for much more in their celebrated success than any subtlety of mind or force of intellect.

All around, just below the weighty man of affairs, are his technical lieutenants of power who have been assigned the role of knowledge and even of speech: his public relations man, his ghost, his administrative assistants, his secretaries. And do not forget The Committee. With the increased means of decision, there is a crisis of understanding among the political directorate of the United States, and accordingly, there is often a commanding indecision.

The lack of knowledge as an experience and as a criterion among the elite ties in with the malign ascendancy of the expert, not only as fact but as a defense against public discourse and debate. When questioned recently about a criticism of defense policies made by the leader of the opposition party, the secretary of defense replied, "Do you think he is an expert in the matter?" When pressed further by reporters he asserted that the "military chiefs think it is sound, and I think it is sound," and later, when asked about specific cases, added: "In some cases, all you can do is ask the Lord."[9] With such a large role so arrogantly given to God, to experts, and to Mr. Wilson, what room is there for political leadership? Much less for public debate of what is after all every bit as much a political and a moral as a military issue?

Beyond the lack of intellectual cultivation by political personnel and advisory circles, the absence of publicly relevant minds has come to mean that powerful decisions and important policies are not made in such a way as to be justified and attacked, in short, debated in any intellectual form. Moreover, the attempt to so justify them is often not even made. Public relations displace reasoned argument; manipulation and undebated decisions of power replace democratic authority. More and more, as administration has replaced politics, decisions of importance do not carry even the panoply of reasonable discussion in public, but are made by God, by experts, and by men like Mr. Wilson.

And more and more the area of the official secret expands, as well as the area of the secret listening in on those who might divulge in public what the public, not being composed of experts with Q clearance, is not to know. The entire series of decisions concerning the production and the use of atomic weaponry has been made without any genuine public debate, and the facts needed to engage in that debate intelligently have been officially hidden, distorted, and lied about. As the decisions become more fateful, not only for Americans but literally for mankind, the sources of information are closed up, and the relevant facts needed for decision, and even of the decisions made, are, as politically convenient "official secrets," withheld from the heavily laden channels of information.

In the meantime, in those channels, political rhetoric continues to slide lower and lower down the scale of cultivation and sensibility. The height of such mindless communications to masses, or what are thought to be masses, is the commercial propaganda for toothpaste and soap and cigarettes and automobiles. It is to such things, or rather to Their Names, that this society sings its loudest praises most frequently. What is important about this is that by implication and omission, by emphasis and sometimes by flat statement, this astounding volume of propaganda for commodities is often untruthful and misleading; and is addressed more often to the belly or to the groin than to the head or to the heart. And the point to be made about this is that public communications from those who make powerful decisions or who would have us vote them into such decision-making places, competes with it, and more and more takes on those qualities of mindlessness and myth which commercial propaganda or advertising have come to exemplify.

In America today, men of affairs are not so much dogmatic as they are mindless. For dogma usually meant some more or less elaborated justification of ideas and values, and thus has had some features (however inflexible and closed) of mind, of intellect, of reason. Nowadays what we are up against is precisely the absence of mind of any sort as a public force; what we are up against is a lack of interest in and a fear of knowledge that might have liberating public relevance. And what this makes possible is the prevalence of the kindergarten chatter, as well as decisions having no rational justifications that the intellect could confront and engage in debate.

It is not the barbarous irrationality of uncouth, dour senators that is the American danger; it is the respected judgments of secretaries of state, the earnest platitudes of presidents, the fearful self-righteousness of sincere young American politicians from sunny California, that is the main danger. For these men have replaced mind by the platitude, and the dogmas by which they are legitimated are so widely accepted that no counterbalance of mind prevails against them. Such men as these are crackpot realists, who, in the name of realism have constructed a paranoid reality all their own and in the name of practicality have projected a utopian image of capitalism. They have replaced the responsible interpretation of events by the disguise of meaning in a maze of public relations, respect for public debate by unshrewd notions of psychological warfare, intellectual ability by the agility of the sound and mediocre judgment, and the capacity to elaborate alternatives and to gauge their consequences by the executive stance.

III.

In our time, all forms of public mindlessness must expropriate the individual mind, and we now know that this is an entirely possible procedure.[10] We also know that ideas, beliefs, images—symbols in short—stand between men and the wider realities of their time, and that accordingly those who professionally create, destroy, elaborate these symbols are very much involved in all literate men's very images of reality. For now, of course, the live experience of men falls far short of the objects of their belief and action, and the maintenance of adequate definitions of reality is by no means an automatic process, if indeed it ever was. Today that maintenance requires intellectuals of quite some skill and persistence, for much reality is now officially defined by those who hold power.

As a type of social man, the intellectual does not have any one political direction, but the work of any man of knowledge, if he is the genuine article, does have a distinct kind of political relevance: his politics, in the first instance, are the politics of truth, for his job is the maintenance of an adequate definition of reality. In so far as he is politically adroit, the main tenet of his politics is to find out as much of the truth as he can, and to tell it to the right people, at the right time, and in the right way. Or, stated negatively: to deny publicly what he knows to be false, whenever it appears in the assertions of no matter whom; and whether it be a direct lie or a lie by omission, whether it be by virtue of official secret or an honest error. The intellectual ought to be the moral conscience of his society, at least with reference to the value of truth, for in the defining instance, that *is* his politics. And he ought also to be a man absorbed in the attempt to know what is real and what is unreal.

Power and authority involve the actual making of *decisions*. They also involve the *legitimation* of the power and of the decisions by means of doctrine, and they usually involve the pomp and the halo, the *representations* of the powerful.[11] It is in connection with the legitimations and the representations of power and decision that the intellectual—as well as the artist—becomes politically relevant.

Intellectual work is related to power in numerous ways, among them these: with ideas one can uphold or justify power, attempting to transform it into legitimate authority; with ideas one can also debunk authority, attempting to reduce it to mere power, to discredit it as arbitrary or as unjust. With ideas one can conceal or expose the holders of power. And with ideas of more hypnotic though frivolous shape, one can divert attention from problems of power and authority and social reality in general.

So the Romantic poets symbolize the French Revolution to an English public and elaborate one strain of its doctrinal legitimation; so Virgil as a member of the Roman ruling class writes his *Georgics*; so John Reed reports to America the early phase of Bolshevism; so Rousseau legitimates the French Revolution, Milton the regime of Cromwell, Marx—in vulgarized form—the Russian revolution.[12]

And so, in an intellectually petty way, do the U.S. intellectuals now embraced by the conservative mood—whether they know it or not—serve to legitimate the mindless image of the American ascendancy abroad, and the victory of the silent conservatives at home. And more important than that: by the work they do not do they uphold the official definitions of reality, and, by the work they do, even elaborate it.

Whatever else the intellectual may be, surely he is among those who ask serious questions, and, if he is a political intellectual, he asks his questions of those in power. If you ask to what the intellectual belongs, you must answer that he belongs first of all to that minority which has carried on the big discourse of the rational mind, the big discourse that has been going on—or off and on—since western society began some two thousand years ago in the small communities of Athens and Jerusalem.[13] This big discourse is not a vague thing to which to belong—even if as lesser participants—and it is the beginning of any sense of belonging that is worthwhile, and it is the key to the only kind of belonging that free men in our time might have. But if we would belong to it, we ought to try to live up to what it demands of us. What it demands of us, first of all, is that we maintain our sense of it. And, just now, at this point in human history, that is quite difficult.

IV.

The democratic man assumes the existence of a public, and in his rhetoric asserts that this public is the very seat of sovereignty. We object to Mr. Wilson, with his God and his Experts, because in his assertion he explicitly denies two things needed in a democracy: articulate and knowledgeable publics, and political leaders who if not men of reason are at least reasonably responsible to such knowledgeable publics as exist. Only where publics and leaders are responsive and responsible, are human affairs in democratic order, and only when knowledge has public relevance is this order possible. Only when mind has an autonomous basis, independent of power, but powerfully related to it, can it exert its force in the shaping of human affairs. Such a position is democratically possible only when there exists a free and knowledgeable public, to which men of knowledge may address themselves, and to which men of power are truly responsible. Such a public and such men—either of power or of knowledge, do not now prevail, and accordingly, knowledge does not now have democratic relevance in America.

NOTES

1. A modified version of this essay was presented to a joint meeting of the William A. White and the Harry S. Sullivan Societies in New York City, February 1955.

2. Cf. Mills, "Liberal Values in the Modern World," *Anvil and Student Partisan* (Winter 1952): 5.

3. Although this interpretation is now widely published, Paul Sweezy's and Leo Huberman's original article remains the most forthright account of it: "The Roots and Prospects of McCarthyism," *Monthly Review* (January 1954): 417–434.

4. *Atlantic Monthly* (August 1949): 20.

5. Examples of The American Celebration are embarrassingly available. Unfortunately no one of them is really worth examining in detail: In order that the sort of thing I have in mind may be clear, by all means see Jacques Barzun, *God's Country and Mine* (Boston: Little, Brown, 1954). Mr. Barzun believes that "the way to see America is from a lower berth about two in the morning," and so far as I can tell from his book, he really means it. For a less flamboyant example, done at least in dim daylight, see Daniel J. Boorstin, *The Genius of American Politics* (Chicago: University of Chicago Press, 1953); and for a scatter of celebrants, see *America and The Intellectuals* (New York: PR series, Number Four, 1953).

6. *The New York Times*, January 31, 1954, editorial page.

7. *The New York Times Book Review*, August 23, 1953.

8. In *Perspectives, USA*, No. 3, Mr. Lionel Trilling has written optimistically of "new intellectual classes," and has even referred to the Luce publications as samples of high "intellectual talent." What lends his view its optimistic tone, I believe, is less the rise of any new intellectual classes than (1) old intellectual groups becoming a little prosperous, even successful, in a minor way, on American terms, and, (2) of course, the confusion of knowledge as a goal with knowledge as a mere technique and instrument. For an informed account of new cultural strata by a brilliantly self-conscious insider, see Louis Kronenberger, *Company Manners* (Indianapolis: Bobbs Merrill, 1954).

9. Charles E. Wilson, cf. *The New York Times*, March 10, 1954, 1.

10. See Czeslaw Milosz, *The Captive Mind* (New York: Knopf, 1953), which is surely one of the great documents of our time.

11. Cf. Gerth and Mills, *Character and Social Structure* (New York: Harcourt Brace, 1953), 413 ff. for a further discussion of these three aspects of authority.

12. Cf. Gerth and Mills, *Character and Social Structure*.

13. Cf. Joseph Wood Krutch, *The Measure of Man* (Indianapolis: Bobbs-Merrill, 1954).

The Reith Lectures:
Speaking Truth to Power

Edward Said*

In last week's lecture I spoke about the way an intellectual can become a professional who specialized in one bit of turf, accredited, careful, speaking not the general language of a wide audience but rather the approved jargon of a group of insiders.

As an alternative, I suggested that as a way of maintaining relative intellectual independence, having the attitude of an amateur instead of a professional is a better course. But let me be practical and personal here.

In the end, one is moved by causes and ideas that one can actually choose to support because they conform to values and principles one believes in. I do not therefore consider myself bound by my professional training in literature, consequently ruling myself out from matters of public policy just because I am only certified to teach modern literature. I speak and write about broader matters because, as a rank amateur, I am spurred on by commitments that go well beyond my narrow professional career. Of course, I make a conscious effort to acquire a new and wider audience for these views, which I never present inside a classroom.

But what are these amateur forays into the public sphere all about, really? Is the intellectual galvanized into intellectual action by primordial, local, instinctive loyalties—to one's race, people, or religion—or is there some more universal and rational set of principles that can, and perhaps do, govern how one speaks and writes? In effect, I am asking the basic

---

*This article first appeared in *The Independent* (London), July 22, 1993, 12. Reprinted with permission of *The Independent*.

question for the intellectual: how does one speak the truth? What truth? For whom and where?

Unfortunately, we must begin by saying that there is no system or method broad and certain enough to provide the intellectual with direct answers to these questions.

Take as a starting point the whole, by now extremely disputatious matter of objectivity, or accuracy, or facts. In 1988 the American historian Robert Novick published a massive volume whose title dramatized the quandary with exemplary efficiency. It was called *That Noble Dream* and subtitled *The 'Objectivity Question' and the American Historical Profession*. Drawing on materials taken from a century of historiographic enterprise in the United States, Novick showed how the very nub of historical investigation—the ideal of objectivity by which a historian seizes the opportunity to render facts as realistically and accurately as possible—gradually evolved into a mass of competing claims and counterclaims. All of them wore down any semblance of agreement by historians as to what objectivity was to the merest fig leaf, and often not even to that. Objectivity has had to do service in the Cold War as "our" (i.e., American as opposed to Communist) truth; in peacetime as the objective truth of each competing separate group (women, African-Americans, Asian-Americans, gays, white men, and so and on) and each school (Marxist, establishment, deconstructionist, cultural). After such a babble of knowledges, what possible convergence could there be? Novick asks, and he concludes mournfully that "as a broad community of discourse, as a community of scholars united by common aims, common standards, and common purposes, the discipline of history had ceased to exist. . . . The professor of history was as described in the last verse of the Book of Judges: 'In those days there was no king in Israel: every man did that which was right in his own eyes.'"

One of the main intellectual activities of our century has been the questioning, not to say undermining, of authority. So to add to Novick's findings we would have to say that not only did a consensus disappear on what constituted objective reality, but a lot of traditional authorities, including God, were in the main swept away. There has even been an influential school of philosophers—among whom Michel Foucault, the French thinker, ranks very high—who say that to speak of an author at all (as in the author of Milton's poems) is a highly tendentious, not to say ideological, overstatement.

In the face of this formidable onslaught, to regress either into hand-wringing impotence or into muscular reassertions of traditional values, as characterized by the global neoconservative movement, will not do. I think that the critique of objectivity and authority did perform a positive service by underlining how, in the secular world, human beings construct their truths, so to speak, and that, for example, the so-called objective truth of the white man's superiority built and maintained by the classical European colonial empires also rested on a violent subjugation of African and Asian peoples and they, it is equally true, fought that particular imposed "truth" in order to provide an independent order of their own. And so now everyone comes forward with new and often violently opposed views of the world: one hears endless talk about Judaeo-Christian values, Afrocentric values, Muslim truths, Eastern truths, Western truths, each providing a complete program for excluding all the others. There is now more intolerance and strident assertiveness abroad everywhere than any one system can handle.

The result is an almost complete absence of universals, even though very often the rhetoric suggests, for instance, that "our" values (whatever these may happen to be) are in fact universal. One of the shabbiest of all intellectual gambits is to pontificate about abuses in someone else's culture and to excuse exactly the same practices in one's own. For me, the classic case is that of the brilliant nineteenth-century French intellectual Alexis de Tocqueville, who to many of us educated to believe in classical liberal and Western democratic values, exemplified those values almost to the letter.

Having written his assessment of democracy in America, and having criticized American mistreatment of Indians and black slaves, Tocqueville later had to deal with French colonial practices in Algeria during the late 1830s and 1840s, where, under Marshal Bugeaud, the French army of occupation undertook a savage war of pacification against the Algerian Muslims. All of a sudden, as one reads Tocqueville on Algeria, the very norms with which he had humanely demurred at American malfeasance are suspended for French actions. Not that he does not cite reasons: he does, but they are lame extenuations whose purpose it is to license French colonialism in the name of what he calls national pride. Massacres leave him unmoved; Muslims, he says, belong to an inferior religion and must be disciplined. In short, the apparent universalism of his language for America is denied, willfully denied, application to his own country, even as his own country, France, pursues similarly inhumane policies.

It must be added, however, that Tocqueville (and John Stuart Mill, for that matter, whose commendable ideas about democratic freedoms in England he said did not apply to India) lived during a period when the ideas of a universal norm of international behavior meant, in effect, the right of European power and European representations of other people to hold sway, so nugatory and secondary did the non-white peoples of the world seem. Besides, according to nineteenth-century Westerners, there were no independent African or Asian peoples of consequence to challenge the draconian brutality of laws that were applied unilaterally by colonial armies to black- or brown-skinned races. Their destiny was to be ruled. Frantz Fanon, Aime Cesaire, and C. L. R. James—to mention three great anti-imperialist black intellectuals—did not live and write until the twentieth century, so what they and the liberation movements of which they were a part accomplished culturally and politically in establishing the right of colonized peoples to equal treatment was not available to Tocqueville or Mill. But these changed perspectives are available to contemporary intellectuals who have not often drawn the inevitable conclusions, that if you wish to uphold basic human justice, you must do so for everyone, not just selectively for the people whom your side, your culture, your nation designates are OK.

The fundamental problem is therefore how to reconcile one's identity and the actualities of one's own culture, society, and history to the reality of other identities, cultures, peoples. This can never be done simply by asserting one's preference for what is already one's own: tub-thumping about the glories of "our" culture or the triumphs of "our" history is not worthy of the intellectual's energy, especially not today when so many societies are composed of different races and backgrounds as to beggar any reductive formulas. As I have been discussing it here, the public realm in which intellectuals make their representations is extremely complex, and contains contradictory features. But the meaning of an effective intervention there has to rest on the intellectual's unbudgeable conviction in a concept of justice and fairness that allows for differences between nations and individuals, without at the same time assigning them to hidden hierarchies, preferences, evaluations. Everyone today professes a liberal language of equality and harmony for all. The problem for the intellectual is to bring these notions to bear on actual situations where the gap between the profession of equality and justice, on the one hand, and, on the other, the rather less edifying reality, is very great.

This is most easily demonstrated in international relations, which is the reason I have stressed them so much in these lectures. A couple of recent examples illustrate what I have in mind. During the period just after Iraq's illegal invasion of Kuwait in 1990, public discussion in the West justly focused on the unacceptability of the aggression, which, with extreme brutality, sought to eliminate Kuwaiti existence. And as it became clear that the American intention was in fact to use military force against Iraq, the public rhetoric encouraged processes at the United Nations that would ensure the passage of resolutions—based on the UN Charter—demanding sanctions and the possible use of force against Iraq. Of the few intellectuals who opposed both the Iraqi invasion and the subsequent use of largely U.S. force in Desert Storm, none to my knowledge cited any evidence or made any argument excusing Iraq for what it did.

But what I think was correctly remarked at the time was how weakened the American case against Iraq was when the Bush administration, with its enormous power, pressed the UN toward war, ignoring the numerous possibilities of a negotiated reversal of the occupation before 15 January, when the counter-offensive began, and also refusing to discuss other UN resolutions on other illegal occupations and invasions of territory that had involved the United States itself or some of its close allies.

The real issue in the Gulf so far as the U.S. was concerned was oil and strategic power, not the Bush administration's professed principles. But what compromised intellectual discussion throughout the country, in its reiterations of the inadmissibility of land unilaterally acquired by force, was the absence of universal application of the idea. What never seemed relevant to the many American intellectuals who supported the war was that the United States itself had recently invaded and for a time occupied the sovereign state of Panama. Surely if one criticized Iraq, it therefore followed that the United States deserved the same criticism? But no: "our" motives were higher, Saddam Hussein was a Hitler, whereas "we" were moved by largely altruistic and disinterested motives, and therefore this was a just war.

Or consider the Soviet invasion of Afghanistan, equally wrong and equally condemnable. But U.S. allies such as Israel and Turkey had occupied territories illegally before the Russians moved into Afghanistan. Another U.S. ally, Indonesia, has massacred hundreds of thousands of Timorese in an illegal invasion during the middle 1970s; there is evidence to show that the U.S. knew about and supported the horrors of the East Timor war, but few intellectuals in the United States, busy as always with the crimes of the Soviet Union, said much about that. And looming back in time was the enormous American invasion of Indo-China, with results in sheer destructiveness wreaked on small, mainly peasant societies that are staggering. The principle here seems to have been that professional experts on U.S. foreign and military policy should confine their attention to winning a war against the other superpower and its surrogates in Vietnam or Afghanistan, and our own misdeeds be damned.

For the contemporary intellectual, living at a time that is already confused by the disappearance of what seemed to have been objective moral norms and sensible authority, is it acceptable simply either blindly to support the behavior of one's own country and overlook its crimes, or to say rather supinely "I believe they all do it, and that's the way of the world"?

Most, if not all, countries in the world are signatories to the Universal Declaration of Human Rights, adopted and proclaimed in 1948, reaffirmed by every new member state of the UN. There are equally solemn conventions on the rules of war, on treatment of prisoners, on the rights of workers, women, children, immigrants and refugees. None of these documents says anything about disqualified or less equal races or peoples. All are entitled to the same freedoms. Of course, these rights are violated on a daily basis, as witness the genocide in Bosnia today. For an American or Egyptian or Chinese government official, these rights are at best looked at politically, not from a consistently moral standpoint. But those are the norms of power, which are precisely not those of the intellectual whose role is at very least to apply the same standards and norms of behavior now already collectively accepted on paper by the entire international community.

Of course, there are patriotism and loyalty to one's people. And, of course, the intellectual is not an uncomplicated automaton, hurling mathematically devised laws and rules across the board. And, of course, fear and the normal limitations on one's time and attention and capacity as an individual voice operate with fearsome efficiency. And no one can speak up all the time on all the issues. But I believe there is a special duty to address the constituted and authorized powers of one's own society, which are accountable to its citizenry, particularly when those powers are exercised in a manifestly disproportionate and immoral war, or in deliberate programs of discrimination, repression, and collective cruelty.

In all these instances the intellectual meaning of a situation is arrived at by comparing the known and available facts with a norm, also known and available. This is not an easy task, since documentation, research, probings are required in order to get beyond the usually piecemeal, fragmentary and necessarily flawed way in which information is presented. But in most cases it is possible, I believe, to ascertain whether in fact a massacre was committed, or an official cover-up produced. The first imperative is to find out what occurred, and then why, not as isolated events but as part of an unfolding history whose broad contours includes one's own nation as an actor. The incoherence of the standard foreign policy analysis performed by apologists, strategists, and planners is that it concentrates on others as the objects of a situation, rarely on "our" involvement and what it wrought. Even more rarely is it compared with a moral norm.

The goal of speaking the truth is, in so administered a mass society as ours, mainly to project a better state of affairs, one that corresponds more closely to a set of moral principles—peace, reconciliation, abatement of suffering—applied to the known facts. This has been called "abduction" by the American philosopher C. S. Peirce, and has been used effectively by the celebrated contemporary intellectual Noam Chomsky. Certainly in writing and speaking, one's aim is not to show everyone how right one is, but in trying to induce a change in the moral climate whereby aggression is seen as such, the unjust punishment of peoples or individuals is either prevented or given up, and the recognition of rights and democratic freedoms is established as a norm for everyone, not invidiously for a select few.

Admittedly, however, these are idealistic and often unrealizable aims; and in a sense they are not as immediately relevant to my subject here as the intellectual's individual performance when, as I have been saying, the tendency too often is to back away or simply to toe the line.

Nothing in my view is more reprehensible than those habits of mind in the intellectual that induce avoidance, that characteristic turning away from a difficult and principled position which you know to be the right one, but which you decide not to take. You do not want to appear too political; you are afraid of seeming controversial; you need the approval of a boss or an authority figure; you want to keep a reputation for being balanced, objective, moderate; your hope is to be asked back, to consult, to be on a board or prestigious committee, and so, to remain within the responsible mainstream; someday you hope to get an honorary degree, a big prize, perhaps even an ambassadorship. For an intellectual these habits of mind are corrupting par excellence. If anything can denature, neutralize and finally kill a passionate intellectual life, it is these considerations, internalized and so to speak in the driver's seat.

And finally a word about the mode of intellectual intervention. One doesn't climb a mountain or pulpit and declaim from the heights. Obviously, you want to speak your piece where it can be heard best; and also you want it represented in such a way as to affiliate with an ongoing and actual process, for instance, the cause of peace and justice.

Yes, the intellectual's voice is lonely, but it has resonance only because it associates itself freely with the reality of a movement, the aspirations of a people, the common pursuit of a shared ideal.

Let's look at an example. Opportunism dictates that in the West, much given to full-scale critiques of, for instance, Palestinian terror or immoderation, you denounce them soundly, and then go on to praise Israeli democracy. Then you must say something good about peace. Yet intellectual responsibility dictates, of course, that you say all those things to Palestinians, but your main point is made in New York, in Paris, in London, around the issue which in those places you can most affect, by promoting the idea of Palestinian freedom and the freedom from terror and extremism of all concerned, not just the weakest and most easily bashed party. Speaking the truth to power is no Panglossian idealism: it is carefully weighing the alternatives, picking the right one, and then intelligently representing it where it can do the most good and cause the right change.

All the Presidents' Brains

Tevi Troy*

If intellectuals can learn one lesson from the past forty years of American politics, it is that they matter. They help shape the perception of elected officials, both short term in the media, and long term in the history books. It is in politicians' interests to woo them, but intellectuals often do not realize this. So the other key lesson intellectuals should take from history is that they should not sell themselves too easily to the presidents who turn to them.

John F. Kennedy realized and capitalized on the potential of America's intellectuals. In 1960, he won the support of Harvard professors such as Arthur Schlesinger and John Kenneth Galbraith to secure the Democratic presidential nomination, despite competition from liberal icons Adlai Stevenson and Hubert Humphrey. As president, Kennedy hired Schlesinger as a special assistant, and Schlesinger served as ambassador to the liberal and intellectual communities. In that role, Schlesinger kept Kennedy abreast of developments among intellectuals, promoted his boss among the nation's literary elites, and, eventually, wrote the first draft of history in the award-winning Kennedy hagiography *A Thousand Days*.

Kennedy deserves credit for recognizing the increasing importance of intellectuals in American life, but in many ways he had it easier than his successors. The 1960s began with most intellectuals belonging to the consensus school of liberal anti-communism. As a result of social and political tensions, the intellectual community split into conservative and liberal

---

*This article first appeared in the *Times Higher Education Supplement*, July 5, 2002, 21. Reprinted with permission.

wings in the 1960s. This made things both easier and more difficult for politicians interested in intellectual support. More difficult because the concept of one-stop shopping for intellectual support, in Cambridge, Massachusetts, or anywhere else, could no longer work, but easier because fragmentation opened new opportunities for intellectuals and politicians frozen out of the monolithic liberal model.

Intellectuals today are far more numerous, better compensated, and more influential than in the past. But as they have become more influential, they have also become more ambitious. And ambition makes them a potentially easy target for presidents.

Bill Clinton often recognized and exploited this. First, Clinton read a lot, as much as four books a week. But he did not change or even create policy as a result of his reading. Clinton, it seems, read for effect at least as much as to affect change. He was quite clever in his choice of reading material, and often used books successfully to woo the books' authors. According to Princeton historian Fred Greenstein, Clinton once conspicuously placed behind his desk Richard Reeves's book *President Kennedy: Profile of Power*, which discussed the disorganization of the Kennedy White House. According to Greenstein: "When that book was published, Clinton had invited its author to meet with him and never touched on the theme of White House organization, which is one of the weak points of Clinton's leadership."

Although there is nothing wrong with succumbing to a presidential charm offensive, there is a potential problem of compromised analysis, an extreme example being *New Yorker* writer and later Clinton aide Sidney Blumenthal. It is a problem that affects both sides of the aisle. The rise of ideology over independent analysis has led to the development of two cadres of intellectual round-heels, who can largely be counted on to adhere to their party's line on any issue. Such a development is useful for the parties, but potentially worrisome for the cause of independent scholarship.

While intellectuals need to be careful around presidents, presidents cannot just ignore intellectuals at their whim. Jimmy Carter thought he could go it alone, and he did so throughout his successful campaign for the presidency. He relied heavily on his Georgia mafia of campaign staffers, and he believed that he did not need eastern intellectuals to tell him what to do. Subsequently, he became the first president since Kennedy without a full-time ambassador to intellectuals on staff. But when his administration floundered with the Iran hostage crisis and a double-dip recession, Carter could have used the support of America's literary and academic elites. After three years of ignoring intellectuals, however, it was too late and he bowed out in the 1980 election.

Despite the growing influence of intellectuals in U.S. politics, it is a safe bet that they do not see themselves as sufficiently influential. Even when they serve in high office, they have relatively little influence. Yet they can help create a positive perception, within the media, among party activists and, ultimately, with voters. Mismanaging or, worse, ignoring them, as Carter did, can contribute to the perception of a president lacking in conviction or in vision.

UNEASY BEDFELLOWS

Lyndon B. Johnson—who served from 1963 to 1969—was uncomfortable with Kennedy's success with intellectuals—the "Harvards," as Johnson called them. Nevertheless, Johnson still craved the accolades Kennedy received from the academic community. Johnson resented the fact that his aides, such as Jack Valenti, did not get the same kudos as Kennedy aides such as Arthur Schlesinger and Ted Sorensen. According to Johnson: "Jack is really an intellectual. People would admit it if he didn't come from the wrong side of the Mason-Dixon line."

Johnson did hire Princeton professor Eric Goldman as his ambassador to intellectuals, but he never really trusted him. Their relationship deteriorated when the White House Festival of the Arts, which Goldman organized, became an albatross after numerous intellectuals boycotted the event in protest against the Vietnam war.

Even worse, some of the festival-goers circulated an anti-war petition. Charlton Heston blasted petition ringleader Dwight MacDonald for his behavior, saying that, "having convictions doesn't mean that you have to lack elementary manners. Are you really accustomed to signing petitions against your host in his home?"

Goldman, for his part, was largely silent about the misbehavior of his friends, as Johnson fumed. Unsurprisingly, he left the White House a scant ten weeks after the fiasco. Later, he wrote a bitter memoir of his time in Johnson's White House. Johnson suffered poor relations with intellectuals throughout the rest of his presidency.

IN THE WRONG CAMP

When Richard Nixon—1969–1974—won the presidency in 1968, he selected former Kennedy and Johnson staffer Daniel Patrick Moynihan as his ambassador to intellectuals largely because of the dearth of conservative intellectuals who could fill such a position.

Although Moynihan was a committed Democrat, he was disliked by most liberals for his critique of liberal excesses in the 1960s. He felt strongly that old-line Democrats had no home in the elite institutions increasingly populated by radicals.

For example, Moynihan told Nixon that *New York Times* editor Abe Rosenthal oversaw "(a news room) still predominantly made up of old-time liberal Democrats who can be counted on to report a story in a straightforward manner." Unfortunately, Moynihan reported, "every time one of (the veterans) goes and is replaced by a new recruit from the *Harvard Crimson* or whatever, the Maoist faction on West 43rd Street gets one more vote. No one else applies."

Despite his critique of radicals, Moynihan still found himself mistrusted by Republicans, including fellow White House staffers, because of his party affiliation. To his credit, he recognized the untenable nature of his position and recommended that Nixon hire and nurture conservative intellectuals of his own. This foreshadowed the flowering of conservative intellectuals in the Reagan administration, as Reagan reached into the newly developed conservative think tanks to help staff his administration.

FRUSTRATED FRIENDS

Bill Clinton—1993–2001—was keenly aware of the intellectual community. From the start of his campaign, when he cultivated the centrist intellectuals in the Democratic Leadership Council, through the depths of his impeachment trial, when much of the intellectual establishment rose to defend the president, Clinton consistently used his good relations with intellectuals to his advantage.

Early in his presidency, he let slip the fact that he tried "to read at least 30 minutes a day." He often strategically placed recently written books on his desk, which endeared him to their authors. But things did not always work out in favor of the intellectuals charmed by Clinton. Al From of the DLC boasted that his organization would help shape the administration, but Clinton spent much of his first two years edging leftward, away from the DLC's centrist ideas. Labor secretary Robert Reich, a committed liberal, was frustrated too. His attempts to introduce liberal ideas were often stymied by Clinton pollster and political guru Dick Morris, who would tell Reich things like: "I tested your ideas. One worked. Two didn't."

Although Clinton disappointed many of his intellectual backers, they backed him in his darkest hours—412 intellectuals signed a petition saying his impeachment was unconstitutional. And in the impeachment hearings, judiciary committee chairman Henry Hyde said that the panel had "heard from so many college professors that I think I'm going to ask if we can get college credit for attending the seminars."

About the Contributors

Paul Berman is a Senior Fellow at the World Policy Institute specializing in American Foreign Policy. He is also a contributing editor for *The New Republic* and a member of the editorial board of *Dissent* magazine. His books include *Terror and Liberalism* (2003) and *Power and the Idealists* (2005).

Daniel C. Brouwer is Assistant Professor of Communication at Arizona State University. His research focuses on public sphere studies, rhetorical criticism, the rhetoric of social movements, the rhetoric of HIV/AIDS, and cultural performance. He is the co-editor of *Counterpublics and the State* (2001).

Lewis Coser (1914–2003) was a founding editor of *Dissent* magazine, founding chair of the sociology department at Brandeis University, and professor of sociology at the State University of New York in Stony Brook. His books include *The Functions of Social Conflict* (1956), *Men of Ideas* (1965), and *Masters of Sociological Thought* (1971).

Ellen Cushman is Assistant Professor of English at Michigan State University. Her books include *The Struggle and the Tools: Oral and Literate Strategies in an Inner City Community* (1998).

Sidney I. Dobrin is Associate Professor of English at the University of Florida. His books include *A Closer Look: The Writer's Reader* (with Anis S. Bawarshi, 2003) and *Saving Place: An Ecocomposition Reader* (2004).

Theodore Draper is best known for his writings on the American Communist Party. He is a fellow of the American Academy of Arts and Sciences and a member of the Council on Foreign Relations. His books include *The Roots of American Communism* (1957) and *A Struggle for Power: The American Revolution* (1996).

Jean Bethke Elshtain is the Laura Spelman Rockefeller Professor of Social and Political Ethics at the University of Chicago. Her books include *Public Man, Private Woman: Women in Social and Political Thought* (1981), *Democracy on Trial* (1995), and *Just War Against Terror: The Burden of American Power in a Violent World* (2003).

Joseph Epstein is a member of the literature faculty at Northwestern University and a Trustee of the Hudson Institute. His books include *Envy: The Seven Deadly Sins* (2003) and *Fabulous Small Jews* (2003); he is editor of *Portraits: A Gallery of Intellectuals* (1997).

Amitai Etzioni is founder and director of the Communitarian Network and University Professor at The George Washington University. He has served as a senior advisor to the White House and president of the American Sociological Association. He is the author of twenty-two books including *The New Golden Rule* (1996), *My Brother's Keeper: A Memoir and a Message* (2003), and *From Empire to Community: A New Approach to International Relations* (2004).

Frances Ferguson holds the Mary Elizabeth Garrett Chair in Arts and Sciences at Johns Hopkins University. Her books include *Solitude and the Sublime: Romanticism and the Aesthetics of Individuation* (1992) and *Pornography, The Theory* (2005).

Irving Howe (1920–1993) was founding editor of *Dissent* magazine and Distinguished Professor of Literature at the City University of New York. His books include *Politics and the Novel* (1957), *World of Our Fathers* (1976), and *Socialism in America* (1985).

Russell Jacoby is Professor in Residence of History at the University of California, Los Angeles. His books include *The Last Intellectuals: American Culture in the Age of Academe* (1987) and *The End of Utopia: Politics and Culture in the Age of Apathy* (1999).

Merle Kling was a professor and administrator at Washington University from 1946 until his retirement in 1983. He is a scholar of the governments and politics of Latin America. His books include *A Mexican Interest Group in Action* (1961).

J. Hillis Miller is Distinguished Research Professor of English and Comparative Literature at the University of California, Irvine. His recent books include *Speech Acts in Literature* (2001) and *Others* (2001).

C. Wright Mills (1916–1962) was an American sociologist whose work often emphasized the responsibilities of scholars in a post-World War II society. He was a member of the sociology department at Columbia University from 1946 until his death. His works include *White Collar* (1951), *The Power Elite* (1956), and *The Sociological Imagination* (1959).

Richard A. Posner is a judge on the Seventh Circuit Court of Appeals and a senior lecturer at the University of Chicago Law School. His recent books include *Law, Pragmatism, and Democracy* (2003) and *Preventing Surprise Attacks* (2005).

Edward Said (1935–2003) was a renowned literary theorist, critic, and Palestinian activist. His books include *Orientalism* (1978), *The World, the Text, and the Critic* (1983), and *Culture and Imperialism* (1993).

Patrick Saveau is an assistant professor of French at Franklin College. His research focuses on autobiography and autofiction, with an emphasis on the work of Serge Doubrovsky.

Catherine R. Squires is Assistant Professor of Communication and of Afroamerican and African Studies at the University of Michigan. Her research focuses on the interactions between racial groups, mass media, and the public sphere.

Tevi Troy served as a campaign strategist for George W. Bush's 2004 re-election campaign. Previously he worked under President Bush as a Deputy Cabinet Secretary and as the White House liaison to the Jewish community. He is the author of *Intellectuals and the American Presidency: Philosophers, Jesters, or Technicians?* (2001).

Alan Wolfe is Professor of Political Science and Director of the Boisi Center for Religion and American Public Life at Boston College. His recent books include *The Transformation of American Religion: How We Actually Practice our Faith* (2003) and *Return to Greatness: How America Lost Its Sense of Purpose and What It Needs to Do to Recover It* (2005).

Howard Young is Professor Emeritus of Modern European Languages at Pomona College. His books include *The Victorious Expression: A Study of Four Contemporary Spanish Poets* (1966) and *The Line in the Margin: Juan Ramon Jimenez and his Readings in Blake, Shelley, and Yeats* (1980).